Home Possessions

Home Possessions

Material Culture behind Closed Doors

Edited by
Daniel Miller

Oxford • New York

First published in 2001 by
Berg
Editorial offices:
150 Cowley Road, Oxford, OX4 1JJ, UK
838 Broadway, Third Floor, New York, NY 10003-4812, USA

Berg is an imprint of Oxford International Publishers Ltd.

Library of Congress Cataloging-in-Publication Data
A catalogue record for this book is available from the Library of Congress.

British Library Cataloguing-in-Publication Data
A catalogue record for this book is available from the British Library.

ISBN 1 85973 580 0 (Cloth)
1 85973 585 1 (Paper)

Typeset by JS Typesetting, Wellingborough, Northants
Printed in the United Kingdom by Biddles Ltd, Guildford and King's Lynn

Chang-Kwo's parents, Stephen Frosh, Helene,
Jef and Mariette, Joseph Kushner, George and Katy,
Orange, Skien Friends, Susannah

Contents

List of Figures

Acknowledgements

This book is intended as a sequel to *Material Cultures*, edited by me and published in 1998. In this second volume we have the advantage of greater cohesion amongst the projects being undertaken, which quite easily transcend their individual case studies to become a sustained analysis of the material culture of the home. So whereas the previous volume was concerned with ethnographic studies of material culture in general, the present volume is more focused and narrower in its scope. Both books were constructed through the process described in the acknowledgements of the previous volume: a monthly round of drinking and gossiping (that counts for us as methodology training) followed by the discussion of a pre-circulated paper. All the contributors to this volume are currently my PhD students. There is only one overlap amongst the contributors to this and the previous volume, which I am glad to say attests to the speed with which each project has been completed. The exception represented by Alison Clarke is understandable given her achievements over the last few years including a highly successful book on Tupperware.

Although I am the sole editor, all these papers were produced within a collective environment of mutual assistance and critique amongst all the contributors. Contributions from co-students present at the evening drinking sessions included Pat Berhau, Mark Mullen, Kaori O'Conner and Andrew Skuse, as well as an ex-member, Sophie Chevalier. In particular, two newcomers who are also conducting research on the topic of the home, Heather Horst on Jamaican returned migrants and Laurence Faure on establishing homes in London, have looked at many of the chapters and have made comments, as has my colleague Victor Buchli, the most recent recruit to the material culture team at UCL.

Daniel Miller

Behind Closed Doors
Daniel Miller

In industrialized societies, most of what matters to people is happening behind the closed doors of the private sphere. The home itself has become the site of their relationships and their loneliness: the site of their broadest encounters with the world through television and the Internet, but also the place where they reflect upon and face up to themselves away from others. For this reason it is likely that people are paying increasing attention to their relationship to their own home, to its structure, its decoration, its furnishing and the arrays of objects that fill its spaces, and that they reflect back on it their agency and sometimes their impotence. It is the material culture within our home that appears as both our appropriation of the larger world and often as the representation of that world within our private domain. Yet precisely because it is a private sphere, an investigation that studies such an intimate relationship, a sharing that can only take place if we are ourselves are present inside these private homes, seems intrusive. Every chapter in this book is written on the basis of just such an experience: they are ethnographic encounters that took place behind the closed doors of domestic homes. We justified these, even where they were clearly experienced as intrusive, on the grounds that we need to understand, through empathy, the diverse ways in which this intimate relationship is being developed as the foundation to so many people's lives.

As such this is not merely 'another book about the home'. It is a volume that attempts to change our understanding of the significance of the home as a route to social and cultural analysis and to question some assumptions about what might have been thought to be the 'obvious' nature and implications of the home. It does so through developing and extending certain key insights and new perspectives. Given the multitude of books that have already been published on the topic of houses and homes, the primary purpose of this introduction is to highlight the several ways in which this particular book is an original and distinctive contribution to the topic. The book does not aim to be comprehensive; it is complemented by many other recent works on the home, some of which also emphasize material culture. It does not, for example, provide the same attention to the development of domesticity found in some of the contributions to Cieraad (ed.) (1999), or examine the house as instrumental in the localization and appropriation of global forms as found in some contributions within Birdwell-Pheasant and Lawrence-Zúñiga (eds) (1999), or consider the relationship to state and private institutions found in Chapman and Hockey (1999), or emulate the social–psychological approaches that range from Csikszentmihalyi and Rochberg-Halton (1981) to Steedman (1992). Instead it concentrates on directly observing the processes by which a home and its inhabitants transform each other.

The study of home life is hardly new to anthropology. Indeed it is probably its core. Typically, in the 'classic' period of ethnographic enquiry, supervisors would instruct their graduate students that it was essential that they live in the homes of their informants, at the heart of a community. Not surprisingly the families that hosted them often became primary informants. Indeed the problem was often that they became the gatekeepers in determining the ethnographer's relationship to other households. So observing the intricate details of such homes was central to fieldwork. But in most of the societies deemed appropriate to ethnographic study, homes were, relatively speaking, public places. In some cases male anthropologists may have had more difficulty gaining access to female 'quarters' that lay at the back of the house, but there was considerable fluidity between the world of work and the home. Artisan and agrarian activities often happened within the home and family life often took place in the public domain. So the study of the home could remain integral to the holistic ambition behind the classic ethnographic study.

Today, however, anthropologists find themselves increasingly exposed to quite different situations. One reason has been the rise of anthropology 'at home', which has required a meeting point with both the tradition of ethnology in continental Europe, but also of indigenous anthropology in countries such as Japan. Another was the increasing reciprocal exchange of anthropologists between all countries, and a third a growth of suburban-style private housing within regions of more traditional anthropological enquiry, and the spread of the 'modern' professionally constructed home (see Birdwell-Pheasant and Lawrence-Zúñiga 1999: 19–25). This volume and that which preceded it (Miller [ed.] 1998) contain several examples of anthropology 'at home'. These include a Greek anthropologist studying Greeks, a Taiwanese anthropologist in Taiwan, and a French-Canadian working in Montreal. On the other hand they also include a French anthropologist carrying out fieldwork in England, an Irish anthropologist studying in Norway, and a Belgian anthropologist studying in Japan. But even anthropologists who were once situated in societies where residence for some might be in long houses complemented by menstrual huts, such as in New Guinea, now find they have to contend with the local rotary club and a suburbia marked by fences and guard dogs (for example, the recent work of Gerwertz and Errington 1999).

Contemporary material culture studies have placed themselves in the vanguard of anthropological acceptance of these changes. What they strive for is the maturity of true comparative studies, which does not separate out the study of Toyotas in

Australian Aboriginal society as somehow more exotic than the study of Volvos in Sweden (see Miller 2001), and where any easy dualism of simple and complex but also colonial and colonized are transcended. The problem indeed is not that privatized households are new. Abundant historical and ethnographic research in Britain (for instance McKibben 1998) has shown that for some considerable time the working-class house has been rigorously privatized, and apart from kin, entry into the private home has been highly restricted. This separation of the private is, however, exacerbated when so much of the encounter with the larger world is through television and now the Internet: encounters that take place mainly within the home (see Morley 1992).

Ethnographers working in such environments often respond by carrying out their researches in a very different situation from traditional ethnography. Usually they do not live with a family, but visit. They find there is no particular community and there is no reason to expect that knowing one family will lead to an acquaintance with its neighbours. Indeed the relationship between neighbours may be cursory or antagonistic. In the absence of community there are fewer cross-references in the gossip and exchanges that take place. The home may have developed historically to become systematically opposed to other arenas such as work (Davidoff and Hall 1987, but see Nippert- Eng 1996). But if this is where and how life is lived, it is very hard to see a future for an anthropology that excludes itself from the place where most of what matters in people's lives takes place. Furthermore there seems no likelihood that any other discipline will take up this challenge. For example, there has been a vast increase in media studies, which acknowledge the role of the home as the site of consumption (for example, Morley 1992), but these still largely rely on the focus group and questionnaires (methods that often produce quite the opposite results from ethnography; see Miller, Jackson, Thrift, Holbrook and Rowlands 1998: 79–89), and so the sense of both the experience and consequences of media consumption may be limited (with exceptions such as Hirsch 1992; Lull 1988). Early studies of the Internet that call themselves ethnographic actually just mean the experience of being on-line, rather than the relationship between that and off-line life (compare Markham 1998 with Miller and Slater 2000). The topic of consumption ought to raise the same issue, but while, for example, Clammer (1997) provides a highly informative book on consumption in Japan, what is missing is a sense of the private life of households.

Much of the motivation behind the contents of this volume and Miller (ed.) 1998 was the feeling that this is the single most important site for material culture studies. Tacchi (1998) for example, did not just accept the challenge of media studies within the home; she took the most private example of that encounter: the very personal relationship between individuals and their radios. In this volume it is not just that most of the papers include material from behind these closed doors but they include case studies from Norway and Japan, which present two of the most extreme national stereotypes of the intensely private domain. Nor was it regarded as sufficient just to have occasional access. Chapters such as those by Garvey and by Daniels depend on coming to know the strains and contradictions of household relations behind the apparent tight normative order of home life. In these as in other chapters this knowledge was obtained vicariously but effectively through a study that focused on the precise implications of the material culture within the home.

As will be evident in the chapters in this book, working behind closed doors does not constitute a simple dichotomy between the private and the public, which itself has been subject to a complex history (for example Sennett 1976, and Attfield 2000: 177–201 who consider the implications for material culture). Clarke's chapter demonstrates that the relationship between these two is found to be far more complex, with each having a place inside the other, and this theme of projection and interiorization is continued throughout. Furthermore, within the home there are equally complex relationships, because we cannot equate the private with the personal. There are many conflicts between the agency expressed by individuals, by the family, the household, and not least as we shall see the house itself, that make the private more a turbulent sea of constant negotiation rather than simply some haven for the self. This becomes clear precisely because all the chapters use ethnography to immerse themselves in the particularity of individual houses.

The study of the home from the perspective of material culture is not new to anthropology. There were many influential examples during the heyday of structural analysis and many since then. But the emphasis was on the home as a representation of normative order through symbolic contrast. The architectural structure of the home was found to have a shadow in its symbolic structure. Other approaches at that time emphasized the home as a stable foundation or anchor to kinship and domestic life. The first part of this book overturns the concomitant assumptions behind such approaches. By contrast these chapters emphasize the home as both the source and the setting of mobility and change. The second part of this book in turn acts as a critique of the dominant thrust of the literature that followed the decline of structuralist perspectives in the 1980s. That literature turned to the active agency of the occupants of the home: the home as a site of consumption and the 'do-it-yourself' process of people transforming their homes. Instead of looking at what we do with homes, the second part of this book examines what the home does with us. The concern is with the agency of the home itself. How this is conceptualized and made manifest.

The third part of this book uses both these previous insights to examine the dynamics of processes in which the transformation of the home is integral to the transformation of social relations, and shows how these develop in tandem. But it also highlights the messy and often contradictory nature of such processes. After considering each part, this introduction will conclude by returning to this initial concern with the significance of ethnographic work carried out in the private sphere. What this book demonstrates is what can be achieved through the focus upon the material culture of homes. But the promise it holds for anthropology as a whole lies in the degree to which so many other topics, from the organization of budgets to the process of socialization might be built upon the ethnographic foundations that are being laid.

Part One: Mobile Homes

If there was a pivotal study that re-launched the material culture of the home as a core topic in the development of modern anthropology it was surely the study of the Kabyle house by Pierre Bourdieu (1970). Although Bourdieu stressed the degree to which he was transforming the legacy of Lévi-Strauss by emphasizing practice and thereby time, contingency and strategy as against what were already by then coming to be seen as the more formulaic and static aspects of Lévi-Straussian structuralism (for example Bourdieu 1977), the study of the Kabyle house harks back to the core of structuralist teaching. In a sense it almost outdoes Lévi-Strauss himself in demonstrating how a series of core symbolic oppositions constitute the unspoken foundation for how a people express their beliefs about the world in material culture. For Bourdieu this habitat appears central to what he termed habitus. In the Kabyle house culture as a normative structure reproduces itself through a social order that is present more in the externalized order of the house itself than through some cognitive order inside the minds of its inhabitants.

Bourdieu's was not the only example. Other anthropologists influenced by structuralism looked for homologies between the order of the house and other domains (for example Tambiah 1969). Indeed, so pervasive has this style of analysis become, that even a text by Weiner (1991) that announces itself as the absolute enemy of structuralist analysis through a claimed affinity with Heidegger is actually a fine piece of micro-structuralism delving into the precise symbolic oppositions constituted by the material culture of the house that would sit well alongside the Kabyle study, since it takes the structural order of the house as the basis for homologies with other expressive systems such as that of poetry.

If there has been a more progressive element to later studies of material culture and the home it has tended to be through a more traditional route of deeper and more subtle ethnography. Vom Bruck (1997) would be a case in point in her analysis of the Yemenite house. Along with this has been some repudiation of the 'neatness of fit' that came with Bourdieu's homologies (for instance Halle 1993) and an emphasis on contradiction and the way the house may not reflect other domains but may itself become an instrument in resolving moral and other dilemmas. So amongst the best studies are Gell (1986) showing the house being used to avoid what is expressed in other domains or Wilk (1984, 1989) revealing the dynamics whereby the house might at one point express individualism within a collective ethos but later on be used in an attempt to suppress rising individualism. There has also been a considerable rise in feminist approaches. These tended first to follow from structuralism (and associated anthropological Marxism) in that they showed how oppressive structures of patriarchy were naturalized as ideology in the taken-for-granted order of the home (for example Ardener 1981) while later stressing the possibility for alternative sites of resistance (Moore 1986).

A greater sense of the house as a dynamic rather than a synchronic figure in the landscape has developed in part through recent historical research. For example, work in the Netherlands (see Cieraad 1999; de Mare 1999; Schama 1987) renders the architecture and material culture of the house as critical to the development not only of current concepts of domesticity but also civil society more generally (see also Frykman and Löfgren 1987 for Sweden; Comeroff and Comeroff 1997: chapter six for colonial Africa). In addition there has developed a greater attention to the intricacies of material culture (for instance Bryden and Floyd 1999) and the details of both provisioning of furniture (for example Auslander 1996) and the influences of states and commercial bodies on home interiors (for example Buchli 1999: 77–98; Forty 1986; Löfgren 1994; Zukin 1982).

In all these respects historians are developing perspectives that were already accepted in archaeology where house foundations are central to what survives. Archaeologists therefore tend to assign the house considerable significance in understanding long-term change . In addition the relationship between the house and associated material culture (such as tombs) has been central to archaeological methodology (see, for instance, Bradley 1996; Hodder 1984). What the chapters in this first part add to this trajectory is an appreciation of this same sense of the dynamic nature of houses as excavated from the more synchronic snap shot of ethnography. By emphasizing the house and its contents as a source and instrument of mobility and change the ethnographic evidence is rendered more compatible with the findings of historians and archaeologists.

In Clarke's chapter the home is evidently more a process than a place. As such she is able to take apart one of the most simplistic and generalized clichés about the home that sees us as all involved in 'keeping up with the Joneses', that is to say a site of aspiration based on emulation of neighbours, in the context of a rise of privatized and more materialistic lifestyles. Clarke replaces this cliché with a far more informed and complex understanding of what the house performs in mediating the relationship to others. The context for her studies, that of working-class households within a British council estate, presents an initial paradox. On the one hand there is a clear concern with neighbours, 'the Joneses', and with what other people might think about one's home. But in accordance with historical traditions there is almost no actual visiting of homes by neighbours. So the Joneses could never be based on an actual comparison or emulation.

What Clarke discovers is that, in practice, the home itself carried the burden of the discrepancies between its actual state at a given time and a wide range of aspirational 'ideal homes' that are generated out of much wider ideals that a household might have for itself (see also papers in Chapman and Hockey [eds] 1999). These range from immigrants' aspirations towards assimilation, through aspirations of a single woman towards an ideal partner, or aspirations for the future of one's children. As such the home becomes not an expression of other people's 'gaze', but rather an interiorized and more controlled replacement of those absent others. It becomes in and of itself the effective 'other' against which one judges oneself. So through the ethnographic study of detailed strategies of home improvement, placed back into the context of the narrative history and narrated futures of the households, Clarke finds a much more profound role for the home itself. In turn she can then confront an often simplistic representation of the politics of 'do it yourself', which has tended to dismiss this core household activity as a kind of superficial expression of 'cheap' emulation. Instead it re-emerges as a profound process of mediation within the contradictions of the household's encounters with wider society.

If Clarke demonstrates what can be achieved through an ethnographic focus upon the house as a process, the chapter by Garvey shows what is gained by taking us to a still more fine-grained perspective on this process. Her chapter corresponds to what has a become a 'classic' mode within modern material culture studies, one that is pivoted upon the term 'inconsequential'. That is to say we tend to divide our actions and possessions between that which we recognize as having important implications and the minor routines, practices or objects that we regard as having little or no consequence. For Garvey the division between major and minor actions is important, but precisely because the consequences of the latter are often hidden and disregarded despite being just as significant. We might assume that moving house or major acts of refurbishment are important, but separate these off from minor, often spontaneous, attempts to simply move a bit of furniture around to give a room a slightly different feel.

Garvey's observations on working-class women in Norway suggest that, whereas the major acts of refurbishment have acknowledged consequences for the presentation of the home to others, it is the small, easily undertaken forms of reordering that bear most on personal and intimate feelings where decorative order becomes a mirror for the self. So far from being the same (but smaller) kind of action as home refurbishment, moving things around may have quite the opposite effects. For example the former is costly, the latter is costless. Garvey concludes that in stark contrast to the act of home decoration within which it would normally have been subsumed, reordering the furnishings becomes a means by which the individual escapes from the arena of social positioning, or explicit narrations of the self.

Garvey's use of material culture to clarify the precise relationship between the private and public domain is of particular significance within the ethnography of Norwegian society. Most commentators have noted the centrality of privacy in Norway as compared to many other regions, but what exactly makes the sense of privacy and its domain different is much harder to determine. Yet it is at this subtle level that a core to an ethnographic account of Norwegian society might be formed. This is why Gullestad's (1984, 1992) earlier work on the home and home decoration was so pathbreaking both in studies of the home and in studies of Norwegian society, and Garvey provides further nuance and depth to Gullestad's observations.

Clarke and Garvey render suspect any assumption about the stability and unchanging nature of the home, and this opens the path to a more direct confrontation with the process of actually moving home, which is the subject of a study by Marcoux. They show the value in regarding the house as a dynamic process rather than a static backdrop, and Marcoux shows that when it comes to the actual movement of people, the tension between the change in the home itself and the movement of the material culture becomes critical in the same kind of realignment of person with their possessions that is the concern of the two previous papers. Indeed for Marcoux's chapter more than for any other chapter, the title of this book implies not the home as material culture so much as the relationship between mobile objects and the immobility of the place they reside in. In the case of Marcoux it is not just the ethnographer who focuses upon material objects that normally work best as the silent backdrop or frame to everyday life; it is the householders themselves who are faced by the way the presence of these things is made explicit by the decisions that have to be made as to what should be brought to the new home and what should be discarded.

What Marcoux demonstrates is the way in which this confrontation between people and their possessions is also an opportunity to reconfigure both the repair and rewriting of the narratives of their own personal biography and also the way their relationship to others has formed part of this biography. This is because the objects of the home are the mementoes and reminders of the past, and so the decision to discard some and retain others when moving house becomes the active management of one's own externalized memory. We are forced to confront directly the detritus that is left in the wake of our passage through life.

Finally in Petridou's chapter the issues raised are taken to a kind of extreme because her study is concerned with people who are not just moving house but moving country. If the previous papers help us to confront a myth of stability, the Greek students she studies have to create one. Food is often used for this purpose. For example Knight (1998) shows the importance for the urban Japanese of country food that brings them the taste and smells they associate with an idealized rural other. In Petridou's case there is paradox in that it is the very mobility of food, the fact that it can be easily transferred from one country to another, which makes it suitable as their means to stabilize their sense of home. Food is often intimately associated with both the particular cooking and smells of one's natal home and more generally the 'taste' of one's homeland. By virtue of this redolence it helps people to constitute a 'home from home' at a time when people are increasingly having to live with a more portable concept of their home (see Rapport and Dawson 1998 for the possibilities of an anthropology of more mobile and mediated experiences of home).

While the mothers who send this food are thereby attempting to reproduce at a distance the relationship of power and dependency that pertains within home family life, the students in turn use it to recast their understanding of the English people around them in terms of the perceived tastelessness of the latter, which implies a lack of sociability that is assumed to be true of the English home. This in turn allows the Greeks to constitute themselves as a homogenized representation of the positive qualities of their homeland. Food becomes the basis of a process including the social relations of preparing food, cooking and eating, which turns the superficial quality of taste into something that is sufficiently profound and rooted that it can appear as a more solid version of the home than the mere house or flat in which they reside. So in this case a taste of home that has itself become fully mobile can in turn be mobilized in the defensive constitution of identity. There is a final virtue to this chapter with respect to the volume as a whole in that there is a danger when analysing the material culture of the home that this will of itself generate too close an identification with the physicality of the house. Here we can see the sense of home emanating not from a house but from mobile material culture.

Petridou's chapter reinforces the insights of the previous papers into the nature of home as a process rather than just a place. Together, these chapters amount to a refusal of any assumption that the study of the home would have to be the study of some sort of concrete foundation or stable entity against which we can contrast the mobility and agency of the persons who sometimes dwell there. By contrast, these four chapters demonstrate that both the home and its attendant material culture can be central to the practices that make people mobile and able to reconfigure their relationships and indeed themselves in tandem with the changes that take place in the contexts within which they live.

Part Two: Estate Agency

If the main thrust of anthropological work on the material culture of the house in the 1960s and 1970s was based on structural and symbolic analysis, in the 1980s and 1990s there arose a new wave of studies (mainly arising from inter-disciplinary contexts) which emphasized the house as a point of consumption, with more emphasis on domesticity and the home. The home was the locus for the 'do-it-yourself' activity by which people transformed their home interiors as a mode of self expression. The home came to be seen less as a backdrop or reservoir of an almost unconscious habitus constructed out of order and relations. Instead, partly in the light of new gender studies that emphasized the agency of women (and subsequently also gays) in the home, it became a mode of expression, a means by which people constructed themselves and their ideologies (see, for example, contributions in Attfield and Kirkham 1989; Putnam and Newton 1990; Segelan and De Wita 1993; Sanders 1996).

As this work has progressed, however, the model of a semiotic home that occupants could use to create meaning has had to contend with the contradictions and complexities of the substantive results of the studies inspired by this approach. Indeed the chapters in the first part of this volume act in part as a critique of any simple reading of the home as expressive. Most of these chapters emphasize problems of contradiction and dissonance in the relationship between people and their homes. This becomes part of the explanation for the stress laid in those papers upon mobility and change. Other studies have shown the way the occupants themselves respond to their need for the home to represent both longer and short-term ideals by separating the home into two opposed units, for example the inalienable possession of the family lineage represented by the second, often rural, home in much of Europe as against the mere occupancy of the present family (see Chevalier 1998 for France) or the home reflecting the high speed of urban life as against the rural idyll (Hirsch 1992 for England). Where the state and commerce might favour a shift to the expression of modernism and change, this could be assimilated by populations who find ways of appropriating modernism within less disruptive and more inclusive agendas (see, for instance, Attfield 1997).

The chapters in the second part of this book contribute an extension of this growing realization that there are clear constraints to regarding the home as an expressive genre. Against the grain of an increasing emphasis upon what people are able to do with their homes, these chapters take up the opposite perspective of how far people are thwarted by the prior presence of their houses and the orders of their material culture. In addition they consider how people come to see their lives as formed through the influence of the home itself, and their role as serving in the reproduction of that historical legacy. If the house is accepted as something that reflects a long term or set of historical processes, then any present occupant has to contend not only with the agency of the previous occupants but increasingly with the house itself as an agent. As Birdwell-Pheasant and Lawrence-Zúñiga note (1999: 9), the degree to which the house becomes taken for granted accentuates rather than detracts from this effect.

In Chapter 6 I contend that there are times when we do indeed objectify our sense of the house possessing agency. This can be found in the traditional figure of the ghost within the haunted house. This act of projection anthropomorphizes our sense that the house may actually be a good deal older and have developed more 'personality' than its mere occupants. In coming to terms with the ghost that haunts the house the occupants have to acknowledge this history and its consequences for the present. The ghost of a haunted house is in effect the original 'estate agent'. This is the most extreme end of a sensibility that in more attenuated form 'haunts' most ordinary householders. In moving in and maintaining a home we have constantly to contend with the pre-given decorative and other ordering schemes of the house. Although we may seek to overthrow these, more often we develop a kind of negotiated compromise between that which is expressed by the house and that which we seek to express through the medium of the house. As such the house comes to occupy us as we come to occupy it, and, as the chapter concludes, what we may not be able to fully possess comes to some degree to possess us.

Hecht's study takes us from the implications of the longevity of the home itself to the longevity of persons. But the implications are quite similar. In contrast to an emphasis upon what people have done to their homes, Hecht presents us with an individual who has become increasingly conscious of what homes have done to her. Having become engaged as a museum volunteer with the task of illustrating history through the material culture of the home, she has come to reflect on her own legacy as the repository of the material objectifications of her own family history. This in turn leads her to see the successive homes she has lived in as central to the development of her own identity. Her biography is narrated as a sequence from the home of her childhood, which originally gave her (and remains as witness to her) continued identity as a working-class Scot. Her biography ends in her present house, which is almost as much a museum as is the actual museum where she works as a volunteer. This provides the backdrop to her present identity as the individual responsible for cultural reproduction by which the younger generation come to understand not just the meaning of the artefacts they see both in the museum and in her house, but also why they should continue to matter. The material culture of the home having served as the agency that gave her own identity is now used as the agent for transcending her life to become her legacy.

Part Three: Building Relationships

The final part exploits points made in the two previous parts and applies them to the central concern of anthropology with the home, which is its place in the development and reproduction of social relations. But precisely because of our emphasis on material culture, this relationship appears somewhat differently from its treatment within more conventional social anthropology. Within anthropology there has developed a considerable literature that attempts to mediate between the analysis of the house itself and that of the social relations of the home. If this literature is examined in detail, however, one finds that, in most cases, a direct relationship between the two is made secondary to a kind of triad, whereby the relationship between people and home is mediated by a third category such as the 'household' in most societies and the 'house society' in some tribal societies.

The household has been understood as a social rather than a physical entity, yet one that because of its stress on residence seems to implicate the house itself. It therefore contrasts with categories such as kinship and the family in according some weight to the physicality of the home in constituting social relations. For this reason the term household seemed to 'do the trick' of creating a non-reductionist approach to this relationship between the home and those who dwell there (see, for example, Netting, Wilk and Arnould 1984). In a similar vein the book *About the House* (Carsten and Hugh-Jones 1995) attempts to achieve the same result for tribal societies. The term 'household' tends to be used for the more restricted units of, for example, many European societies, but here the discussion is about what Lévi-Strauss has termed 'house societies', which seemed pertinent to larger systems of kinship that are present in South-East Asian and South American tribal societies in particular (although the original model was from European lineages). 'Household' mediates with the concept of family, but 'house society' mediates between the concept of lineage and the longevity of the site of residence.

In some ways, however, the construction of this triad whereby both home and social relations are mediated in their relationship by a third category, that of household and house society, has still led to a playing down of the materiality of the home and its attendant material culture. So, for example, although in their introduction Carsten and Hugh-Jones say they will pay attention to the architectural aspects of the home, this rarely happens in the essays that follow, where the house tends to appear as metaphor rather than substance. But the two previous parts of this book have shown why a focus on this materiality is itself critical to an analysis of the social relations of the home. Once one acknowledges the degree to which the home itself is both a site of agency and a site of mobility, rather than simply a kind of symbolic system that acts as the backdrop or blueprint for practice and agency, then the rewards of this focus upon material culture in trying to understand the social relations that pertain to the home become apparent. Birdwell-Pheasant and Lawrence-Zúñiga (1999: 1–7) also suggest that the materiality of the house can usefully mediate between the concepts of household and family.

Feminism has provided a complementary contribution in mediating our understanding of this basic relationship. Because feminist studies concentrated on the role of the housewife, there has been considerable research on activities such as food preparation (see DeVault 1991) and housework routines such as cleaning (Jackson and Moores 1995). Certainly, by looking at such routines and practices the material culture of the home is implicated, but there is a clear difference of degree between the explicit focus upon material culture within this volume and most previous feminist analysis. What the third part of this book accomplishes as a complementary addition to these feminist works is a sense of how this hybridity between social and material relations can be better achieved if the house is taken as a more equal partner. Of course the separation of this volume into three parts is in many ways artificial. The previous chapters in the volume mostly include the same attention to the detail of the material culture of the home and the subtlety of its place in those processes that also develop social relations.

Tan's chapter focuses upon one particular relationship, that between developing one's house and one's marriage. The argument follows from an insight of Bloch (1995) that in many 'house societies' the construction of the home is understood as both a reflection of and a medium for the construction of a marriage. Both are seen to begin as relatively insecure and fragile structures that gradually acquire solidity and foundations. The increasingly 'concrete' house and marriage thereby become the solid basis for the core task of reproduction. Tan starts with an exploration of the close correspondence between building a house and marriage within the non-Christian Paiwan (of Taiwan). But in the second half of the paper he demonstrates how under Christianity, although the close symbolic associations are often repudiated, what develops is a syncretic alignment with the equivalent ideals within Christianity where again building up a home and building up a marriage are seen as complementary aspects in the ideal of Christian domesticity. As a result Christian households may engage in practices that, for them, express Christian compassion such as showing forgiveness through giving away possessions, that while entirely compatible with Christian teaching, are not usually found in other Christian communities. They are, however, entirely comprehensible here in the light of the particular way the material culture of the house had already been seen as a medium of conjugal relations in non-Christian practices.

It is fascinating to contrast Tan's chapter with that of Drazin. In the case of Tan there is a transition between two relatively clear normative structures within which marriage and home building can be aligned. In the case of Drazin there might once have been such an alignment, but the last few generations have turned the establishment of normative culture itself into a struggle, so that what happens within the home is a process developed in direct negation to and often negotiation with what happens outside the home. The startling aesthetic contrast between the grey and crumbling concrete of Soviet-system blocks of flats with the emphasis on wooden furniture and infrastructure within their warm interiors, objectifies two histories: that of the public and the state on the one hand and a domestic situation that has tried to reconstitute itself in defiance of the constraints that were imposed.

The constraints may have changed from lack of products to lack of money, but they establish the degree to which, in the inside of the home, wood itself has become the objectification of care for the family. In the local context the appropriation of furniture from production to consumption signifies what the private household has been able to wrest from what has been historically an alienating state. Although the process within which care has been associated with furnishing is basic, the particular goals, for family and furnishing, that households strive for are much less certain. Drazin can observe how the criteria for success and display are themselves being reinvented in the new material circumstances of post-socialist society. We can perceive a struggle to re-link the wider idea of being Romanian with what remains of the normative behind such everyday practice of caring and furnishing; or we can see the recreation of Romanian norms within emerging routines of everyday domestic consumption. So if in the case of Tan we see the Paiwanese striving to develop practices that will objectify their ideals, in the case of Romania we see people formulating and negotiating normative orders that will build upon their practices.

This dichotomy between normative orders projected in this case as an ideal and the practice of domesticity becomes, in the final paper by Daniels, the central tension that pervades both the relationships of the household and their expression as material culture. The possibilities given by Daniels' title are delicious. Not only does her encounter with a series of rather ordinary Japanese home interiors make nonsense of the constant reification of an ur-Japanese aesthetic as though it is seamlessly embedded in everyday practice, but in a way this become symptomatic of this book's attempt as a whole to confront the 'neatness' of certain theoretical assumptions and show how we can ground ourselves in the complexities and contradictions of the ethnography but still emerge as theoretically ambitious.

Daniels first has to mark the ubiquity of the assumptions she confronts as emblematic within orientalism. She exposes the way this ideology made the house a foundation for similar assumptions about the aesthetic harmony of 'tidy' Japanese domestic relations. This leads to an ethnographic encounter in which she can reaffirm the close relationship between domestic interior arrangements and social relationships, but this time through the way they are being contested. The idealization of the tidy house is seen to be part of state as well as foreign stereotypes, such that feminism and other expressions of modernity have to contend with this same homology of material and social practice. As in so many of the contributions to this volume, a closing down of the ethnographic lens to focus on the finer detail of household material culture tells us a story about the conflicts and transitional state of domestic relationships that a 'landscape' shot that typifies most Japanese studies has tended to leave hazy and out of primary focus.

Concluding with Tan's and then Daniels' contributions creates one further argument against an assumption often made about the contemporary home. The stress on the problem of ethnographic work inside the home and the rise of privacy could have led to a conclusion that what was at issue was an aspect of 'Westerniza-tion' created by a simple transition from a public sphere to a private sphere. In Tan's chapter we do see a transformation from houses based around lineages to houses based on a more nuclear family, but as in his case of the Pastor there remains a more complex relationship between these spheres, because the interior decoration is intended in part for public display. If his chapter thereby suggests the need for studying the private sphere for insights into the public sphere, there is some symmetry with the chapter by Clarke, where the home is used as a mode for the imagination of the occupants' relationship to the public sphere whether or not many other people actually visit it. Nor is there some simple evolution from public to private. In the working-class homes Clarke was studying there has been a tradition of privacy that historical records show is certainly not a recent invention. Taking the book as a whole the most extreme examples of privacy come from Norway and Japan. In both cases this has much more to do with the longer historical trajectory of the particular regions. This is all quite contrary to any glib notion of privacy as a sign of Westernization.

Conclusion

What emerges as a collective conclusion from these chapters is a claim. We have shown that our focus on the fine-grained relationship between people and the material culture of the home tends to work, in the sense that it leads to powerful insights into the societies in question. This is at least in some measure because the people being studied are themselves playing out their relationships through the very same material culture and experiencing the same contradictions that emerge in our respective analyses. If home is where the heart is, then it is also where it is broken, torn and made whole in the flux of relationships, social and material. Obviously we do not claim to be alone here; there are many other exemplary studies for almost any region (such as Humphrey 1998; Buchli 1999 for Russia) that in a similar fashion pay attention to the materiality of homes both in relation to domestic relations and in articulation with wider forces such as states and commerce. Equally, there are other approaches to the home that complement rather than contradict those explored here, such as the vast literature on home ownership and renting, which on the whole we do not try to reproduce.

It will be evident, even from the summaries that have been given above, how dependent this volume has been upon ethnography, which largely takes place within the home itself. An anthropology that thinks that sensitivity about being too intrusive is demonstrated by remaining outside and respecting the distance of conventional social proxemics is a dead anthropology, that loses its humanity in the very moment that it asserts it in this claim to sensitivity. The life of anthropology comes from its insistence in seeing the world through perspectives we would never have even imagined if we had not forced ourselves into the site from which other people view their worlds. For this reason material culture studies that focus on the fine-grained developments in material and social relations of the home become once again the vanguard for contemporary anthropology. This vicarious route to the intimacy of relations may well be preferable for both informants and ethnographers to an approach that separates off social relations from the agency of the material worlds within which they occur. Instead of confronting people with questions about love and jealousy we are exploring with them the ways these are experienced as grounded in processes such as decorating and moving home.

I can attest from the approaches that are increasingly made to me that commercial and marketing research is becoming increasingly concerned to find the means for working inside the home, because this is as critical to topics such as budgeting, or e-commerce as it is to material culture. Such highly focused research will certainly increase in the future, but it is important that applied and commercially driven projects are complemented by the kind of academically driven studies that are represented by this volume. These are long-term studies that do not assume prior to fieldwork what any particular practice pertains to. A study of food did not expect to be about the mobility of identity, nor a study of soap in Romania to be about caring, nor a study of rice scoops in Japan to produce a paper on the untidy house. This is why this book does not study objects such as homes and take social relations as its context. It does not 'reduce' things to their correlations with prior social parameters such as gender, class and ethnicity. Rather, social and material divisions emerge to the degree that they appeared salient in the fieldwork. What is at stake then is not just the future of studies of material culture and the home. The centrality of the home to contemporary life means that we are concerned with the future of material culture studies and of anthropology more generally. Either to become a romantic elegy for claims to the lost authenticity of public life – in Sennett's (1976) terms The Fall of Public Man – or to become the only discipline that retains at its core the sense of humanity and empathy that comes from being in the presence of ordinary life at the place where it is increasingly lived.

References

Ardener, S. (ed.) (1981) *Women and Space: Ground Rules and Social Maps.* London: Croom Helm.

Attfield, J. (1997) 'Design as a practice of modernity: a case for the study of the coffee table in the mid Century Domestic Interior'. *Journal of Material Culture* 2/3: 267–89.

—— (2000) *Wild Things: The Material Culture of Everyday Life.* Oxford: Berg.

—— and P. Kirkham (1989) *A View from the Interior: Feminism, Women and Design History.* London: Women's Press.

Auslander, L. (1996) *Taste and Power*. Berkeley: University of California Press.

Birdwell-Pheasant, D. and D. Lawrence-Zúñiga (eds) (1999) *House Life: Space, Place and Family in Europe*. Oxford: Berg

Bloch, M. (1995) 'The resurrection of the house amongst the Zafimaniry of Madagascar'. In J. Carsten and S. Hugh-Jones (eds) *About the House*. Cambridge: Cambridge University Press.

Bourdieu, P. (1977) *Outline of a Theory of Practice*. Cambridge: Cambridge University Press.

—— (1990 [1970]) 'The Kabyle house or the world reversed'. In *The Logic of Practice*. Cambridge: Polity Press.

Bradley, R. (1996) 'Long houses, long mounds and Neolithic enclosures'. *Journal of Material Culture* 1: 239–56.

Brydon, I. and J. Floyd (1999) *Domestic Space: Reading the Interior in Nineteenth Century Britain and America*. Manchester: Manchester University Press.

Buchli, V. (1999) *An Archaeology of Socialism*. Oxford: Berg.

Carsten, J. and S. Hugh-Jones (eds) (1995) *About the House: Lévi-Strauss and Beyond*. Cambridge: Cambridge University Press.

Chapman, T. and J. Hockey (eds) (1999) *Ideal Homes?* London: Routledge.

Chevalier, S. (1998) 'From woollen carpet to grass carpet'. In D. Miller (ed.) *Material Cultures: Why some Things Matter*. Chicago: University of Chicago Press.

Cieraad, I. (ed.) (1999) *At Home: An Anthropology of Domestic Space*. Syracuse: Syracuse University Press.

Clammer, J. (1997) *Contemporary Urban Japan*. Oxford: Blackwell.

Comaroff, J. and J. Comaroff (1997) *Of Revelation and Revolution*, Vol 2. Chicago: University of Chicago Press.

Csikszentmihalyi, M. and E. Rochberg-Halton (1981) *The Meaning of Things: Domestic Symbols and the Self*. Cambridge: Cambridge University Press.

Davidoff, L. and C. Hall (1987) *Family Fortunes: Men and Women of the English Middle Class 1780–1850*. London: Hutchinson.

De Mare, H. (1999) 'Domesticity in dispute: a reconsideration of sources'. In I. Cieraad (ed.) *At Home: An Anthropology of Domestic Space*. Syracuse: Syracuse University Press.

DeVault, M. (1991) *Feeding the Family: The Social Organization of Caring as Gendered Work*. Chicago: University of Chicago Press.

Forty, A. (1986) *Objects of Desire*. London: Thames & Hudson.

Frykman, J. and O. Löfgren (1987) *Culture Builders: A Historical Anthropology of Middle-Class Life*. New Brunswick: Rutgers University Press.

Gell, A. (1986) 'Newcomers to the World of Goods'. In A. Appadurai (ed.) *The Social Life of Things*. Cambridge: Cambridge University Press.

Gewertz, D. and F. Errington (1999) *Emerging Class in Papua New Guinea*. Cambridge: Cambridge University Press.

Gullestad, M. (1984) *Kitchen Table Society: A Case Study of the Family Life and Friendships of Young Working-Class Mothers in Urban Norway.* Oslo: Universitetsforlaget.

—— (1992) *The Art of Social Relations: Essays on Culture, Social Action and Everyday Life in Modern Norway.* Oslo: Scandinavian University Press.

Halle, D. (1993) *Inside Culture: Art and Class in the American Home.* Chicago: University of Chicago Press.

Hirsch, E. (1992) 'The long term and short term of domestic consumption: an ethnographic case study'. In E. Hirsh and R. Silverstone (eds) *Consuming Technologies: Media and Information in Domestic Spaces.* London: Routledge.

Hodder, I. (1984) 'Burials, houses, women and men in the European Neolithic'. In D. Miller and C. Tilley (eds) *Ideology, Power and Prehistory.* Cambridge: Cambridge University Press.

Humphrey, C. (1998) 'The villas of the "New Russian": a sketch of consumption and cultural identity in post-Soviet landscapes'. *Focall* 30/31: 85–106.

Jackson, S. and S. Moores (eds) (1995) *The Politics of Domestic Consumption: Critical Readings.* London: Prentice Hall.

Knight, John (1998) 'Selling Mother's Love?' *Journal of Material Culture* 3/2: 153–75.

Löfgren, O. (1994) 'Consuming Interests'. In. J. Friedman (ed.) *Consumption and Identity.* Chur: Harwood Academic Press.

Lull, J. (ed.) (1988) *World Families Watch Television.* Newbury Park, CA: Sage.

Markham, A. (1998) *Life Online.* New York: Sage.

McKibben, Ross (1998) *Classes and Cultures: England 1918–1951.* Oxford: Oxford University Press.

Miller, D. (ed.) (1998) *Material Cultures: Why some Things Matter.* Chicago: University of Chicago Press.

—— (ed.) (2001) *Car Cultures.* Oxford: Berg.

—— and D. Slater (2000) *The Internet: An Ethnographic Approach.* Oxford: Berg.

—— P. Jackson, N. Thrift, B. Holbrook and M. Rowlands (1998) *Shopping, Place and Identity.* London: Routledge.

Moore, H. (1986) *Space, Text and Gender.* Cambridge: Cambridge University Press.

Morley, D. (1992) *Television Audiences and Cultural Studies.* London: Routledge.

Netting, R.McC., R.R. Wilk and E.J. Arnould (1984) *Households: Comparative and Historical Studies of the Domestic Group.* California: University of California Press.

Nippert-Eng, C.E. (1996) *Home and Work.* Chicago: University of Chicago Press.

Putnam, T. and C. Newton (eds) (1990) *Household Choices.* London: Middlesex Polytechnic and Futures Publications.

Rapport, N and A. Dawson (eds) (1998) *Migrants of Identity.* Oxford: Berg.

Sanders, J. (ed.) (1996) *Stud: Architectures of Masculinity*. Princeton: Princeton University Press

Schama, S. (1987) *The Embarrassment of Riches*. London: Fontana.

Segalen M. and B. De Wita (eds) (1993) *Chez Soi-Objets et decors: des creations familiales*. Autrement, série Mutations no. 137.

Sennett, R. (1976) *The Fall of Public Man*. Cambridge: Cambridge University Press.

Steedman, C. (1982) *The Tidy House*. London: Virago.

Tacchi, J. (1998) 'Radio textures: between self and others'. In D. Miller (ed.) *Material Cultures: Why some Things Matter*. Chicago: University of Chicago Press.

Tambiah, S. (1969) 'Animals are good to think with and good to prohibit'. *Ethnology* 8: 424–59.

Vom Bruck, G. (1997) 'A house turned inside out'. *Journal of Material Culture* 2: 139–72.

Weiner, J. (1991) *The Empty Place: Poetry, Space and Being among the Foi of Papua New Guinea*. Bloomington: Indiana University Press.

Wilk, R. (1984) 'Households in process: agricultural change and domestic transformation among the Kekchi Maya of Belize'. In R.McC. Netting, R.R Wilk and E.J. Arnould (eds) *Households: Comparative and Historical Studies of the Domestic Group*. Berkeley: University of California Press.

—— (1989) 'Houses as Consumer goods'. In H. Rutz and B. Orlove (eds) *The Social Economy of Consumption*. Lanham, MD: University Press of America.

Zukin, S. (1982) *Loft Living: Culture and Capital in Urban Change*. Baltimore: Johns Hopkins University Press.

Part I
Mobile Homes

–2–

The Aesthetics of Social Aspiration
Alison J. Clarke

The British boom in home improvement during the 1980s was associated, by many academics, with the broader conservatism and materialism of Thatcherite politics (Hall and Jacques 1983; Forrest and Murie 1984). Home ownership, considered as a petty capitalistic venture, was aligned directly with the demise of class consciousness, a view encapsulated in sociologist Alan Tomlinson's disdainful tone: 'Do it yourself, then. Build your own cultural environment. Thematize all your spare time activity. Express your familiarity with and ease in consumer culture by the choices you make in this sphere: and, also, with d-i-y [Do-It-Yourself home improvement], make some canny investment decisions' (Tomlinson 1990: 69). Sociologists and geographers alike have identified the increasingly privatized and home-bound condition of the working class as a symptom of powerlessness and alienation in the public realm and workplace (Marshall, Newby, Rose and Vogler 1988; Saunders 1990). In particular, such theories have highlighted the aspirant privatism of the post-war British working class as indicative of a shift 'away from a broadly based identification with work, and the issues and activities which stem from the workplace, towards greater home-centredness and self-identification with a domain of control which lies in the home and consumption' (Franklin 1989: 93).

The proliferation, from the mid-1990s onwards, of a range of home-improvement media suggests a continued shift towards privatized leisure and consumption in both western Europe and the US. From the mysticism of monthly feng shui advice journals (offering wealth and happiness through the rearrangement and decoration of household interiors) to the stencilling techniques of US home-making guru Martha Stewart, the transformation of the home as a site of aspiration abounds. The market for home-oriented lifestyle media has expanded several-fold over the last decade; in Britain, this phenomenon is epitomized by the pragmatism of television programmes, offering practical refurbishment tips to enhance the property value of owners' homes, and spin-off publications (Walton and Walton 1997, 1998). The diminishing use of professional painters and decorators as a class-wide service industry has been coupled with the increased availability of an expanded range of wallpaper, paint, stencils, design sources, tools and advice (Gershuny 1985). The friction between investing in the house as inalienable environment and realizable commodity value is an increasingly prominent feature of home ownership mediated largely through the mass consumption of visual and material culture: 'newspapers, magazines, catalogues, television and even the internet are part of the global marketplace where people now shop for the latest houses, furnishings, and ideas and values regarding home and family life' (Birdwell-Pheasant and Lawrence-Zúñiga 1999: 27). Homes and gardens are presented as transient aesthetic entities, requiring regular 'makeovers' in keeping with the vagaries of fashion (Bhatti and Church 2000).

Historically, the construction of the household as an expressive form has been associated with the consolidation and formation of middle-class identity, as described by Victoria de Grazia in *The Sex of Things:* 'the pattern of expenditure for the bourgeoisie reflected considerable individuality, especially with regards to socially strategic commodities such as home furnishings, decoration, and charity, even when the family fortunes were in decline' (de Grazia 1996:153–4). By the nineteenth century, the furnishing and decoration of the bourgeois domestic interior in Europe and the USA had taken on a new significance as a form of expressive cultural practice: 'As never before, families invested time, money and a burning interest in designing their domestic tableau, creating impressive landscapes and special atmospheres in room after room' (Frykman and Löfgren 1987: 126). The masculine pursuits of collecting and the feminine activities of home-crafts, indicative of bourgeois leisure, were displayed within a carefully articulated schema promoting the home as both 'showcase and shelter' and 'civilizing' space. The domestic sphere became increasingly understood as a moral endeavour as expressed by the author of a typical contemporary publication titled *Artistic Homes or How to Furnish Them with Taste* (1881): 'There can be but little doubt that the surroundings of our daily life are largely instrumental, not only in affording pleasant sensations. . . but in actually moulding our natures and characters in many important respects' (cited in Pacey 1989). The ornamentation, decoration and conviviality associated with the middle-class parlour epitomized the notion of home decoration as an expressive (if highly prescriptive) practice perpetuating bourgeois values of social aspiration, material comfort and lineage (Ames 1992; Grier 1988; Davidoff and Hall 1987). In contrast, working- and lower middle-class home making has been considered as a 'normative' and instrumental practice prompting, by the late nineteenth century, the scrutiny and intervention of State, government and social reformers (Lubbock 1995).

In Britain, by the first half of the twentieth century, government organizations such as the Design and Industries Association (DIA) used didactic displays to educate the mass consumer of the appropriate and 'modern' ways to furnish and decorate their homes using 'tasteful' and non-imitative styles in keeping with modernist ideologies. Social reformers, such as Elizabeth Denby, went as far as condemning specific material-culture forms, such as the three-piece suite and bedroom ensemble readily embraced by working-class couples of the 1930s, as indicative of their uneducated and restricted lifestyles (Morley 1990: 95). Similarly, Richard Hoggart in *The Uses of Literacy* (1957) identified the normativity of working-class home furnishing, in particular the arrangement and use of the three-piece suite, the occasional table and the bedroom set, as a consolidating element of class identity. While the stark normativity of lower-class consumption attracted the condemnation of design and social reformers, the overtly aspirational bent of celebratory events such as the *Daily Mail* Ideal Home Exhibition (an immensely popular annual exhibit featuring fantasy homes and the latest in modern gadgetry and home-decoration styles) attracted condemnation from both sides of the political field. Sponsored by a newspaper renowned for its female-dominated lower middle-class readership, the spectacle of the Ideal Home Exhibition challenged the positive aspects of class consolidation identified by figures such as Hoggart while simultaneously undermining the home as a place of enduring bourgeois values. Like suburbia, the Ideal Home Exhibition offered a vision of modernity, mass consumption and class aspiration that caused much disquiet in academic, high-cultural quarters (Oliver, Davis and Bentley 1981; Ryan 2000).

The modern household, then, defined as a site of provisioning, social relations and economic management, holds a vital historical position in relation to the modern State and class politics (de Grazia 1996: 153). This chapter uses ethno-graphic examples to explore how the increasing emphasis on home decoration as a practice, its intersection with class, gender and ethnicity, is related to the construction of ideal and actual contemporary social worlds. It does not simplistic-ally suggest that the external abstract forces such as 'class' and 'the State' are countered through the appropriation of domestic environments. Rather, it considers 'home' as a process, as opposed to an act of individual expressivity, in which past and future trajectories (inseparable from external abstractions such as 'class') are negotiated through fantasy and action, projection and interiorization. The house-holders in this study are representative of the broader section of informants in that their home making marks a particular stage in the life cycle of the family (and the individual women concerned). Whether physically or mentally transforming or transposing their homes, the process in which they are engaged is socially aspirant, not merely in terms of accumulating and articulating cultural capital (Bourdieu 1979), but in terms of the ambitions and projections of ideal social relations.

The study is based on ethnographic research concerning the provisioning of households in north London. The initial stages of the ethnography were shared with Daniel Miller (whose work concerned formal modes of shopping [Miller 1998]) and combined preliminary interviews and participant observation involving seventy-six households. This section of the research arises from a separate aspect of the ethnography that considered a range of informal, non-retail or alternative means of acquisition including home decoration, second-hand purchase, home-made goods, gift giving and mail-order catalogue and Internet shopping (Clarke 1998, 2000). The ethnographic site in north London consisted of a street referred to as Jay Road, with a cross-section of housing: 1960s blocks of council (State owned) flats and maisonettes; semi-detached 1930s homes; Edwardian rented and small owner-occupied maisonettes as well as larger Victorian family houses occupied predominantly by middle-class families on adjoining streets. The ethnic groups found in the area and included in the study range from those of Greek Cypriot, West African, Jewish, Asian, South American, West Indian and Irish descent. The main street in the study was selected because it lacked any outstanding features although it does have an array of particularly mixed housing types. In short, the street is typical of north London in being cosmopolitan but manifestly ordinary.

Day Dreaming Ideal Homes: The Process of Envisaging

Home decorating in north London takes on numerous forms. Some homes on the street have remained decoratively unchanged for over fifteen years, while others are altered yearly to match, for example, pieces of new furniture purchased by a householder. The birth or death of a family member instigates many redecorating schemes. Similarly, 'moving in' to a home frequently warrants decorating as part of the process of cleansing the property of its previous owners' presence. Occupants also embark on home decorating in preparation for passing on their home to a new owner or marking particular seasonal events, such as Christmas and spring. Many households take part in sporadic bouts of home decoration directly linked to material or perceived changes in household circumstance (for example, a financial windfall or, as with some elderly residents, in preparation for death). Home decoration, though tied to key life cycles and events, is the principal means by which members of households attempt to invert, reinvent or perpetuate their material worlds. The physical act of 'decorating' requires the household to draw on (or negate) both traditional and contemporary cultural, social, aesthetic and technical knowledge to varying degrees. But crucially, it also requires a process of envisaging or imagining even at its most basic level.

Walking along Jay Road, in the shadows of blocks of council flats, maisonettes and Victorian terraced houses, there are Devonshire fisherman's cabins, baronial mansions and rose-covered country cottages that thrive in the imaginations of the street's householders. These imaginings are not merely 'dream homes', plucked from the pages of lifestyle magazines and used as a blueprint for home decorating choices, rather they act as conceptual and value-laden configurations informing or undermining everyday household decisions. While the single occupant of a spacious three-bedroom 1930s semi-detached house on Jay Road conjures up a fantasy seaside residence to explain her taste in fabrics, the occupant of a cramped one-bedroom maisonette on the other side of the street talks of the garden she would have at 'her' rambling imaginary home in southern Ireland.

'Ideal homes' are not just escapist fantasy spaces conjured up to deal with the limitations of the materiality of 'real' homes, but rather are used as measures or as proactive forces that intermittently meld with or mock the reality of lived experience. One of the research techniques used in the ethnography was to ascertain the 'biography' and provenance of particular objects in the home (Appadurai 1986). In this way, informants provided narratives regarding the ways in which items were obtained and came to be in the place they presently occupied. As well as tracing how people came to own these goods this approach also highlighted subsequent issues over how these goods should be consumed or understood in the longer term. Jane's description of one of her favourite objects, placed prominently in the living room of her one-bedroom owner-occupied Victorian flat, reveals how material culture simultaneously embodies the ideal and the actual:

> I never use that massive candelabra, hardly ever, it drips all over the floor but I loved it, I thought it was brilliant because I always fancied that one day I would live in the sort of house that had a baronial hall and I would have this massive candlestick or I would be walking through this huge house waving this candlestick, but its never happened, its just sat there quite sadly. I did trot it out for a dinner party but, as I said, all the wax dripped on the floor.

Even informants with the economic and cultural means at their disposal to realize their 'ideal' home are confronted by the lag between the 'ideal' and 'actual'. Joanna and Ben, two professional designers living on two full-time incomes, had originally envisaged a minimalist décor for their marital home and decorated in a stark modernist style. A decade after their marriage, however, collections of china, floral upholstery and a traditional Welsh dresser haunt them as markers of how, to quote Ben, their 'taste fell apart'. Despite their earliest attempts at living out a decorative scheme deemed most representative of the couple and their peer group, the house and its objects have taken on an agency of their own:

> We made a wedding list which involved setting up a home, as we needed stuff. Cutlery you know, we were very specific then – but it just shows how our taste changed – or how our taste fell apart – because we had this very specific Danish Cutlery from Arne Jacobsen and we wanted eight sets but we managed to get five [laughing] we gave up because they were too expensive. We have a table cloth that Polly got especially, it's white damask she got it from Liberty's [designer department store] – we wanted something – well at that time we did a lot of entertaining for friends – you know suppers and things, and we just wanted something crisp and clean. But we don't do much entertaining now.

These 'ideal homes' conjured up by middle-class home owners, are not just trivial fantasies about a perceived aesthetic style or associated social aspiration, rather they offer an idealized notion of 'quality of life' and an idealized form of sociality. Furthermore, these daydreams directly inform the construction, provisioning and aspirations of the lived home, allowing the occupants to begin to actualize beyond the limitations of their particular domesticity.

The late 1990s proliferation of publications and television programmes dealing with aspects of interior and garden design have drawn heavily on the fantasy element of home-making as a crucial aspect of its newly valorized status. The period of ethnographic study (1994–7) on which this paper is based coincided with a visible increase in the media, particularly in the form of prime-time television programmes, directly addressing issues of home decoration as a leisure pursuit. In a particularly popular series, named *Changing Rooms*, couples (friends or neighbours) swap houses and, with the aid of a professional interior designer and 'handy man', set to work redesigning and redecorating a room nominated by the householders and envisaged by the friends. The weekly programme places design and decoration firmly within the context of social and friendship (as opposed to kinship) relations. Each couple is limited to a tight schedule of forty-eight hours in which to transform the other's rooms. At the end of this hectic period they offer back the redecorated rooms as gifts to each other; for the refurbished interiors meld imagination, caring, labour and, ideally, a taste consensus generated through the friendship. As well as providing DIY tips and practical information the excitement of the programme revolves around the risk of allowing good friends or neighbours to potentially destabilize their relationships by completely misinterpreting each other's tastes and fantasies, or worse still, blatantly implementing their own. Couples are led blindfolded back to their own residences and filmed taking in with pleasure, shock or dismay the other couple's decorative scheme. More often than not, couples are seen accepting each other's designs with pleasure, suppressed shock or good grace. For they are making a direct exchange of each other's homes, taste knowledges and aesthetic fantasies mediated by design experts.

In contemporary Britain, then, the representation of home decorating as a widely accessible, playful and celebratory leisure pursuit has become commonplace but it remains implicitly tied to property ownership. In May 1998, a television viewer made an official complaint of discrimination (enthusiastically followed up by the tabloid press) against the BBC (British Broadcasting Corporation) charging that *Changing Rooms* had never featured a council or State-rented home in the full four years of its transmission. The production team defended themselves by arguing that, to date, no volunteers from State housing had offered their homes for interior redecoration.

Whether or not there is any truth in the producer's claim of mass antipathy towards home decoration in British council estates, there clearly remains a strong cultural assumption regarding the relationship between middle-class home ownership and home decoration as an expressive practice. While the middle-class home is seen as a place of fantasy making and fashionability, the notion of normative working-class home furnishing prevails (Gurney 1999). By contrast the following section focuses on the decoration of State-designated homes, namely a council housing estate in north London, named Sparrow Court, in order to place the home-making activities of its occupants in the context of a local and class-specific housing culture. Do the inhabitants of State housing use home decorating any less than their middle-class counterparts as an activity of creativity, day-dreaming and expressivity? In a strictly delineated, State-designed environment, where the interior and exterior world of the households is standardized and regulated by an external entity (the council/State) the ethnography goes on to reveal the ways in which the occupants appropriate, interpret and generate agency through their standardized spaces. In so doing, it challenges the understanding of home decoration and consumption as a merely expressive or normative activity. Rather, the interior worlds of these households, although they may remain to all intents and purposes physically private, are used as projections of very real relations with the larger external world.

Sparrow Court: Behind Lace Curtained Windows

Sparrow Court council estate was built in the mid-1960s and is situated along one side of Jay Road opposite a row of late Victorian terraced maisonettes and 1930s semi-detached houses. Although the estate is an integral part of the street there is a vivid conceptual divide between the mainly owner-occupied properties on the other side of the road and Sparrow Court. Organized in three-storey blocks of approximately thirty units as it is, access to the upper stories of the estate is made by ascending a central stairwell leading to an open balcony, running to the right and left, overlooked by the kitchen windows of each unit. This relatively narrow balcony with open railings is the only thoroughfare, and it allows little room for external storage, decoration or individual exterior customization of flats.

The block of housing is easily identifiable as State housing. It has uniform green/blue PVC doors and standardized external fittings, but it is a relatively low-density, well-maintained and neighbourly housing arrangement with an ethnically diverse range of households ranging from five-children families to single elderly-person households. It is common for neighbours in Sparrow Court to recognize and greet each other, but this is usually the limit of their intimacy. Despite this semblance of community and the comparatively small scale and green setting of the housing block, inhabitants view the estate as an ostensibly urban dwelling with the associated problems of theft and the protection of privacy.

Only in exceptional circumstances do neighbours actually see the contents of each other's homes. The ability to contain 'domestic dramas' within the walls of individual households is considered paramount for the smooth running of everyday life on the estate. Incidents that involve the spectacle of police intervention generate notable exceptions and warrant widespread inter-household communication. Rumours and gossip endure for several years. Consequently, unless a household is fearless of ostracism, maintenance of privacy becomes paramount. In this sense a form of conservatism, which undermines liberal individual self-expression associated with middle-class home decoration, prevails. The notion of 'the neighbours' acts as a form of 'super-ego' through which the estate is controlled (Miller 1988).

Estates such as Sparrow Court are suspended between a constant tension of privacy and sociality that impacts on the broader moral economy of households (for contrast see Gullestad (1986) for the actual sociability of Norwegian house-wives where the home is constantly 'primed' for potential neighbourly visits). Suzy, a mother in her late thirties, consciously maintains an aloofness from her neighbours. Her husband Jim, who is out working most of the day, views the boundaries of his home more protectively than Suzy who spends a considerable amount of her time alone in Sparrow Court;

> Jim is one of those people who likes to keep himself to himself and he doesn't like to interfere in anybody's life or them interfere in his but I'm more like, I'm not saying gossipy but I have a chat and I like talking to people. I invite people round for a coffee sometimes and he'll say, 'what did you invite her in for? You have her in every week.' But I say, 'I'm here half the time on my own!'.

The negotiation of living inside and outside, for retaining autonomy and maintaining sociality, is a tentative and on-going process particularly for women raising children on the estate. While it is unusual for adult neighbours to speak to one another, let alone be welcomed into each other's flats, it *is* deemed acceptable for children to congregate on the estate and occasionally enter each other's homes in the summer months. But even this can cause tension. Lola, a new tenant of South American origin on the lower floor of the block, has two daughters aged seven and eleven who play with the daughters of a next-door-but-one neighbour. Lola was initially happy to see the girls making friends with their neighbours and 'fitting in' even though she admitted to having little in common with the girls' Irish mother. However, after an incident in which the neighbour's children 'stole' toys and helped themselves to large amounts of drinks and provisions from the refrigerator, Lola is reluctant to be 'taken advantage of'. Now the daughters are dissuaded from playing in the public area at the front of the flat and their parents have purchased a swing for private use in their own small back garden.

There is a clear paradox in terms of the sociality aspired to by most of the residents and the actual sociality of their private domains. In exceptional circumstances there is a limited amount of public sociality though this may be heavily discouraged by spouses wary of protecting their own reputations and privacy. Jenny, despite her normal reserve feels justified in getting involved in neighbourly incidents on the estate much to the consternation of her husband:

> If something happened everyone would be out and I would go out and he would say, 'don't go out Jenny keep your nose out of it, stay in!' And I'd be peeping through the keyhole then somebody would come and tell me 'oh did you hear that last night?' and I'd say 'well I heard it but I didn't see'. Then they'll start telling me and I'll say 'oh terrible'. And these could be people that I've never spoken to before but they'll come and kind of tell me, so yeah, you get to know people through the gossip.

Although households are separated by thin walls, and literally built one on top of the other, the layout of the flats and the positioning of the windows make it impossible for passers-by to casually glance inside a tenant's flat. Despite this and the studied distancing from each other's affairs (with the exception of overtly public incidents) informants frequently try to envisage the interiors of one another's homes. The flats in Sparrow Court do not vary from a standardized layout of rooms, but this seems to add to, rather than detract from, neighbourly interest in specific individual's interpretation of household space, as revealed in the informants' following conversational extracts:

> Yeah the girl next door, have you seen it? She's done her loft and she sews up there and everything. She's boarded it all out. Her boyfriend did it before he went to Africa. . . but mine is twice as big as hers, it covers the whole flat

> Well, she's got two kids cos' I think the little one's room is there [pointing to neighbour's flat above] and they moved their living room to the big bedroom as far as I can tell.

> Well she had a big sofa and chairs moved in from the catalogue [mail-order purchase], and her washing machine was out on the landing so I think they're having a clear out.

Despite this interest in neighbours' private domains there is very little in the way of formal or informal sociality conducted in each others' homes. Mail-order catalogues might be passed from door to door for shared perusal but it is rarely anticipated that neighbours will step beyond each other's thresholds.

Getting your House in Order: Strategies for Sociality and Aspiration

The isolation and oppression of the domestic sphere is a familiar aspect of feminist discourse regarding the home (Oakley, 1976). Similarly, women's historical relation to 'home' as the focus of social reproduction and the role of their labour and emotional investment within it is well documented (DeVault 1991; Madigan and Munro 1983; Franklin 1990). How, if at all, do women appropriate this potentially oppressive space called 'home', as subjects in their own right? How do women with comparatively limited resources identify and mobilize their aspirations as individuals and mothers through the aesthetic construction of home? The following case studies focus on the distinctiveness of the home decorating activities of three women bringing up families on low incomes in Sparrow Court. They highlight the ways in which home decorating and interior decoration are used to establish relations with an outside and ideal social world. Rather than construct their homes as 'havens' these households use 'home', and its provisioning, to project themselves beyond their immediate surroundings. The informants share identical spatial layout. Their flats comprise an entrance hall leading to a central living room, kitchen, bathroom and two or three bedrooms.

All three households have a steady but minimal income supplemented by sporadic cash injections from entrepreneurial activity or members of family outside the immediate household. But, as Sandra Wallman's pioneering study of urban households in south London revealed, economic measures of capital, land and labour do not alone explain the diversity of households in industrial societies and the range of resources they deploy:

> The livelihood of a London household involves all kinds of work. It depends on the achievement of a sense of identity and belonging; on its ability to differentiate between us and them in apparently transient and impersonal urban settings; and on its capacity to manage social relationships and information, as much as it depends on informal economic organisation and on some member of the household having a job in the formal economy. (Wallman 1984: 23)

While Wallman treats consumption as a by-product of employment and services rather than as an integral or productive aspect of household resourcing, in the following case studies, consumption, in the form of home decorating is seen as a focal point, rather than a 'reflection', of the construction and negotiation of 'household philosophies'. Historical narratives and future trajectories, revealed through the ethnographic detail of home-decoration practice, highlight the home as process.

1. Kelly: 'A Man about the House'

The first case study considers the role of home decoration in the life of a woman running a household as a single mother. Aged around forty years old, Kelly relies on social welfare and sporadic cash supplements from her ex-partner, casual work and occasional entrepreneurial activity. She has rented her three-bedroom flat on the Sparrow Court council estate for over ten years and lives there with her two children aged seven and fifteen years. Kelly has no savings and would only ever be able to move house by taking part in the council-housing exchange scheme, which would be unlikely to benefit her because her flat is extremely large and well situated in comparison to other council properties in the borough. Her ex-partner, the father of her children, makes very occasional visits to the family's home (he now lives abroad) but he generally acts as an absent but much-loved father figure. Towards the end of the three-year span of the ethnography his visits had decreased dramatically and after several years' work as the sole childcarer Kelly has begun to reconsider the direction and future of her own life, as well as her children's. As both children are settled at local schools Kelly has become determined to pursue a new social life. As a first-generation black British woman she has relatives in the West Midlands and Jamaica. Her older sister, whom she stays in contact with by telephone, is a solicitor. She does not regularly meet any members of her extended family, and she moved to London more than fifteen years ago when she met her ex-partner. Kelly openly seeks to detach herself from what she describes as her 'traditional Jamaican working-class roots' and considers herself middle class even though, unlike her sister, she has no formal college education or qualifications. In this context, several years ago Kelly changed her Christian name from what she considered to be an 'old-fashioned' form to a more suitable and trendy version more indicative of her own self-image.

For Kelly, then, a woman all too aware of the constraints of externally imposed definitions, aspiration is an empowering concept. Despite her comparatively friendly relations with neighbours, her reliance on State housing, and the stigma associated with council estates is a constant source of unease for Kelly, which she counters through her interior-design schemes. Kelly last fully decorated her flat in 1989 and describes it as an 'oasis of tranquility'. Situated on the upper storey of Sparrow Court at the point furthest from Jay Road it is protected from the noise of passing traffic. Although Kelly is conscious of her flat as a council property she consistently counterbalances her antipathy towards Sparrow Court with the 'specialness' of her specific flat and its interior design. In order to feel confident about the prospect and ambition of leaving behind her home of over ten years by meeting a new partner, she goes through a process of re-amelioration regarding her flat and prepares to spring clean and refurbish the living room:

> Honestly I mean even when it's hot outside it's cool in here. It's just so nice in the winter I mean it's not that cold I can economize on bills heating and that, but if I can find myself someone... I'm going out now because I'm going to find myself a partner. Yeah this is what it's all about!

Kelly stands apart from other informants in the street due to the overwhelming enthusiasm she expresses for formal principles of interior decoration. Her living room has a white fitted carpet, white walls, a white leather three-piece suite and a mirrored rear wall which, she says, is used to accentuate a 'monochrome feeling'. She made the rouched curtains herself, 'before everyone else had them', in shiny pale pink using exclusive cut-price designer fabric from a friend working in a prestigious fabric shop in the West End. Previously, the room had been decorated in an even more extreme monochromatic style with a black ceiling:

> Yes it looks incredible [with a black ceiling] it's amazing it looks so different you wouldn't believe it's the same room and the carpet was a grey with it. It had black in it, it wasn't plain but it wasn't a pattern, anyway everything else was white. I had a white suite but the same kind of colours because most designers work with black and white [the effect] is really funny, strange.

Although the living room is the largest single space in the flat, which she shares with her two children, it is very much designated and decorated as an adult space. A large coffee table, a gift from Kelly's ex-partner, with a bevelled glass top, chinoiserie engraving and Egyptianesque legs stands in the centre of the room. In the corner an ornate flower stand features a climbing plant. A bookcase hidden around the corner from the doorway in a recess holds a pile of *Hello!* photo-gossip magazines, the stereo system, paperbacks and a selection of school and family photographs. The room has a palatial feel of relaxed and modern luxury. There are no toys or children's items present.

Kelly sees the room as an expression of her talents as a designer, the one room she has managed to completely redecorate in her 'own taste' according to sound decorative principles since she moved to Sparrow Court. While expressing dismay at the state of her unfinished kitchen (she paid the next-door neighbour to install shelves last winter but still has not finished decorating) Kelly views her living room as a testament to her 'know-how' and individual artistic flair. She also couches the significance of the room in spiritual terms:

> most people wouldn't think of doing a room like this because it could be clinical. When it was just done it just looked so therapeutic. Colours are really important we take it for granted but it really is important about how we feel about things, you know, and so most of these colours together could look clinical but it's funny it just opens it up and makes it look airy.

Unfortunately, the 'purity' of the room has more recently been marred by 'wear and tear' and the decorative scheme has been turning from white to off-white. Due to her extremely restricted income Kelly intends to refurbish the room 'on a shoe string', making white Velcro-attached throw covers for the suite and hiring an industrial vacuum cleaner to clean the carpet.

The white, spatial living room of Kelly's flat stands in stark contrast to the clutter of the rest of the house. The other rooms have been left unaltered since moving to the flat over ten years earlier. The children have attached posters to their bedroom walls but Kelly points out that they are still waiting to decorate these rooms. The bathroom also remains unchanged since the beginning of the tenancy and Kelly is concerned about a rising-damp patch in the corner. Rather than rely on the council to deal with such problems Kelly waits until her ex-partner makes one of his sporadic visits and hopes that he will take on some home-improvement tasks. She has occasionally 'borrowed' her next-door neighbour's husband, to move heavy household items, but is weary of over-stretching this relationship. Without 'having a man about the house' Kelly has confined her efforts to the living room, and her effort to spring clean and refurbish the living room coincides with a determined decision on Kelly's part to find a new partner:

> I've just got myself together I've started going out again and if I go out I'd like to entertain, right? So if I start [decorating] then I feel comfortable when I go out. It's no good projecting this image and then you invite people back and 'oh!' [feigns shocked disappointment] because I hate pretending. When I decorated three years ago I didn't even finish the kitchen so I've got that to do, the bathroom and everything and then I'll feel comfortable about myself. I've got to take them down [looking at the curtain pelmets] and clean everything.

Kelly is detached from her extended family but has a large network of friends across London. Several years ago she began a dress-designing company with a best friend. They turned their own experience making clothes in the home into a made-to-measure 'couture clothes' business. Specializing in glamorous party dresses the two women rented a small shop and used contacts at fabric shops to support their enterprise. Despite a certain amount of success the enterprise folded when her business partner 'found herself a nice rich man friend' and left the shop. Since then Kelly has intermittently used her home dressmaking skills to make one-off party dresses for paying friends and contacts.

As well as refurbishing her white, spacious living room, for the possibility of increased home entertainment, Kelly has begun to make a range of short and clingy 'club' dresses for dancing. Browsing through *Hello!* magazine (a popular photographic gossip publication) she picks out designs that she finds potentially flattering and adapts them to her own taste. She has also installed a miniature trampoline for home-based exercise in order to improve her muscle tone. The design of her new made-to-measure dresses (the refurbishment of her body) and the cleaning of her white living room mark the beginning of her self-conscious pursuit of a life outside Sparrow Court.

Alison J. Clarke

Kelly is openly instrumental in pursuing her new life. She is quite happy, for example, to date men she considers inappropriate as long-term partners in order to gain access to a new group of friends and escape the limitations of life as a single mother in Sparrow Court. While Kelly's flat acts as a testament to her artistic home-making skills, getting 'her house in order' would offer a springboard to a new life – ideally a home with a garden for the children, and a 'man around the house'. Kelly's aspirations are underpinned by imaginings, that manifest themselves in the decoration and refurbishment of the household and ultimately have real implications.

2. Lola: Assimilation and Aspiration in 'Bring a Bottle' Culture

Lola, her husband and three children share exactly the same layout of rooms as their neighbour Kelly in their three-bedroom flat in Sparrow Court. They are comparatively new residents and after living in the property as council tenants for a year took the option of purchasing the flat by taking on a large mortgage. This home marks, for Lola and her husband, a major life transition. Prior to living in Sparrow Court they shared a multiple-occupancy house with several other immigrant families in Camden, London. When the couple first arrived in the UK they had few possessions with which to construct a home; 'When I came from Chile I didn't bring any special things just my clothes and bed linen as I didn't know where I was going to sleep and I decide [sic] to bring those.'

Over a ten-year span Lola and her husband have moved from sleeping on friends' floors, to bringing up their new babies in communal homes, to sharing a co-op house, to renting a council flat that has finally become 'their own home'. This process has involved decisions, conscious and otherwise, over the extent of their Anglicization. By moving to Sparrow Court they have severed many of their ties with their ethnic community which initially facilitated their lives in a new host country. Although they regularly attend Chilean party events their decision to make Sparrow Court their permanent home has had direct consequences for their everyday social lives, as Lola points out: 'None of my friends live around here – none of them. I don't know any Chileans living around here. I say hello to the neighbours and that but we are not really friends – my friends live south of London or at Camden.'

Lola is a full-time house parent and, except for occasional visits to friends' homes at weekends, spends each day at Sparrow Court alone while her children attend local Catholic schools. Since moving to the area her husband, Philipe, who works in south London, has had to work longer hours to increase his training as an electrician and earn more money to cover new living costs. Initially he spent most weekends studying but more recently spends an increasing amount of time involved in home-improvement projects. It is principally Lola, then, who has become the member of the family responsible for acquiring information about local amenities and for making friends on the estate. Lola is not at all confident in this position. She is reluctant to leave the house alone and limits her provisioning to one weekly shopping trip to the supermarket. Although Lola's children are becoming increasingly involved in school and social activities (such as attending friends' birthday parties) Lola herself remains relatively isolated.

While the children gain confidence in their new social groups, their parents work on transforming their home, and through the negotiation of objects and styles struggle to make an appropriate home for their first generation Chilean/British children. The children instruct their parents in the mores and nuances of British taste and culture, which they bring home daily from their peers and apply when flicking through the pages of furnishing catalogues together. Lola and her husband mediate their children's new values and tastes and try to combine, through the provisioning and decoration of the home, some version of Anglo-Chilean identity.

In this sense, the children become the driving force behind Lola's and her husband's most recent spate of home decoration. Unlike their neighbour Kelly, the couple cares little for their living room or its potential for home entertainment. While their Chilean friends frequently host extravagant house parties, the Santoses, aware of the importance of 'not upsetting the neighbours' or drawing undue attention to themselves in Sparrow Court, feel that such festivities are an aspect of culture they left behind in their ethnic community in Camden along with the associated social relations. Now 'out of the circuit' Lola explains that in her own culture the home would be decorated and furnished almost exclusively through gifts from friends and family rather than through private consumption. Similarly, the English 'bring a bottle' culture (whereby a guest is expected to make a contribution to their host's hospitality) is anathema to Chilean sociality and hospitality:

> If I had house parties I would receive lots of gifts but I can't. The Chileans are always having houseparties to early in the morning – but now they are learning they must hire a hall or a place because of the noise. They play the music very loud and until 5 o'clock in the morning and they have trouble with the neighbours so now they hire a place. Chileans like parties and they spend a lot of money and they invite you and give you food and you don't have to buy anything like an English party where you bring a bottle – not Chileans they spend hundreds.

The living room, the most public room, has changed little since the Santoses arrival at the flat three years earlier, even though they are buying the property through the 'right to buy' scheme. There are dust patches on the walls where the previous occupants hung their pictures. It contains only an ageing television, a makeshift table and two pieces of flimsy garden furniture. There are no comfortable seats and few ornaments. Lola disassociates herself from many of the objects in this room, as they are 'hand-me downs' from a series of other Chilean families setting up home in Britain. In a complete inversion of Kelly's home it is the private rooms, in particular the children's bedrooms, which have received maximum decorative attention.

While the living room has an air of neglect and aesthetic indifference, on entering the children's bedrooms one is struck by the immaculate, 'show-home' finish of newly decorated and refurbished rooms. The wall-to-wall fitted carpets have been replaced by shining wood-effect laminate. The bedroom doors have been removed and re-hinged to allow room for hand-made customized louvred cupboards. The bed linen matches a set of stencilled toy boxes and the walls are covered with bright wallpaper co-ordinated with pretty swagged curtains in modern plaid fabric.

In the bathroom the entire bath suite has been replaced by a large walk-in shower. Like the bedrooms, the bathroom features hand-made cabinets crafted by Philipe. The windows have been fitted with double-glazing and ceramic tiles have replaced the linoleum flooring. Gradually, then, beginning with the children's rooms and bathroom, the flat is being overhauled and modernized in a style most appropriately described as modern European.

The Santoses want their children to have opportunities equivalent to or better than their English peers and are very aware of their own children's perception of deprivation (the older child, for example, complains that English families all own cars). This move towards a more materially comfortable lifestyle has to be weighed tentatively against a loss of core 'Chilean values' as perceived by the parents. Since they embarked on the refurbishment of their home the girls have become, Lola believes, unappreciative of the 'value of things': 'We just bought a new bedroom suite and Susannah [the eldest child] started saying she wanted this she wanted that. I told her, I said "this is the first piece of new furniture I've had in fifteen years of marriage, things just don't come to you like that".'

Their newly decorated house is defiantly non-traditional British, with its non-carpeted floors, walk-in shower room and café-style kitchen. But it also defies the lavishness or 'Dynasty style' Lola associates with her Chilean friends in Camden. Rather they have created a metropolitan style that brings together homecrafts (cabinetry, home sewing, hand painting) and modern design styles. Although much of the furniture is brand new, Philipe customizes the items, including especially designed cupboards and lamps for the children's rooms, and Lola makes the bed linen and curtains herself from Ikea fabric. While Philipe is solely responsible for home improvement, Lola spends much of her time at home adapting patterns from women's magazines to make linen items for the home and the children. This home is indeed a labour of love.

The Santoses, while steadfastly focused on the significance of their own home, are largely unaware of its meaning within the broader context of property value in the area. Home decorating between the normativity of two disparate cultures may have undermined their expenditure as a viable financial investment, particularly as the property is problematized by its ex-local authority status. Within the British housing market, to remove a traditional bathroom suite is, for example, likely (according to popular wisdom) to alienate potential buyers and diminish the value of a property by several thousand pounds. Similarly, the home's bright modern style, incorporating non-traditional surfaces and non-neutral colours, contradicts the perceived wisdom of maintaining neutral tones (such as 'magnolia' and 'beige') to enhance resaleability. Despite the major aesthetic and structural changes made to the home, which firmly delineate it as a non-State property, the Santoses have not necessarily maximized their very limited economic resources (in terms of resaleability). Neither is this their imperative. Rather their home and its improvement becomes the material context for an envisaged aim of family and a new sociality. Despite the diminishing ties to their ethnic community the Santoses are not merely undergoing a process of assimilation into British culture, with its crudely reciprocal 'bring-a-bottle' sociality. Rather, Lola orchestrates a carefully managed syncretism where 'home-making' operates as the key form of identity construction easing the way of her first generation British-Chilean children into their new social worlds.

3. Sharon: 'The Creative Home and the Ideal of Mothering'

Sharon and her partner David have two younger children and a teenager who has left home to live with his grandmother (following a family argument). They are both in their early forties. They have an identical space to that of Kelly and Lola with a large living room, medium-size kitchen and three bedrooms. They are situated on the upper storey of the block. The family are very settled in their home, and Sparrow Court in general, having lived in the flat for over fifteen years. Unlike many of the families on the estate they use their garden plot (situated some distance for the dwelling) regularly as a place to keep the pet rabbit and hang a hammock in the summer. Their children are well known on the estate as they frequently play outside. The couple rent their flat and live largely on Dave's casual income as a part-time painter and decorator.

As in their neighbour Kelly's flat, the kitchen is the least decorated room, serving as a place of functional tasks rather than aesthetic interest or coherence. The living room is the centre of the home. It contains a deep, green velveteen three-piece suite, a worn shag-pile carpet, a large television/home entertainment centre, wall display units and cupboards, a dining table and four chairs, and an enormous American juke box. On the living-room wall, as well as pictures acquired from car-boot sales, are old sepia photographs of Dave's great-grandparents and elderly West Indian relatives displayed in a prominent, symmetrical composition. As

Sharon has become estranged from her own mother, Dave's family have become the closest extended kin. She frequently expresses love and admiration for her mother-in-law who has been teaching her traditional feminine skills that she did not acquire herself as a child, such as home dressmaking.

Since buying her first sewing machine three years ago Sharon has dreamed of having her own space, a sewing room up in the loft, where she could embark on a home-craft pursuit that she could return to without clearing from the dinner table when the kids get home from school. In the drawers of the living-room cabinets Sharon keeps all of her home-making magazines and books that she buys at the local newsagent or as offers from the cable daytime television 'homecraft' shows she loves to watch. She also has an extensive collection of unused home-craft materials such as ribbons, threads and hooks that she picks up at car-boot sales and '50p shops'.

Over the last decade Sharon has consistently tried to implement a series of home-improvement schemes. She has, for example, been stripping the paint from the doors and banister. This process has taken so long she worries that by the time she finishes bare wood 'will be out of fashion again!' This home-improvement scheme is at the focus of a running joke and playful antagonism between Sharon and her husband, Dave. Sharon does not work outside the home and the family relies on Dave's part-time employment in the building trade for most of their income. Sharon's paint-removal task falls within the realms of Dave's paid expertise but he never gets around to doing their own home improvement. Sharon complains that she is full of ideas and schemes for home decoration but because of the kids she never has time to carry any of them through: 'you've got to stop to go shopping and stop to get the kids dinner ready. And I couldn't just stop and leave it I had to stop and clean up all the dust and everything, so it was taking me forever.'

As well as using a converted loft as a creative space for making clothes and homecrafts for the children and their bedrooms, Sharon envisages it as a useful storage area. If she could move extraneous furniture into the loft she could complete her bedroom design (another project in progress for over ten years). If her husband had not mismeasured the cabinet units he finally got around to making for the bedroom, it would not be necessary for the radiator to be moved and extra furniture to be stored in the loft that he has been promising to convert for ten years. Similarly Sharon would like a dishwasher in the kitchen, but her husband argues that until he moves the kitchen doorway to another position there will not be enough room for the plumbing. Until he moves the doorway Sharon cannot redecorate the kitchen and introduce her ambitious wall-of-glass-bricks idea inspired by the television home-decorating programme *Changing Rooms*.

Within the household a 'circular logic' operates preventing the successful completion of the home as a coherent project of redecoration. Encompassing all rooms in the house, Sharon's role as would-be home maker and Dave's role as provider and facilitator, this 'circular logic' revolves around a pivotal character — a rogue squirrel. Dave will not rearrange the kitchen until he has completed the loft idea they have been discussing for years. But he refuses to do this as a rogue squirrel has made a nest in the roof and 'it gives him the creeps'. While Sharon uses this in defence of her husband's inactivity (along with the fact that he does home improvement as a job outside the home), she is quick to guard against any sense of emasculation she may be conferring on him: 'He's not really sacred of it [the squirrel]. It's just that it might jump out at him and you know [mock scream]! I rang the council but they want twenty-five quid to come out and I thought "bugger that".'

Over the three-year period of the ethnography Sharon repeatedly mentions the 'bloomin' squirrel' in relation to her thwarted ambitions for the home: 'cos when I get around to converting my loft I'll have some where — the only thing that's stopping me is the squirrel up there'. Sharon and David's home could not be described as a haven of coherent home decoration or aesthetic normativity. Despite Sharon's consistent desire and efforts to transform the home through her own labour, time and creativity, the home seems to have reached a happy but static situation (see Figure 2.1). The 'would-be' loft has become the most important, if conceptual, space in the home. It is the focus of much hope for change in terms of Sharon's own personal fulfilment, her commitment to the kids as a 'better' mother and the family's overall improvement. Here we see vividly the home as process: how its decorative schemes (implemented and failed through a light-hearted play-off of gender relations) are the interiorizations of external concepts such as 'proper' mothering.

Conclusion

The home-improvement aspirations of the above informants clearly challenge the homogeneous and normative models of working-class home-making. While it would be easy to assume that the rise of the 'home' as a privatized arena of consumption exists in inverse relation to a State of declining sociality experienced by the occupants of the housing estate, such an assumption fails to explain the extent or nature of the investment made by the households in their interior worlds. In these particular examples, there is an extraordinary disparity between the amount of attention paid to how a place should look, as if it is firmly within the public domain, as against all evidence which indicates to the contrary that they are very rarely exposed to the view of an outsider. Kelly, Lola and Sharon conjure up their 'ideals' (as manifest in a man, class aspiration, the kids, immigration or home creativity), and it is as though instead of being inspected by actual visitors they are being viewed and judged by these same ideals.

Figure 2.1. Suspension between the 'ideal' and the 'actual' demonstrated in a half-decorated children's bedroom in Sharon's home

This is not to suggest that people have become more materialistic and, having abandoned sociality, merely turn to an 'interiorized' social world. Traditions of working-class sociality have historically revolved around public rather than private domains. Earlier studies of working-class housing, for example, reveal the importance and sanctity of the 'parlour' – a fully furnished formal room preserved for potential, but largely unrealized, visitors. So even in the poverty of the slums most of the home decoration was devoted to a room which was judged as an ideal but was not usually visited or even used. Later sociological studies show that social visits were largely confined to female relatives (Young and Willmott 1957).

Rather, this ethnographic example shows how the ideal home, as used to influence the construction of the actual home, becomes an internalized vision of what other people might think of one. Far from being a site of crude emulation, the house itself *actually* becomes the 'others'. The house objectifies the vision the occupants have of themselves in the eyes of others and as such it becomes an entity and process to live up to, give time to, show off to. As against actual observers it is an interiorized image of the other that can actually be worked on and fed into the aspirations and labour of the occupants. So the proliferation of home decoration and the popularization of design has become a key, contemporary component of a relationship that was never simply between an internal private sphere and an external public sphere, but a more complex process of projection and interiorization that continues to evolve.

References

Ames, K. (1992) *Death in the Dining Room and Other Tales of Victorian Culture*. Philadelphia: Temple University Press.

Appadurai, A. (ed.) (1986) *The Social Life of Things*. Cambridge: Cambridge University Press.

Bhatti, M. and Church, A. (2000) '"I never promised you a rose garden": gender, leisure, and home-making'. *Leisure Studies* 19/2 183–97.

Birdwell-Pheasant, D. and D. Lawrence-Zúñiga (1999) *House Life: Space, Place and Family in Europe*. Oxford: Berg.

Bourdieu, P. (1979) *Distinction: A Social Critique on the Judgement of Taste*. London: Routledge.

Clarke, A. (1998) 'Window shopping at home: classifieds, catalogues and new consumer skills'. In D. Miller (ed.) *Material Cultures: Why some Things Matter*. Chicago: University of Chicago Press.

—— (2000) 'Mother swapping: the trafficking of nearly new children's wear'. In M. Lowe, D. Miller and F. Mort (eds) *Commercial Cultures: Economies, Practices and Spaces*. Oxford: Berg.

Council for Art and Industry, G.B. Board of Trade (1937) *The Working-Class Home: Its Furnishing and Equipment*. London: HMSO.

Davidoff, L. and C. Hall (1987) *Family Fortunes: Men and Women of the English Middle Class 1780–1850*. London: Hutchinson.

De Grazia, V., with E. Furlough (1996) *The Sex of Things: Gender and Consumption in Historical Perspectives*. Berkeley: University of California Press.

DeVault, M. (1991) *Feeding the Family: The Social Organization of Caring as Gendered Work*. Chicago: University of Chicago Press.

Forrest, R. and A. Murie (1984) *Right to Buy? Issues of Need, Equity and Polarisation in the Sale of Council Houses*. Bristol: University of Bristol School for Advanced Urban Studies.

Franklin, A. (1989) 'Working-class privatism: an historical case study of Bedminster, Bristol. *Environment and Planning D: Society and Space* 7: 93–113.

—— (1990) 'Variations in marital relations and the implications for women's experience of the home'. In T. Putnam and C. Newton (eds) *Household Choices*. Middlesex: Future Publications.

Frykman, J. and O. Löfgren (1987) *The Culture Builders: A Historical Anthropology of Middle-Class Life*. New Brunswick: Rutgers University Press.

Gershuny, J. (1985) 'Economic development and change in the mode of provision services'. In N. Redclift, and E. Mingione (eds) *Beyond Employment*. Oxford: Basil Blackwell.

Grier, K. (1988) *Culture and Comfort: People, Parlours and Upholstery 1850–1930*. Rochester, NY: The Strong Museum and University of Massachusetts.

Gullestad, M. (1986), *Kitchen Table Society: A Case Study of the Family Life and Friendships of Young Working-Class Mothers in Urban Norway*. Oslo: Universitetsforlaget.

—— (1992) *The Art of Social Relations: Essays on Culture, Social Action and Everyday Life in Modern Norway*. Oslo: Scandinavian University Press.

Gurney, C. (1999) 'Lowering the drawbridge: a case study of analogy and metaphor in the social construction of home-ownership'. *Urban Studies* 36/10: 1705–22.

Hall, S. and M. Jacques (1983) *The Politics of Thatcherism*. London: Lawrence & Wishart.

Hoggart, R. (1957), *The Uses of Literacy: Aspects of Working Class Life*. London: Chatto & Windus.

London, J. (1997) *Bright Ideas: Dining Areas*. London: Merehurst.

Lubbock, J. (1995) *The Tyranny of Taste: The Politics of Architecture and Design in Britain 1550–1960*. New Haven, Yale University Press.

Madigan, R. and M. Munro (1993) 'Gender, house and "home": social meanings and domestic architecture in Britain'. *Journal of Architecture and Planning Research* 8: 116–31.

Marshall, G., H. Newby, D. Rose and C. Vogler (1988) *Social Class in Modern Britain*. London: Hutchinson.

Miller, D. (1988), 'Appropriating the State on the council estate'. *Man* 23: 353–72.

—— (1998) *A Theory of Shopping*. Cambridge: Polity.

Morley, C. (1990) 'Homemakers and design advice in the postwar period'. In T. Putnam and C. Newton (eds) *Household Choices*. Middlesex: Polytechnic and Futures Publications.

Oakley, A. (1976), *Housewife*. Harmondsworth: Penguin.

Oliver, P., I. Davis and I. Bentley (1981) *Dunroamin': The Suburban Semi and its Enemies*. London: Barrie & Jenkins.

Pacey, P. (1989) *Family Art*. Cambridge: Polity Press.

Ryan, D. (2000) 'All the world and her husband: the *Daily Mail* Ideal Home Exhibition 1908–1939'. In M. Andrews and M. Talbot (eds) *All the World and her husband: Women in Twentieth Century Consumer Culture*. London: Cassell.

Saunders, P. (1990) *A Nation of Home Owners*. London: Union Hyman.

Tomlinson, A. (1990) 'Home fixtures: doing it yourself in a privatised world'. In A. Tomlinson (ed.) *Consumption, Identity and Style.* London: Comedia.

Wallman, S. (1984) *Eight London Households.* London: Tavistock.

Walton, S. and S. Walton (1997) *The 'Home Front' Guide to Doing up your Period Home.* London: BBC.

—— (1998) *'Home Front': Children's Rooms.* London: BBC.

Young, M. and P. Willmott (1957) *Family and Kinship in East London.* London: Routledge & Kegan Paul.

Organized Disorder: Moving Furniture in Norwegian Homes
Pauline Garvey

Of all modern notions,
the <u>worst</u> is this; that domesticity is dull.
Inside the home, they say, is dead decorum and routine;
outside is adventure and variety.
But the truth is the home is the only place of liberty,
the only spot on earth where a man can alter arrangements suddenly,
make an experiment or indulge in a whim.
The home is not the one tame place in a world of adventure;
it is the one wild place in a world of rules and set tasks.

G.K. Chesterton

Introduction

The use of the home for purposes of 'self-presentation' is not a new concept to the study of domestic interiors. Within the academic literature the home is often posited as a key arena in transmitting and codifying an image of oneself to others, through the appropriation of the material environment. Indeed, these associations are so innately tied that one might expect that 'home decoration' as a single topic covers the spectrum of practices involved in self-expression or presentation. This paper draws a critical distinction between decoration and reordering furniture, and argues that each relates to different if not opposing domestic strategies. The material on which this paper is based draws from sixteen months' fieldwork in the town of Skien, located in south-east Norway.[1]

The Home as Self-Decoration: Presentation – and Display

Much is made of home decoration (see McCracken 1989; Miller 1990; Putman and Newton 1990; Chevalier 1996, 1998; Cieraad 1999), not least in Scandinavia

1. I gratefully acknowledge the Research Council of Norway for financial assistance during my fieldwork period.

as a whole (Löfgren 1984, 1994a, 1994b) and Norway in particular (Gullestad 1984, 1992, 1993; Reme 1994; Bergan and Dysthe 1994). The popularity of domesticity is due, perhaps, to its 'polysemy' (Wilk, Netting and Arnould 1984: 1). This quality also relates to the ambiguity of the home, where a vast spectrum of approaches and emphases are considered under one subject heading of 'home decoration', and in which a huge range of individual and social strategies are played out.

The argument of this chapter is posited on the distinction between redecoration on the one hand and rearranging furniture on the other. The salience of the distinction emerges in an analysis of both activities, which despite being employed in the elaboration of the household stem from different motives and fulfil contrasting needs. The approach I adopt here recasts the significance of home decoration from the *results* of home decoration to the *processes* of these routines. This emphasis contributes to an academic trend which has moved from the study of the home as a reflection of the 'generational grammars' of social order (see Buchli 1999: 9) to an emphasis on the material culture and more particularly to the activities which engage with the domestic environment and make it meaningful. For example, early approaches to domestic material culture focused on 'prized possessions' or key objects within the household. Csikszentmihalyi and Rochberg-Halton (1981) provided one such approach based on the idea that *homo faber*, as a self-reflexive animal, would invest proportionate 'psychic energy' in an object depending on its personal worth. They argued that an object would thereby become 'charged' or cultivated when greatly esteemed by the social actor and therefore this process would be illustrative of individual priorities. These priorities also followed trends which could be placed in generational or gendered categories (for example men and technology). One of the key premises of Csikszentmihalyi and Rochberg-Halton's argument, was the correlation of physical materiality with a social or meaningful 'permanence': '[v]iewed as signs, objects have the peculiar character of *objectivity*, that is, they tend to evoke similar responses from the same person over time and from different people. Relative to other signs such as emotions, or ideas, objects seem to possess a unique concreteness and permanence' (ibid. 14, emphasis in original). This idea of objectivity, concreteness and permanence has significant implications. First it suggests 'stability' – a householder's long-term appreciation of his/her material environment. From this perspective the longevity of the household and the materiality of its possessions necessarily favoured the diachronic over the transient and assumed meaningless. Also the investment of time in prized possessions therefore was valorized in cultivating a sense of self to the neglect of banal household routines which leave little physical trace.

One of the important advances of this literature on the home was to focus attention on the textured strategies at play behind the appropriation process. The complex and contradictory meanings of material culture became apparent.[2] Material culture could be seen as a tool for self-actualization, and practices such as re-decoration illustrated the importance of personal engagement with the domestic environment or the concretization of domestic relationships (Gullestad 1993). Studies of home decoration became relevant to ideas of gender, individual agency and empowerment (Miller 1990). The result of such studies led to the recognition that far from being 'conspicuous consumption', practices involved in the organiza-tion of the domestic interior have the capacity to relate to an overt or latent sense of self which transcends an image of home as purely a presentational field (see Hecht, Chapter Seven of this volume). In such studies, however, focus has favoured the material reality of home decoration and refurbishment, often as a couple or family commitment, to the neglect of the ephemeral decorative activities which leave little lasting trace. Therefore while anthropology might be criticized for the 'prevailing preoccupation with the ethnographic and synchronic moment' (Buchli 1999: 6) to the neglect of the dynamics of long-term change, this study provides one illustration of how transient and discontinuous preoccupations can have long-term relevance.

The aim of this paper is to argue that banal routines located in the home are fundamental in understanding the relationship between domesticity and self-identity. It does this by distinguishing ephemeral strategies of agency and individual introspection from long-term collective narratives at play within the domestic space. To illustrate this I emphasize transience over permanence, insignificance over investment. The reorganization of furniture is one such 'incidental' routine, which I suggest stems from different motives and fulfils more 'individualizing' needs than home decoration. This can be seen in the case of Beate.

Beate

Beate is in her mid-fifties and has one adult son. She does not redecorate often, but moved into her present house in the mid-1980s, and other than purchasing some new furniture about ten years go, much has remained the same. Reasons for this relate partly to a lack of disposable funds but more importantly to a lack of interest in changing her home by purchasing novelties. Beate is very conscious of waste. This rationale impinges on all her domestic choices and is intermingled with a fascination for the past, and both, perhaps, relate to her avid support and participation in local auctions.

On one occasion, I visited Beate to find her and a friend rearranging her living-room furniture and talking with great animation. Everything was in disarray and

---

2. Halle, for example, argues that art-works in a domestic environment may have 'little to do with aesthetics' (1993: 169).

the two women stood in the middle of the room, looking intently at the spaces they had just created. It seemed as if Beate's friend, a woman named Grette was chief adviser while they discussed plans for change. When I arrived they were both taking it very seriously – deep in conversation and negotiation. Beate's house is organized so that it has two reception rooms: one is a large carpeted sitting room which spans the length of the house, and another is a room which one enters after crossing the front hallway, and is alternatively a dining room or small informal living room. One passes through this room to get to the rest of the house. The staircase to the basement and bedrooms upstairs is in one corner, with the entrance to the kitchen and sitting room along the adjacent and opposite walls. Because this room is small, fronting onto the kitchen and with a fuel stove warming the rooms overhead, it is used during the winter months with the main sitting room left cold and vacant until spring. The only exception to this is at Christmas when the sitting room is reopened and warmed with small electric heaters. Because of these changes, marked by the approaching drop or rise in temperature, Beate is provided with a reason or excuse to complement the realignments with other domestic changes. The dining table, a large, heavy birchwood piece with six matching chairs, is shuffled from one side of the sitting room to the other or alternatively taken from the sitting room to the living room – or back again. During my year of fieldwork I saw these heavy and cumbersome pieces of furniture in both rooms and on both sides of the spacious sitting room.

On the evening in question, Grette had just moved the dining table into the sitting room and consequently was obliged to rearrange the sofa which had occupied that position. Meanwhile Beate found an extra sofa in her son's room which would suit the informal living room. She wanted to place it along the wall under the window, but Grette suggested that it would be more cosy (*koselig*) if they turned it to face the sitting room so that one could sit there and see in. Every decision was taken after much discussion and they compromised on those areas where they differed. My advice was also requested and my help recruited – although I was somewhat peripheral to the occasion. Grette won out on the dining-room arrangement, depositing the dining suite in front of the piano. Everything else had to be moved: lamps no longer suited the arrangement; taller ones were positioned in some places and smaller ones in others. Paintings and photographs were blocked by newly positioned bookcases and therefore necessitated a novel orchestration. 'This is all part of it', explained Grette, 'once you move the furniture, everything else has to be moved, it is like getting a new house.' She also added 'I have moved everything around in my apartment so many times, although I am somewhat limited because I have a slanted roof, so I have to take that into account.' She continued:

It is such fun, don't you think so, I think I would die of boredom if my flat was always the same, you need a change, now and again, a renewal, it is such fun. Like sometimes I might think of a more practical way of putting things, so I do that.

Meanwhile, Beate pottered around, making small changes, while they talked and laughed. When it came to the radio, Beate wanted to place some old photographs in its place. After some discussion they decided that 'ugly technical things' shouldn't be on view and so the radio was put in the corner. In addition to Beate's uncertainty with the radio and television, all her prints and paintings were now out of place. In her sitting room a blue velveteen low-backed sofa replaced a set of polished wooden drawers. For this reason, three items, including a hand-woven rug are placed high on the wall to accommodate the drawers. Now they look odd and uneven over the blue sofa. Some other problems include the present position of her son's portrait, which is now blocked by the television. And so it continues, the small readjustments seem endless. Everything has to be positioned and repositioned accordingly.

The main reason given for the propensity to rearrange the domestic interior relates to 'feelings of newness' or 'difference'. That is, while an informant might say that he/she couldn't afford to change their interior completely, often the purchase of some small items, such as a candlestick or a tablecloth provided the impetus to refashion the environment into which these objects would be placed. Changes of this sort could vary; in some houses a few items of light furnishings, coupled with a change of table cloths and ornaments could effect this change. For others, depending on the need and time available the movement could involve and extend to every item in the room, in order to complete the sensation of a totally new environment. To a degree, routines of this sort have become structured in social life and follow seasonal changes: summer and winter curtains are common and to others a collection of curtains to suit one's mood is a popular pursuit. As Karina expressed it, 'I have a whole cupboard of curtains, I save them up, I just can't help myself buying them when I am out shopping and see something I like — but I don't use them. I change from summer to winter curtains but I don't use the others, they just sit there.'

In the example of Beate it is not the efficacy of 'prized possessions', individual items or decorative schema which are important in conjuring emotions, so much as the processes of their organization. Through such practices Beate and Grette contemplate and order emotional states as much as domestic paraphernalia. The home is an intersubjective space, a catalogue of memories and emotions, some of which can be accentuated and others cast into the material background. Banal routines such as moving furniture provide an atmosphere of change or newness to a home owner distinguishing it from more elaborate and labour-intensive decorative schemes.

Moving Furniture: 'Order can stand as a metaphor for order'

It is, for many, common to arrange and rearrange one's domestic environment. One might view it as tidying up, restoring order, and therefore a necessary chore in the upkeep of a family home. Especially when children are present, the necessities of maintaining order often appear as both particularly difficult and frequent. But it is not this quick tidy-up that I am describing here. The routines which I explicate are not undertaken in a rush in order to make the home presentable for residents and visitors. Rather I refer to a more processed reflexive motive, which is more in keeping with Gombrich's statement that 'order can stand as a metaphor for order; perhaps we have the disposition to accept degrees of order as potential metaphors for inner states' (1984: 247).

Unlike other aspects of decoration, reordering one's home holds slightly different connotations than refurbishment. It entails a suggestion of work yet is more often approached in a positive light, as a response to an emotive stimulus, such as boredom. Reordering furniture therefore is most commonly an emotional response to an emotional condition. Lacking any prescribed template on how it should be accomplished, the homeowner can engage in this activity as his/her mood dictates. And because it is an informal practice, involving little manual or fiscal outlay, it tends to be overlooked as unimportant. As Putman and Newton's edited volume on *Household Choices* (1990) illustrates, life circumstances have an impact on experience of place. But while certain chapters (for example Sixsmith and Sixsmith) stress intentionality on the part of the householder in reflecting 'the intentions of the dweller' in the domestic context, the mutual transaction between both agent and material domain is not emphasized.

Renewal can take a number of forms, varying from minor alterations to complete expulsion of existing aesthetic genres. Often very small alterations are adequate. Common responses detail the advantages of rearranging one's existing furnishings and possessions, so that one is left with a totally different 'feel' to the living room. As Maj said, 'I just replace the red towels with yellow and purple ones and buy a similarly coloured rug and the bathroom suddenly looks completely different.' This involves no waste, minimal consumption yet gives an impression of change and renewal. One common example of this is in living-room interiors, as expressed by Karina as she explains that she wanted something 'new' and 'different' in her home:

> I move the furniture around a lot. But now I can't move the sofa because it is so big, which is a bit stupid. But when I had a regular sofa, I used to move everything around; the TV, the chairs and the things on the wall, I organise everything and then I move it all again. So when people come they would wonder at how everything is changed. I have to organize it and I would sit here and think about what would it look like if. . . then I can't relax until I have seen what it looks like.

More often, however, the explanation proffered by informants refers to feelings of boredom and imagination. As Grette expressed it 'it is amazing when you use your imagination, that is why it is such fun, because you have to fantasize about it and imagine new things and how it might be, it is using you imagination which is such fun'. Therefore, while reordering might be discussed in terms of tidying up, moving furniture as a form of redecoration is an attempt to reinvigorate a perception of staleness or impose a missing dynamism. On some occasions this lack is something which informants feel about themselves, and the engagement with this domestic routine can be explained as almost a surrogative response. Take Lise, for example, in her discussion of her bedsit:

> Lise: I change the furniture around, not the decoration so much but I do move the things around, it is moved around, I need that. First I had the bed here and then I moved it under the window and then I had it as I have it now and I like it best this way – a distance from the living area.

> Researcher: Do you feel better when you change things around?

> Lise: When I feel depressed it feels good to move things around. There are some people who have a very clear mind but have very untidy homes. . . when you have a lot to think about it can help to move things around and clean up or throw things out, and in a way you are also sorting things out in your brain. That's a kind of psychological reason, I don't know why I do it. I just become tired of the way I have it, its good not to be used to things for so long, right?

With the manipulation of her environment, Lise reorders her feelings and draws comparisons between the mental and physical forms of organization. Through her involvement in these routines, she exerts a feeling of agency over her emotions. Her home is not incidental but holds a dynamic, even interactive, role in this process.

Rearranging one's material environment establishes a feeling of newness in an environment which is otherwise characterized by a large degree of normativity. While the majority of interviewees claim to be roughly satisfied with their domestic environment, this claim is made in recognition of the restrictions imposed by finances and that their decorative choices comply to a certain price range. The point of rearranging, however, is that it does not involve the restraints and considerations of purchasing, but in some respects provides the feelings of novelty and self-expression which this ordinarily provides. To others, a degree of domestic sameness was attractive and formed the backbone of feelings of security that the home engendered. Unlike the considered attention that much interior purchasing seems to assume, the value of moving furniture is that it allows the homeowner to impress a feeling of newness and change on his/her domestic environment as the need arises.

As we have seen in the case of Beate, reorganizing furniture gives her an opportunity to delve into a creative, imaginative space. The frequency with which this happens and, for some informants, its habitual nature earns the title 'routine' for a practice which is marked by its customary, albeit impulsive, nature. Drawing from studies of infants, Giddens (1991) posits that the discipline of routine helps to constitute a framework for existence by cultivating a sense of 'being' in the individual. Through the experience of routine, he suggests, orientations towards aspects of the object world with symbolic residues are carried into the later life of the individual. The relationship is ambiguous, however, as routines also express a deep-rooted ambivalence which the concomitant early involvement with routine-as-discipline suggests. Routine activities are never just carried out in an automatic way, rather 'the maintaining of habits and routines is a crucial bulwark against threatening anxieties, yet by that token it is a tensionful phenomenon in and of itself' (1991: 39, see also Giddens 1990).

The difficulty of such a label lies in the suggestion that it negates spontaneity, which is the lynchpin of this process. Indeed, it is rupture from routine that is precisely its defining characteristic. Routine reminds the individual of stability and permanence which reorganization provides an escape from. However, the rupture effected by change is nevertheless ephemeral, and framed within a domestic setting which by its nature assuages the efficacy of transient challenge. Moving furniture should therefore be explained as a form of 'habitualized spontaneity'. It is spontaneous because it has little to do with necessity and relates more to the householder's wish to engage with the material environment. Yet despite the temporal rupture which it cues, it can become habitual, almost a hobby; as Martha said 'I move it one way and then I decide that it was better the first way and everything gets moved back. It is such fun, I am always changing things in one way or another and eventually they all end up where they originally were.' Repetition does not necessarily defy forms of relaxation, spontaneity or rupture. A tea break is no less significant or efficient in structuring time and mood because it is habitual. Even when rearranging one's environment is enjoyed on a weekly, monthly or seasonal basis, the result of the action is necessarily described in terms of change and refreshment.

The emphasis on freshness and introspection which moving furniture allows, differs from the standard line on presentation and necessitates a more subtle division to be drawn across practices described as 'home decoration'. As one can see in the example of Beate, the impetus behind her wish to reorganize bears little relation to strategies of emulation or display. Equally it can only be minimally attributed to presentation to a perceived audience. The raw materials of the practice remain the same and many homeowners remark how changes made can be undone within a short period of time. It does not therefore involve prior planning or purchasing, and can be undertaken on the spur of the moment. Moving furniture then is about mood, reversal, undoing and imposing order on temporary chaos. It can be described as 'spontaneous' rather than 'continual', 'catharsis' rather than 'narration'.

As I will show below, home decoration relates to narrative and temporality because it fulfils a 'representational' role. This is primarily because of the investment inferred by decoration; it involves considerable fiscal and manual outlay, and incorporates the replacement of furniture, colour schemes and fittings in favour of a fresh appropriation of the domestic environment. In some cases informants are happy to repaint a living room or kitchen, whereas in other cases full-scale changes of furniture, curtains, floor coverings of primary reception rooms are required. Also decorative choices are frequently made in recognition or direct rejection of what is currently seen as fashionable, both by one's social environment and the heavy advertising of national furniture chains. These factors all contribute to the seriousness of 'decorative narratives', the biography of the household through a long-term perspective. 'Narrative' as Giddens defines it (see below) has direct implications on ideas of self, and the portrayal of self to a social audience. Being in fashion and identifying oneself as fashionable is frequently about avoiding the 'wrong' choices, defining oneself by what to dislike and what to consume (Wilk 1997)[3] or responding when decorative choices become 'tackified', 'old-fashioned' or 'comical' (Löfgren 1994a: 55) with the passage of time. The home is pivotal in this process, as O'Dell argues for post-war Sweden '[F]or it was here, in the confines of the home, somewhat protected from the peering eyes of colleagues and mistrusted neighbors, that Swedes were able to experiment with new ideas, designs and identities without the risk of immediate disapproval' (1997: 132).

The idea of the long term is a key point of difference with moving furniture because in most cases the latter is undertaken precisely because there are no long-term implications. Temporality and mood are often linked. Informants describe how engagement with their possessions can momentarily clear their minds of troubles or cares. It creates a medium for emotional expression, even if this is not always consciously registered. One such mundane yet emotional state that is frequently referred to is boredom, a need for change or an awareness of monotony in which a renewed dynamism is the only cure. This unique spontaneous quality allows a degree of introspection which departs from the pressures of decorative display in which domestic narratives are fundamental.

Domestic Narratives

Through the framework of biography maintenance, Giddens argues that self-identity achieves coherence because it allows active and ongoing revision. Home

---

3. Swales' informant, for example, avoided pine because she did not want to be associated with 'that kind of woman' (1990: 16).

decoration is one vehicle through which an individual engages in a continually revised presentational field. In many ways, home decoration is an ongoing process of self-definition through which continuous revision is a necessary factor.

In looking at continual action and ideas of self, Giddens (1991) suggests that mechanisms of self-identity in the modern age must be seen as interactive and mutually constitutive with one's social (and material) environment. The man or woman of the late modern age is, he argues, essentially and reflexively involved in maintaining and revising his/her self-identity. To this end therefore lifestyle becomes central in devising this identity which is forged through the endless choices with which one is presented in everyday life. This is negotiated through the maintenance of a coherent biography – the series of events that are salient in influencing the progression of a person's life. The individual comes to terms with ideas of self through an awareness of continuity over time and space, but this continuity is interpreted and acted upon reflexively. Self-identity is not a distinctive trait, or even a collection of traits, possessed by the individual, but is rather understood in terms of an ongoing biography (ibid.: 53). Coherence is achieved through continuous revision.

Through the notion of biography Giddens takes emphasis off presentation as constituting individual identities and places it on forming a personal story, which is understood and maintained by the self. A person's identity is not, he suggests, to be found as constituted in their behaviour or in the reactions of others but in the ability to keep a particular narrative going. The internal world of the subject interacts with the external, material world as the individual spontaneously sorts aspects of the environment and integrates them into an ongoing story about the self (ibid: 54). As Charles Taylor put it '[I]n order to have a sense of who we are, we have to have a notion of how we have become, and of where we are going' (quoted in Giddens 1991: 54). Similarly, redecoration is continual because it is ongoing; a project one plans, elaborates and saves money towards. Purchasing new furniture frequently involves long-term planning: shops are perused and friends consulted. Fashion trends, social aspirations and individual dispositions all play a part in the decision-making process which both particularize the homeowner while also retaining a vital social role.

Informants deal with home decoration as an ongoing project, renewing perhaps the living room before the kitchen and bedrooms and so on. One corrects past errors, explores new aesthetic options, panders to some fashions, rejects others and makes a mental inventory of future experiments. Creating an environment in which one is comfortable, therefore, is essentially a processual exercise. As long as one has a project in mind, one is always endeavouring to keep up; the project itself assumes a form of agency and social participation. Through the materiality of the home, decorative benchmarks become emblems of the past and projects for the future. Combined with the actual physical features of the domestic sphere are also the projects or decorative schemes which one plans for the future. These encompass both expected changes as well as the ideals which never come to fruition. For some, the ideal home takes the role of an aspiration, a dream which is inviting but unattainable nevertheless. As we will see in the case study of Knut and Dorothy, the 'ideal home' provides an intellectual or emotional space that has little correspondence with their domestic situation. Perhaps in maintaining a very rigid dream of unattainable circumstances, one is acquiescing to their impossibility.

But if the ideal home or the ongoing decorative project often relates to fantasy, vision and identity building, activities that are involved in more immediate quests for self-introspection or exploration of creative abilities lack this narrative quality. One issue that remains unexplored here relates to gendered associations with moving furniture – which emerged as an overwhelmingly female activity – but which also relates to other factors such as associations of home decoration with female activities and also amount of time spent in the home. On one occasion a middle-aged female informant named Else, who is unemployed and spends much of the day at home, acknowledged that numerous arguments arose with her husband who came home from work each day, only to find a new list of heavy pieces of furniture to haul around their flat. His frustration was expressed in his continuous inquiry 'was it not all right as it was?' Through this daily routine, Else created a new exciting environment, an 'other' to the loneliness and boredom of oppressive domesticity and unemployment. Her husband, on the other hand associated home with familiarity, relaxation and stability – the 'other' to his hectic office job, and found the effort of constant rearranging both tiring and disorienting.

The movement of furniture within the home allows for a certain playfulness or spontaneity that can alleviate homeowners' feelings of staleness regarding their home. This in turn rebounds upon feelings of self. As we have seen in Beate's example, moving furniture has a cathartic quality in taking control of the material environment. It was neither sequential nor continual because it is not approached as building upon former undertakings; new arrangements could be dissolved as quickly as set in place. On some occasions informants confessed that they embarked on new decorative schemes with resigned recognition that everything would probably revert to its original position; 'I am sitting there and I think what would it look like if that was there and then I have to try it out, but often things were better as they were.' Moving furniture is referred to in playful terms 'I just do it for fun', 'I get bored with looking at everything in the same place so I change everything around!' Motivated primarily by mood and feelings of boredom, the movement of furniture relates to personal wishes where issues of display are often secondary. This can be placed in direct contrast to the following case studies where the interviewees seem weighed down by the pressures and commitments that decoration can bring.

Knut and Dorothy

Knut and Dorothy are seventy-nine and eighty years old respectively and live on the third floor of a block of flats. They have been there since it was built in the early 1970s, and when I met them, they had just inherited an apartment and were considering a move. Both Knut and his wife were interesting informants because, unlike most other interviewees, they professed to actively dislike their domestic arrangements. Additionally, unlike many others I spoke to in the blocks, Dorothy and Knut were entirely responsible for their present home interior and perhaps this accentuated even more acutely their recognition of both how their tastes have changed and how their choices are at variance with their articulated ideals. Up to the time of my fieldwork, they had made little headway in changing their domestic circumstances, but the prospect of a new apartment provided them with fresh momentum to discuss their decorative preferences. And while both agreed about ideals such as simplicity and a 'total modern home', how these ideals worked out in practice often proved more difficult.

Throughout our discussion, the prospect of a move provided a mirror image of the couples' ideals as opposed to their present circumstances. Despite the fact that Dorothy is the self-proclaimed more conventional of the two, she does admit that she would happily change everything – 'the wallpaper makes me depressed' – and they muse about how they might effect these changes. Their home is a bricolage of objects and furniture that they have accumulated over the years. When they first got married, the housing crisis was such that they, like many others at the time, were obliged to live with parents until they could become established. Eventually they found a house in the country and settled there, furnishing it with traditional pine furniture befitting to the age and ambience of the building. They moved to the blocks, primarily because Knut grew ill and they needed somewhere small, compact and closer to the town, taking some items of furniture with them and dumping the rest.

Knut is artistic, he likes modern art and owns a number of artworks that were painted by well-known artists. When he was younger he earned a living as a sculptor and sold his pieces. He showed me one of his works, a long elegant figure of a young naked female. It was wooden – carved, sanded and lightly varnished to give a glossy appearance, and smooth to the touch. It sat neatly in Knut's hand and its smoothness seemed to derive more from years of polishing and handling than its original sanding and varnishing. He eulogized the piece in terms of its form and texture, Dorothy says she likes it now but in the beginning she thought it 'a bit pornographic'.

In some ways Dorothy epitomizes conventional expectations which Knut describes as working against the realization of his ideal decoration of a 'total modern home'. As Knut visualizes it, it would fit the minimalist ideal – very simple and without fuss. They would have his modern art on the walls, very little furniture and a few well-chosen items of ornamentation. It would be above all functional, adequately fulfilling the needs of the householders yet with minimal decoration, denoting for Knut both good taste and an austere simplicity. Mentioning the modernist architect Le Corbusier a number of times invoked the functionalist inspiration underpinning his ideals.

Their home exhibits no hint of this, however. When they first moved in, they chose a brown-tinted wallpaper, which was in keeping with fashions at the time. They have since changed the wallpaper once, to a somewhat lighter, monochrome shade, but it is still rather dark, and in referring to it Dorothy snorts in disgust that she finds it 'depressing'. Knut did at one point make gestures towards changing it, and covered one end wall with the same paper but in a lighter hue. That was an improvement Dorothy tells me, but it went no further. The reason they haven't made any additional changes, they admitted, is because they didn't feel like taking the trouble (*vi gidder ikke*). Despite their dislike of their present environment then, Dorothy and Knut seem resigned to accept that that is how it shall remain for the duration of their stay there.

Knut's description of a minimalist dream of stark modern furniture came as a surprise, as their present decoration resembles other flats occupied by elderly residents. Unlike the pine that characterizes the tastes of younger generations in Skien, the couple have surrounded themselves with mahogany and birch furniture and fittings. They have a living- and dining-room area in their flat, with adjoining doors leading to the kitchen and bedrooms. The living room holds a crimson-coloured velour suite, clustered around a mahogany table. Other pieces of hard wood furniture stand in corners, such as a small corner display cabinet filled with glass and porcelain oddments. Bookcases line the walls, along with a piano and television and occasional-tables decorated with plants, candles and photographs. The dark wood-stained furniture and velour suite featured in a number of homes I visited, as did the traditional 'farming culture' emblems, such as spinning wheels and traditional wooden bowls, painted with a design (*rosemaling*) diagnostic to the province.

It is against this setting that we discussed the idea of a 'total modern home'. Knut described his plans with relish, Dorothy being a bit more circumspect in her enthusiasm. In lieu of the environment which Knut imagines, he has set a room apart where he collects his favourite paintings. This room is like the rest in the home, adhering to the same wallpaper and mahogany furniture, but is characterized as unique through the collection of art which it houses. There are five paintings, ranging from oils to charcoal drawings that feature nudes, landscapes and a couple of abstract figures. On his desk sits a piece by the Romanian sculptor Brancusi and a few items of his own sculpted work. It is in this room that Knut can hang his favourite pieces without interference from others, and he is left largely unhindered by Dorothy in his choices.

The reasoning behind this room is born from a marriage of recreation and necessity. For a start, Knut has been ill and relatively housebound for some years. The room and its organization gives him a personal space to appreciate his collection. He doesn't paint anymore and most of his paintings are stacked in the cellar; still, here he has most of his most treasured possessions. There is also a more pragmatic rationale to the room. For a while Dorothy and Knut found that they differed in relation to their approaches to their living room. The images that Knut favoured jarred with Dorothy's ideas of self-presentation. At first, they tried to hang some of his paintings in their living room. As Knut explained to me, 'we had a painting, it was a great painting. It was of three women having a siesta, two with clothes and one without, it was a great painting but later we sold it – which is a real pity.' Dorothy continued: 'we had it in the living room and occasionally it shocked people. Once we had some people over, an old couple and the man was a little senile perhaps and we were sitting here having coffee and he said "what do you think that painting means?"' This was enough to put Dorothy off the painting, the remark reminding her of latent embarrassments and perhaps ambiguous feelings regarding Knut's preferences in art. So it was removed and sold. Knut still regrets this and accuses Dorothy of being 'too conventional' and having 'bad taste', accusations which she seems to accept passively. In general terms their taste or rather their common dislike of their present environment is a point of communion. And when they started discussing a possible move to another flat, they had a lot in common. Dorothy finds the decoration depressing and while she is not opposed to an ultra-modern living room in theory, she argues that they cannot afford a complete refurbishment. Therefore, or perhaps because, both accept the impossibility of realizing this fantasy, they both agree with its attractiveness.

Dorothy and Knut exhibit a number of interesting issues in their approach to their decoration. They are both elderly and therefore lack the energy to attack their wallpaper with the gusto with which they discuss it. They lead a quiet lifestyle and profess to have few visitors. Other than these, and while they are a very amiable couple, they do express a wish to lead a solitary lifestyle. Lacking children and consequently without grandchildren this is relatively easy to accomplish. Energy is a major player in defining what practical changes they can make to their domestic interior. Cost-efficiency is another issue, especially as they are considering making a move. When all is taken into account, it seems unlikely that their proposed changes will materialize, but rather they are manifested as a canvas through which they can compare preferences which they feel mirror their 'true' identity. Discussing 'true' identity when it remains in the realm of fantasy allows Dorothy and Knut to preserve a space for them to picture an ideal. As we have seen from their decorative choices so far, imposing this ideal on their material environment works much better in theory than in practice. In part this relates to the necessary negotiations which one undergoes when coming to terms with the aesthetic temperaments of a cohabiting partner.

Dorothy and Knut are still negotiating between their ideal and actual circumstances, moving between ideas of self-presentation and ideas of appropriate display. And while they expressed frustration during our interview at their lack of domestic accomplishment, the alternative seems beyond their reach. Along similar lines, we can compare this with the case study of Monica. Monica lives alone, and therefore, although her difficulties in deciding appropriate decoration are not the result of a partner, she nevertheless experiences considerable conflict in coming to terms with how she sees herself and how this is presented or misrepresented to those around her. In one particular event, this comes to a head in which she strikes out as 'a forty-year-old woman making a protest' through the medium of her post box.

Monica

Monica is forty years old and lives alone. When I first met her, she had only been settled in her single-storey home for a few years. She was familiar with this area though, having visited it as a child, although she now notes that it was much rougher then. Before her present move, she relocated quite a bit and was settled for a number of years in a block of flats located a small distance outside the town. Having chosen the present house, however, she seemed satisfied to stay there for life. Monica is credited by her friends as being very interested in domestic decoration, which she is, but to a degree this is attributed to her because of the general interest that her home elicits.

Monica's house invites quite a bit of local attention and was frequently described to me as the 'cosy little red house'. Despite its less salubrious location, flanked on two sides by tall buildings and overlooking a disused factory, it manages to convey an impression of traditional charm. The red ochre colour of the house represents a traditional Norwegian home, as does its small size and the carved woodwork around the windows. On the whole the home looks well maintained, and attention to small details such as the candles in the windows and pristine doormat suggests a proud owner – but no more so than most of her neighbours.

Monica works as an administrator in a rehabilitation centre. Living alone and without children, she recognizes that she does not have the same domestic pressures as some of her colleagues. For this reason she works long hours, often sacrificing her holidays for career duties. She claims not to obsess about her home the way some of her neighbours do, and prefers basic, functional and simple styles to give her house a 'homely' feel. Of her collection of furniture, there are a number of pieces that she has picked up informally. Some items such as her pine kitchen table were bought second hand. Additionally, she was given her stereo by a friend, her coffee table by her sister, and some comfortable chairs by her mother. Other items she procured herself: shoe shelves in an Oslo shop now hold her books, and the CD shelves were made by a friend. To some extent, these things were 'happened across', and Monica congratulates herself on acquiring possessions informally and she is satisfied with them.

In part, Monica sees her present attitudes as guided through her experiences as a child. She is aware for example of the difficult financial circumstances of her parents, and this frames her identity as 'working class':

> My father is from this area and I have a lot of relatives here. My grandmother lived here when I was small so I came down here a lot when I was little and I have always lived in a working-class area and that is the same with [the blocks], and that is my background . . . It was the working-class children who lived in the blocks and we used to steal apples from the people who lived in [the adjacent area]. And this area too was nearly a slum, and the council had a lot of houses but it has changed a lot and now is nearly for 'culture snobs'. Perhaps what I react against but follow it too, is how much we spend on houses, in order to have them proper [*ordentlig*], decorating outside and inside, and it is nearly like if the post-box doesn't fit in with the rest, it's like 'are you mad?' People nearly change their post-box from Christmas to Easter.

Monica exhibits some ambiguity in relation to her home and claims that the 'socialist streak' in her causes her to question her own present sense of priorities such as her need, as a single person, to own a house at all. Having resided in temporary accommodation for some time in her youth contributes to her present enjoyment of the autonomy of her own space. Despite these feelings, or perhaps because of them, she questions if she has changed over the years, if her former ideas have relaxed as she approached middle age. In purchasing a house, Monica doubted whether she was complying with social norms that were unnecessary for her situation. She lived alone and expressed concern that she was becoming more materialistic as she grew older.

> I felt it was a paradox for me. I suppose it has something to do with my upbringing or a socialist streak in me, why should I own a house alone. Really I didn't care about such things, but I notice in myself I care more about things which other people think are important. I don't think of myself as materialistic but I know that I am becoming more and more so.

The problem for Monica is essentially an ambivalence towards her shifting ideals, and her home has come to mirror how her expectations and needs have changed with age and improving financial circumstances. This reflection was textured, however and, not wholly negative. It was obvious that she was houseproud; she spoke to me of her hopes of getting planning permission to build a little porch for her front door, and also of the little hedge she had planted around her garden. This pride and enjoyment of her home is not focused on keeping it pristine, but rather a certain relaxed or 'messy' quality is welcomed. On a number of occasions she remarked to me how surprised she was at the interest she was taking in the conversation and how it reflected her changing attitudes. These changing attitudes and her domestic aspirations became obvious through the story of her post box.

When Monica moved into her new house, she was given a gift of a post box painted in blue, with a matching name plate for her door. The giver of the gift had it specially painted so that the name plate stated 'here lives Monica' – as one frequently sees ornamenting Norwegian homes. The post box carried a picture of a small red ochre house, and both were embellished with small painted flowers in a nostalgic style which was common in the area. Other decorative motifs I had seen in the area included name plates with depictions of cows or bells. Monica was initially satisfied with her gifts and started painting the window boxes and window frames of her house in a matching colour. One day, however, she was walking in the area with her sister and she recounts noticing all the houses in the area with similar name plates and registered her reaction:

> . . . and then I suddenly saw that every house had the same sign and everything should look so nice from the outside and I thought, dear god that we should be so occupied with such things, that it doesn't only have to look nice from the inside but from the outside too. All of this on the outside, now style is going too far.

Monica's reaction to this observation was immediate and unrelenting. She painted everything white. The hand-painted motifs on her post-box were obliterated, as was the name plate and the matching colour of her window frames. The obliteration of the name plate, the window boxes, window frames and post-box in a thick white paint was explained to me in terms of a strike against competition between neighbours or attempts to impress others with ornate, impractical details. It also actively removed Monica from participating in popular, local fashions. Now the white post box and window frames are in keeping with the white walls of her kitchen, which Monica suggests jokingly will be fashionable in the near future.

Monica legitimates her decision by framing it in terms of a protest, as an attempt to disparage symbols of conspicuous wealth as embedded in consumption practices; 'a forty-year-old middle-aged woman making a protest, and provoking others by painting everything white'. As she discusses the post-box episode, her home becomes a canvas through which she pictured her 'true' identity. Its remaining an aspiration allows her thus to preserve a space for her to picture an 'ideal' self. However her articulated ideals regarding her domestic decoration are qualified by a number of contradictory factors.

In negotiating between ideas of self-presentation and appropriate display Monica is constructing an 'appropriate' idea of herself through the domestic sphere. It is significant that her choice of white also relates to fashions in that she mentioned in passing that she might be setting trends by returning to decorative simplicity in her home, thus suggesting an actual interest against which she claims to react. This aspect of her decision was underplayed, however, as she stressed the moral dimension to her choices and her own fears of personal compliance with popular materialism. Perhaps the ambivalence of Monica's actions surface in her assertion to me that any guilt which she feels in offending a friend is assuaged by the personal satisfaction she gained by the awareness of the moral correctness of her motive. On the other hand, it could be suggested that if Monica was truly disinterested in these details of home embellishment, it wouldn't have mattered whether her post box remained blue with painted flowers. One-and-a-half years later the doorplate remains white with a darker inscribed 'here lives Monica' in a thick grey paint.

Monica's home feeds her own self image by acting as a carrier for her ideals. It situates her as a key player in a certain subversive relationship with her perception of popular social values:

> She [a friend of Monica's] said to my sister that she was fed up with me for doing it and my sister thought it was stupid herself. And that has been a little ongoing discussion between us and I know that people who go by here discuss it. The same as me, like when I and a friend might walk around and look in houses and see which curtains look nice and which don't. I know that others do that for my house too. And there were quite a lot who have discussed the colour change of the post-box.

Monica's protest is not only a strike against social trends and materialism as she describes it, but she is also repositioning herself in relation to her home and her social environment. While viewing her domestic alterations as the result of self-conscious reflection – which she feels is missing on the part of her neighbours – she is also participating in the construction of her ideal home and her visions of herself as homeowner. In this sense, in choosing white rather than the nostalgic motifs of her neighbours, she is constructing a visionary template of herself through the priorities manifested in her domestic choices.

Conclusion

Henrietta Moore (1993) makes the point that Western ideas have been dominated by certain assumptions regarding personhood since the Enlightenment. She refers in particular to the Western belief in essences, on the self residing in discrete physical bodies, and makes the point that 'in spite of ethnographic data to the contrary, much anthropological writing on the person still proceeds on the implicit assumption that the physically discrete nature of the body is somehow evidence for the unity of the person' (1993: 203). From the idea of the self as constituted and contained in the body is the related notion of the self itself as something coherent, rational and self-determining, a concept that can be traced to the history of Western philosophy on the one hand and to the specific agendas of anthropological scholarship on the other (ibid.: 203).

In illustrating the Western source for these concepts, Moore points to contemporary theorizing in which the 'unity of the subject is illusory or fictive' (ibid.: 203) and therefore questions how this unity is to be created. One perspicacious example is provided by Gullestad (1993) who illustrates how this is achieved through home decoration. That is, 'Norwegians create the experience of a whole person, and of a unified family, through processes of externalising and objectifying the idea of wholeness in the physical arrangements of the house' (Moore 1993: 203). Through the long-term planning and fiscal investment involved in domestic decoration, the biography of its residents are evident. In Chapter Two of this volume, Clarke shows how homeowners on low incomes and living in flats of identical layout can use their decorative skills to mediate a reality that bridges their ideal and actual social worlds. Personal aspirations are manifested in decorative choices such that the ideal home mediates the construction of the actual home. Through such processes, one can trace a domestic narrative, which can create a feeling of 'wholeness' to which Moore refers.

Placed alongside these considerations, is an alternative quality which leaves little lasting trace. It is precisely due to this ephemeral nature that practices such as moving furniture have been overlooked in studies of home decoration. One explanation for this has been the valorization of 'permanence' to which Csikszentmihalyi and Rochberg-Halton (1981) allude, has been sustained in appraising home decoration as a long-term narrative through which residents find self-expression. Moving furniture receives little attention in comparison with other domestic concerns, and yet in the examples given one can see that it is significant in cultivating a sense of domestic empowerment for many informants. In the example of Beate, moving furniture is performed in response to feelings of boredom or apathy. Additionally, it is continuously enacted, soon forgotten and has minimal presentational value. This is one of its prime assets because it is immediate, cathartic and allows a degree of private introspection that is frequently lacking in long-term decorative projects. For others such as Else, who is unemployed, it provides her with a medium to combat the loneliness and monotony of the domestic space and exert control over her environment and circumstances. The value of such a practice is that it is spontaneous, establishing a feeling of newness and difference in an environment that is otherwise characterized by a large degree of normativity. Whilst becoming habitual in some cases, rearranging furniture is characterized by its immediacy and therefore acts as a foil to decorative projects which have more 'aspirational' aims.

Gullestad made the observation in the 1980s that although her informants declared their individuality in decorating their homes, the similarities between houses was marked (1984). Domestic projects are infused with significances that transcend the home itself and comply with various social considerations. In this respects the home is a canvas that mediates between the household and the actual or imaginary visitors, the 'peering eyes' (O'Dell 1997: 132) of the social audience. Monica illustrates this in extrapolating from her post box a 'lost sense of priorities' in which her decorative decisions are as much about presentation *to* herself and self-definition as about presentation *of* herself to others.

However, small incidental routines such as moving furniture allow momentary disarray, and individual empowerment in the face of social conformity. Whilst such practices do not negate the long-term narratives of domesticity, they fracture the narrative sufficiently to provide ephemeral respite. The domestic raw materials that ordinarily feed normative expectations of the social self become suddenly playful and alterable, significant because of their triviality. And yet while they are distinct, they are not mutually exclusive, but illustrate the necessity of the transient and the banal as well as the diachronic and aspirational in cultivating a sense of self. Therefore, much as permanence has been valorized, so too has the coherence of narrative. Much like the layers of Ibsen's onion which peels off layered experiences of Peer Gynt (see Gell 1998: 140), this paper focuses on the incoherence of narrative, on the creation of unity through disjuncture and looks at the home as providing a coherence from layers of fractured experience.

References

Bergan, G.Ø. and T. Dysthe (1994) *Hjemme i Norge: Tradisjon og Fornyelse*. Lillehammer: J.W Cappelens Forlag.

Buchli, V. (1999) *An Archaeology of Socialism*. Oxford: Berg.

Chevalier, S. (1996) 'The domestic as museum'. Barcelona, EASA Conference, unpublished.

—— (1998) 'From woollen carpet to grass carpet'. In D. Miller (ed.) *Material Cultures: Why Some Things Matter*. Chicago: University of Chicago Press.

Cieraad, I. (ed.) (1999) *At Home: An Anthropology of Domestic Space*. Syracuse: Syracuse University Press.

Csikszentmihalyi, M. and E. Rochberg-Halton (1981) *The Meaning of Things: Domestic Symbols and the Self*. Cambridge: Cambridge University Press.

Gell, A. (1998) *Art and Agency: An Anthropological Theory*. Oxford: Clarendon Press.

Giddens, A. (1990) *The Consequences of Modernity*. Cambridge: Cambridge University Press.

—— (1991) *Modernity and Self-Identity: Self and Society in the Late Modern Age*. Oxford: Polity Press.

Gombrich, E.H. (1984) *The Sense of Order: A Study in the Psychology of Decorative Art*. Oxford: Phaidon Press.

Gullestad, M. (1984) *Kitchen Table Society*. Oslo: Universitetsforlaget.

—— (1992) *The Art of Social Relations: Essays on Culture, Social Action and Everyday Life in Modern Norway*. Oslo: Scandinavian University Press.

—— (1993) 'Home decoration as popular culture: constructing homes, genders and classes in Norway'. In T. del Valle (ed.) *Gendered Anthropology*. London: Routledge.

Halle, D. (1993) *Inside Culture: Art and Class in the American Home*. Chicago: University of Chicago Press.

Löfgren, O. (1984) 'Sweetness of home: class culture and family life in Sweden'. *EthnologiaEuropaea* 14/1: 44–64.

—— (1994a) 'Consuming interests'. In J. Friedman (ed.) *Consumption and Identity*. Chur, Switzerland: Harwood Academic Publishers.

—— (1994b) 'The empire of good taste: everyday aesthetics and domestic creativity'. In B. Klein and M. Widbom (eds) *Swedish Folk Art: All Tradition is Change*. New York: Harry Abrams.

McCracken, G. (1989) '"Homeyness": a cultural account of one constellation of consumer goods and meanings'. In E. Hirschman (ed.), *Interpretative Consumer Research*. Provo, UT: Association for Consumer Research.

Miller, D. (1990) 'Appropriating the State on the council estate'. In T. Putman and C. Newton (eds) *Household Choices*. London: Middlesex Polytechnic and Futures Publications.

Moore, H. (1993) 'The differences within and the differences between'. In T. Del Valle (ed.) *Gendered Anthropology*. London: Routledge.

O'Dell, T. (1997) *Culture Unbound: Americanizarion and Everyday Life in Sweden*. Lund: Nordic Academic Press.

Putnam, T. and C. Newton (eds) (1990) *Household Choices*. London: Middlesex Polytechnic and Futures Publications.

Reme, E. (1994) 'Hverdagsbilder–selvbilder: om hjemmet som arena for estetisk praksis'. In A. Strømsvåg and T. Selberg (eds) *Hverdag: Festskrift til Brynjulf Alver. Professor Brynjulf Alver 70 år 28 September 1994*. Stabekk: Vett & Viten.

Sixsmith, J. and A. Sixsmith (1990) 'Places in transition: the impact of life events on the experience of home'. In T. Putman and C. Newton (eds) *Household Choices*. London: Middlesex Polytechnic and Futures Publications.

Swales, V. (1990) 'Making yourself at home: a study in discourse'. In T. Putman and C. Newton (eds) *Household Choices*. London: Middlesex Polytechnic and Futures Publications.

Wilk, R. (1997) 'A critique of desire: distaste and dislike in consumer behaviour'. In *Consumption Markets and Culture* 1/2:175–96.

Wilk, R., R. McC. Netting and E.J. Arnould (1984) *Households: Comparative and Historical Studies of the Domestic Group*. Berkeley: University of California Press.

−4−

The Refurbishment of Memory[1]

Jean-Sébastien Marcoux

'I am unpacking my library. Yes, I am.' These are the opening lines of Walter Benjamin's talk about book collecting. It goes on as follows:

> The books are not yet on the shelves, not yet touched by the mild boredom of order. I cannot march up and down their ranks to pass them in review before a friendly audience. You need not fear any of that. Instead, I must ask you to join me in the disorder of crates that have been wrenched open, the air saturated with the dust of wood, the floor covered with torn paper, to join me among piles of volumes that are seeing daylight again after two years of darkness, so that you may be ready to share with me a bit of the mood. . . which these books arouse in a genuine collector. For such a man is speaking to you, and on closer scrutiny he proves to be speaking only about himself. (Benjamin 1999: 61)

Benjamin wrote these lines in 1931, one year after his separation, after he moved into an apartment in Berlin (Allen 2000), while he was settling. At least, this is what we can suppose. As he unpacks his belongings, he describes the souvenirs and the memories that arise. He refers to the places, the people and the events that the contact with these books evoke for him. He who cherished two passions, reading and travelling, moved frequently during his existence. So did his collection. He moved to Berlin, Frankfurt, Munich and Bern for his studies. He had to leave Germany in 1933, however, after Hitler's accession to power. He then stayed in Paris transitorily, until he was compelled to flee from the threat of the Gestapo in 1940, before he died at the Spanish border that same year. Despite its tragic character, Benjamin's case highlights the role played by mobile possessions in securing memory in motion. This role has also been emphasized by the research on migration, exile and Diaspora. Parkin (1999), for instance, has explored the

1. I would like to thank Daniel Miller for his comments on a draft of this chapter. This chapter was presented at the departmental seminar on material culture at UCL in January 2001. I would like to thank the participants for their valuable insights. I also wish to thank the personnel of the CLSC Côte-des-Neiges in Montreal for their help in the conduct of my research as well as the Social Sciences and Humanities Research Council of Canada for its financial support. Above all, I wish to express my gratitude to my informants.

importance of the things that refugees forced to flight, sometimes from the threat of death, choose to bring with them. And how they use these objects to reobjectify themselves in a new environment. Mehta and Belk (1991) and Belk (1992) have analysed Indian migration in the US as well as Mormons' migration through the possessions that people take with them, whereas Leo Spitzer's (1993) biographical account deals with the transmission of relics among uprooted people. Those works are relevant for an anthropological understanding of the constitution of memory through displacements even though moving occurs in less dramatic circumstances, when it relates to changes of place within the same city, as is the topic of this chapter. I concede from the start that the experience of displacement that I will be describing here hardly compares with Benjamin's exile or the cases of refugees described by Parkin. Having said that, the people on the move that I have accompanied in Montreal are confronted by the same kind of question, that of determining which books or things they would like to take with them or can take with them.

With this in mind, I will explore ethnographically the relationship between memory, material culture and mobility. In doing so, I will examine and analyse what people bring with them when they move, what are the things that matter when the time to move comes, why they matter and how they come to matter. I will devote particular attention to the process of sorting out things which normally accompanies their changes of residence (Desjeux, Monjaret and Taponier 1998; Rautenberg 1989). And I will try to demonstrate that this process is critical in the experience of mobility inasmuch as it metaphorically relates to the sorting out of relations and memories. Indeed, I will argue that the things that people move with them are at the heart of the constitution of a memory which often resists displacements. I will go further by emphasizing how this memory is constituted *throughout* those displacements and how it is often transformed, altered and refurbished by the same token. As such, sorting mediates the relationship between people and things, and in turn that between people and places.

I should say that moving is a feature of Montreal life. Approximately 15 per cent of the city's population changes address annually (Statistic Canada, 1996). In this city where three-quarters of the dwellings are rented (ibid.), and where leases customarily range from the 1 July to the 30 June of the following year, most of the people move at about the same time of the year. They also do so over short distances: on the same street, around the corner, in the same neighbourhood; sometimes into a different one close by. And yet, remaining in place has been institutionalized as a tenant's right in Quebec province's housing legislation since the 1970s. It appears, then, that moving responds to some Bourdieusian-structured set of preferences, which is particularly prominent among tenants who count among the least-advantaged groups (Bourdieu 1979). Given that transition costs are relatively low for tenants as against owners, and that most of the people move by themselves, which keeps the moving costs at a low level; given also that leases are short, moving becomes understandable, not to say rational. At least, it is reasonable to think that in the Montreal context it may become a means for trying to make the best out of renting. In other words, even though the legal system in force protects tenants' residential stability, moving is part of many Montrealers' identity. It is probably also part of a certain idea of what it is to be a Montrealer. As such, it is often characterized humorously – not to say sarcastically – as the Montrealers 'national sport' (*Le Devoir*, 1994, 1997).

In brief, up to now I have emphasized the importance of the tenants as a residential class in Montreal and the importance of moving for that group of people. Most of the people that I have accompanied in the course of my work are tenants. They come from different social classes and different age groups. I now want to focus on the central role played by possessions in these people's displacements. In Montreal, an apartment or a house is usually not furnished. People move with their things: their most cherished possessions as well as the more common ones. They move with the tiniest objects as much as the more cumbersome ones such as the refrigerator and the cooker. In this respect, tenants can probably be said to inhabit their belongings as much as their place. In fact, objects are at the heart of the problematization of the experience of mobility because while these possessions move in relation to a place, they may represent stability in relation to the people. This is probably why we can often hear people saying that things 'accompany' them in their move.

Travelling in Good Company

Many things such as dishes, the utensils and non-perishable food are brought simply because they are taken for granted. They are brought because 'it is obvious', because 'we are not all the same going to leave them there', because 'it is still good'. Many things are brought because they are 'despicably utilitarian', 'functional', not vital or significant. Simply useful. Things of 'little importance' are also brought. These are things that people are not really attached to, but that are nonetheless necessary inasmuch as they aid the pursuit of day-to-day activities: the medicine cabinet, the personal telephone directory and so forth. Other things are brought because they could serve, because they could always be useful in the new place, just in case.

The move is also the occasion to better determine what is useful, as in the case of Mme Cabot. She is a seventy-eight-year-old widow who moved from a three-and-a-half-room apartment into a single room in residential care and who legitimized her choice of objects in functional terms. Mme Cabot surrounded herself with the necessary, only the necessary. She abandoned without any regret all her kitchen appliances and utensils because meals are provided in such institutions.

She decided to bring into her new residence what she considered to be 'handy', 'practical', what was 'functional'. She brought 'just enough to decorate' as she put it. She brought that carpet for 'functional reasons' to 'dress the place a little bit'. She brought this armchair that was 'faded, but still comfortable', her sideboard that used to be in the living room of her apartment and in which she stored her silverware. She brought it into her new room where it became a cupboard in which to put her clothes and on which she displayed her numerous photographs, illustrating Howes' (1996) argument, that things may be reinterpreted in a different context. Mme Cabot brought it, as she explained, because of its 'practical' side. She also brought with her the things that she cherished more: her books that she described as 'the companions filling her evenings', a radio, some cassettes that she used to listen to when reading, her lead-crystal glasses that came from Czechoslovakia and so on.

Mme Cabot's case shows how the move is the occasion to classify things and refocus on those things that are perceived as practical, useful or functional. Those useful things are also, if not mostly, mnemonic objects. They are mementoes as Parkin puts it. The armchair, for instance, was purchased at the beginning of her wedding. The glasses were given to her on the occasion of her fifteen marriage anniversary. Those important things take on their value from their association to events that are constitutive of the person or of the family's history. They take on their value from their association to important persons as well. Things become all the more important when they constitute the sole link with a person, for instance a deceased person: an ancestor, kin, a close friend. As such, Mme Cabot gave away all her coffee sets on the occasion of her move except the one coming from the *Commission des transports* where her late husband used to work. She did not keep it as an object of reminiscence (Thomasma, Yeaworth and McCabe 1990) but as a 'surrogate' (Mehta and Belk 1991) for the person it stands for, in this case her husband. Indeed, elderly people like Mme Cabot often surround themselves with artefacts just as they would attempt to surround themselves with those persons these things relate to. When it became time to move she emphasized how those possessions were important for her. She mentioned, like *all* the other elderly people that I have encountered, that it was important for her to 'remain with her things'. This reminds us that 'loved objects' do not come alive in a person like Mme Cabot. On contrary, as Walter Benjamin puts it, it is the person who lives in them.

This becomes even clearer when the central role played by possessions is pushed to its extreme, when people possess nothing else, when things are the only tangible assets available in the creation of a sense of home. This is the case of Sandra Parent, a forty-one-year-old single mother receiving social benefits. Sandra has experienced domestic violence in the past. She went through a separation and was relocated by the *Office municipal d'habitation* which manages social housing in

Montreal. She was relocated to a smaller apartment situated on the same street, a few hundred meters away. This is where I met Sandra. This woman who moved more than forty times in forty years, most times within the same Montreal neighbourhood, used to move with all that she possessed – the things that she acquired since she has ran away from her parents' home at the age of sixteen. Sandra ran away with nothing. Only a few objects linked her to her past: some cauldrons that her mother gave her on the sly, when she visited her without her father knowing it; a photo of her mother that always accompanied her as she put it, that 'never left her on her own' or abandoned her. Those mementoes became actors, in Latour's (1989) sense, of Sandra's experience of mobility in space as well as in time.

For personal reasons, Sandra put her childhood behind her. The therapy that she was following when I met her was aimed to help her face that past. In the confines of her own apartment, she was rather trying to reinvent herself. In this respect, she devoted particular attention to her collection of unicorns. Sandra lived with unicorns. Unicorns were literally everywhere in her apartment. She had a duvet, key ring, paintings, photographs, T-shirts, even oven mitts emblazoned with images of unicorns; jewels as well. Over the years she also built herself a collection of miniatures. Contrary to those important things that take on their value from their association to other persons, few of Sandra's unicorns related to other people. Some of her unicorns had been given to her by her son; others by her partner. She acquired the majority, however, by herself. For instance, she used the decoration of a new apartment as a pretext for buying new unicorns. She did this to please herself as she put it, because she knew or she thought that she had nothing to expect from other people. She stressed this as if she wanted to show that she owed nothing to anybody, as if she wanted to be the sole tributary of her past. It is not my intention to analyse the symbolism of unicorns. I rather wish to stress that in the absence of enjoying a stable home, Sandra spent a great deal of effort in housing her unicorns adequately. She put them in a case specially adapted by herself for that purpose – a case fitted with a glass that she painted and in which she talked about installing a neon light some day. This case stood at the centre of the living room like a shrine (see Figures 4.1 and 4.2). It nearly took precedence over the unicorns themselves. By sheltering her protégés in this way, and by increasing her collection along with her successive moves, Sandra attempted to transform the compulsion to move into a constitutive event for her. More importantly, she invented herself a memory.

In recapitulating, we could say that the things that people take with them, those 'aide-mémoires' (Rowlands 1993), help preserve a certain consistency and continuity. Going further, we could also say that memory may be constituted in motion through the displacement of objects. Bringing things with oneself, then, is to make the choice of remembering.

Figure 4.1. Sandra's unicorn case in the living room after the move

Heavy Memories and Cumbersome Companions

Mme Lambert, a forty-two-year-old French immigrant who is married to a Canadian citizen and is the mother of two teenage children, dragged many objects of memory from her childhood, along her successive moves. She dragged a whole collection of collections throughout the three places that she and her family have occupied over the last sixteen years since she arrived in Canada. Sometimes, she moved them without even unpacking them: a collection of books, another one of saucepans, china, LPs and so forth. She dragged with her a collection of dolls that she began when she was young, that she kept enlarging since then, and that she moved with the intention of transmitting one day to her grandchildren – those she hoped she would have. She also dragged with her a multitude of sculptural and pictorial ornaments of animals that she consistently, rigorously, arranged in her homes, move after move *(*Figure 4.3). She described one particular ornament, that of a sleeping cat, as a 'piece' of the house. For her it was not a simple brick, as she put it, but 'the soul of the house'. While Bahloul (1996, 1999) emphasizes the importance of recreating the house for Jewish immigrants coming to France from Algeria, here the stress is on the role of the object as a remembrance of the edifice. The object becomes a metonymy. It contains the house. In this respect, things are at the heart of the creation of a sense of place and of its recreation. Far from only

Figure 4.2. Another view of Sandra's unicorn case in the living room after the move

having an instrumental role, they are at the symbolic centre of the house. It is around these things that the home is symbolically recreated and rebuilt.

Mme Lambert's example also demonstrates how objects of memory may be difficult to move. Her possessions that she had taken care to accumulate and to drag with her since her childhood did not only bring her satisfaction and security. She also often complained that these things enslaved her and imprisoned her within the house. Mme Lambert was working part-time as a clerk. Housework was entirely devolved upon her. She hardly received any help from any other member of her family. Mme Lambert did not really want to emulate her mother and her mother-in-law who appeared to her to be ideal 'interior women'. She did not want to

Figure 4.3. Mme Lambert's miniatures

become like them even though this was the wish of her husband. She dreamed of a more public life. She wanted to work more outside, bring in money and help her husband pay for the mortgage. Sometimes, she thought that she could reconcile her public aspirations and her domestic responsibilities by attracting people to her house, by teaching at home for instance. In any case, she realized that she should devote less time to taking care of the house and to the housework. Belongings require care, effort and work. Keeping them calls for attention. She thought that things took too much space, that they were too difficult to keep in order (Figure 4.4). In fact, for Mme Lambert the house was so overcrowded that it was useless to tidy it up (Figures 4.5 and 4.6). She often tried, in vain, to get her husband and

Figure 4.4. A view of Mme Lambert's bedroom before the move

her children to help her in the domestic tasks. So she came to consider that the solution was through a lightening of the burden of her work and a separation from many of her belongings. In other words, after failing to transform the social and political structure of domestic relations that had conspired to disadvantage her, Mme Lambert instead hoped to transform the material structure of those relations.

Getting rid of things was not an easy task, however. It amounted to sacrificing a part of herself. When confronting her things at the time of sorting them, Mme Lambert often recovered a taste of her past just like Marcel Proust recalled childhood remembrances when tasting a madeleine. She ended up keeping things for fear of regretting not doing so. She kept some of her hats hoping that they would be useful some days, some pullovers in case they would go camping. She also kept a 1976 agenda including only one annotation, that of a meeting with friends on the occasion of her birthday. She kept it at least for the moment, without really knowing what to do with it. She just said to herself that it did not take up too much space. In the end, she kept almost everything with her and clearly gave the impression of regretting it. For her, things became cumbersome companions. And they appeared as such on the occasion of the move which revealed the weight of their memory. Indeed, moving brings relations and memories up to date and forces people to do the same. It forces people to think about the objects as we shall see now.

Figure 4.5. Mme Lambert's closet before the move

Repudiating the Normal Life of Things

Moving often gives rise to strong emotions, for it proceeds from the need to face every single object, from the first baby hair lock to those things that are redis-covered, those that had been lost, forgotten, or that one would have preferred to forget. And, through the sorting, it is the souvenirs, the memories and the relations that need to be faced. Sorting out, in a sense, is to engage oneself in an excavation of the memory. It requires us to go into the details, to the heart of things for one cannot content oneself with an overview. Moving does not permit *status quo*. In

Figure 4.6. The Lambert's living room before the move

Miller's (1987) line of thought, we would say then that moving repudiates the normal life of things.

Some people want to take everything with them and keep things at all cost because that is all that they possess, as is the case of the poorest people encountered, like Sandra Parent. Others are simply incapable of getting rid of things, like Mme Lambert who worked on it for three months before the move and for the whole year following it without the anticipated success. In most of the cases, however, people do not move with all their belongings. Sorting is often perceived to be necessary because of the multiplication of things. It accompanies and punctuates the changes of relations that in themselves often give rise to a move. It responds, as in the formation of a couple, from the desire to avoid the repetitions resulting from the pooling of resources and possessions. It responds to the desire to select for keeping what matters, those things that will define the identity of the new place and of the new social entity as well as the exclusion of those that would be incompatible with it. Sorting out things may engender disagreements. One person will wish to keep that wooden fork, that orange couch, whereas another will want to get rid of it. Sorting also calls for compromises. Sometimes sorting even awakes tensions. Mme Lambert recalls how she had to 'fight', to use her own expression, in order to keep a bookcase that her husband considered to be space consuming.

Hence, the difficulty in sorting out things does not only come from the difficulty of separating from an object that may nearly be considered as a part of oneself, but from the difficulty of determining what to begin with, where to start or which priorities to put forth. It also comes from the fact that a person does not always sort out things for herself, as Mme Lambert put it, and that a person is not always alone in doing so. The extreme case is rupture. On such an occasion, the most valuable objects, like the most common ones such as the measuring cup which have no particular economic or sentimental value, easily become the locus of conflict. As one informant moving in the context of a separation put it, what matters is not so much *what* is divided, but *how* it is divided; how the sorting is performed and conducted. The difficulty in sorting out things also arises from the sorting out of social relations that build around those artefacts. If we consider that what gets developed through the sorting out of things is a project of self-construction, we can say that people are rarely alone in the construction of their self-narrative.

Some things are abandoned, sold or thrown away. Others are sent to the charity organizations like the St-Vincent-de-Paul Society, the Salvation Army or the parish's bazaar. Young people and students also often lend or entrust to friends things or furniture that they don't need for the moment, like the refrigerator, the kitchen set and the couch, because their new co-tenant, or their new partner brings their own equipment. Other things are consigned to their parents' cares where they will be secure until one feels 'more settled' as one informant put it. And it seems that keeping those possessions even if in storage becomes, for the parents, a means for coping with the children's departure; an alternative to the preservation of the bedroom in its intact state. People lend, store or entrust those things provided that they may need them in the future. These objects remain important with regard to the potential changes of status, relation or residence in case it does not work out with the new partner or with the new place. In other words, people want to keep these objects as an option for the future and keep their options over them.

On the other hand, elderly people moving from domesticity to care, usually into a smaller place, need to separate from many if not most of their belongings irrevocably. This is what is commonly described as *'casser maison'*. Things are then discarded for fear of lacking space. They are discarded on the advice of the residence authorities or on that of health-care workers, in order to reduce the amount of obstacles, in the hope of reducing the risk of a fall. Moving into an environment in which one is cared for, where meals are provided as in boarding and chamber residences, also makes some things like the cooker and the kitchen sets useless. Getting separated from one's belongings, however, often equates with getting separated from all that appears to be stable and familiar, everything that could be accounted for and mastered; sometimes all that remains. An eighty-nine-year-old single woman declared that she had to move into a residence because she became unable to take care of herself, of her house and of her possessions. 'Elle ne pouvait plus tenir son ménage', as she put it. Discarding things, in this respect, becomes a form of rendition. A form of loss. At least, it is a difficult experience. Hence, it is through the sorting out of the things that the persons can or cannot take that the moving crisis asserts itself, that dispossession and the loss of landmarks manifest themselves grievously.

Elderly people often try to transform this compulsion to empty the home into a constitutive event for the self, how the divestment from the home may become a form of investment into relationships (Marcoux 2001) through the transmission of things in Weiner's sense to related others (Weiner 1992). This contraction of the material environment is not always apprehended grievously. Moving into a smaller place with and within a smaller amount of things is sometimes seen as a relief: less things need to be remembered, dusted, managed or worried about. When one gets older, when one suffers from arthritis as one informant put it, every single task, like reaching the bottom of the sideboard or the top of the cupboard, becomes a complicated one. The symbolic virtues of the separation are not negligible in this respect. As we have seen earlier with Mme Cabot, it can become a way to focus on the relations and memories that matter and devote oneself entirely to those. When pushed to its extreme, discarding things takes on the form of what elderly people sometimes call a 'clean sweep': a move on which occasion they abandon many of their belongings in attempting to free themselves from the burden of their past. As an example, Roger Ricard, a seventy-one-year-old man, moved out of the house he built himself thirty-three years earlier of which the first twenty-three years were spent with his wife prior to her death. Mr Ricard not only moved away from that house, he also left everything behind him. This is unique among my informants. Indeed, most of them wish to move with as well as within their things. Mr Ricard told me that everything in that house reminded him of his spouse: how she had imbued her personality into the place, the life she gave to the place, the objects that she had chosen and that became part of the place. Nothing, according to Mr Ricard, was not hers, nothing was not her. He felt that by taking the furniture with him he would have uprooted her; that he could not do. Moving without his belongings, then, became a means for giving respect to the remembrance of his late wife. As he put it, he cut himself from that place. And he left all those things he was attached to behind. Mr Ricard, a former teacher, had the financial means to start over again. Nonetheless his example is useful because it shows that people may get separated from some things precisely because these are too important. Because the memories are cumbersome.

Sorting may result from the refusal to bring everything into the new place if anything at all, or it may respond from the 'pleasure to throw away' and the 'habit of not keeping everything', as Filiod (1999) puts it. It may express the desire to exorcise the pressure of the abundance of things. It may also respond from the desire to 'change skin', as we often hear. As such, sorting lies at the edge between the ideal of domesticity and its actual realization as Clarke (Chapter Two of this volume) would probably argue. We have seen earlier how Mme Lambert longed, wished, hoped to get detached from the things that weigh upon her. And how this desire to change was related to an ideal of self-construction. Her concrete preoccupation was a lightening of the burden of her housework. Her rationale, however, was an ideal towards which she should tend: what people generally call 'detachment'. Mme Lambert's case is not exceptional. A common motif among the people met in Montreal is that mobility is related to lightness. 'Detachment', understood here as the capacity not to get attached to things, is valorized among the people who valorize mobility, often the younger generation. Indeed, moving is sometimes taken to lead to detachment, as if it were leading to a superior state, nearly a state of spiritual elevation. Detachment is said to provide a feeling of being in control, a feeling of being free to move in the symbolic sense of the term. For instance, one informant, a student in her twenties explained to me that she did not want to 'be stuck with too much furniture' in her new apartment. She used moving to challenge her stability and to force herself to become detached. Another informant, a thirty-seven-year-old woman working as a health-care professional spoke of her need for not feeling 'too much attached' to things. She insisted on the need for her to feel free to go. As such, she admitted she was afraid that 'too much materialism' would 'restrain' her and 'imprison' her. By moving she felt she retrieved her freedom. At least, as she explained, she felt that she was reaching what she called 'the essential'.

At first sight, we find in these remarks the functionalist contradiction between wealth and movement, which is fundamental to the mobility of hunters and gatherers as argued by Sahlins (1972); the idea that objects constitute a curb of moving and the corollary that moving easily is to travel light. This is no coincidence. Montreal movers are often compared to nomads. The real contradiction, however, lies between different kinds of things: between the mass of things and the singularized ones, the alienable world of things and the inalienable ones. Getting detached, in this sense, is to get separated from the material contingencies taken as an enslavement and a burden. It is a way of retrieving or maintaining 'a certain sense of priorities' as one informant put it, a way of 'using things instead of serving them' as another put it. It is a way of focusing on what matters as Mme Cabot's example showed us earlier. Similarly, Mr Ricard did not move because he was detached from the things surrounding him; on contrary. He moved *in order* to detach himself. This is probably why Mme Lambert saw her salvation in the sorting that the move would allow her to achieve. Why she saw her move as the occasion 'at last' to drive 'everything away'. Why it had to be *the* good move.

Even though they define themselves as detached, people tend to remain attached to those things that are personalized, singularized and that therefore represent the opposite to mere materialism. The purpose of sorting is then to impose an order; a topic central to Daniels' and Garvey's contributions in this volume (Chapters Ten and Three, respectively). It is to impose the symbolic over the accumulation of things and on the material world. To paraphrase Rowlands (1993), we could say that out of the move, out of disorder and chaos, a new unity emerges. The question is, now, what kind of principle presides over this new order?

Putting Order in Relations and Memories

Considering that things embody relations and memory (Bourdieu 1972; Chevalier 1994, 1995, 1998; Gotman 1989; Miller 1987) and that memory is selective, it follows almost logically that the sorting out of things becomes a metaphor for the sorting out of relations and memories. In this respect, when facing the difficult task of discarding possessions, Mme Lambert disposed of those belongings associated with the persons she cared for the least. At least, she was easily separated from this deep fryer offered to her by her mother-in-law. She also separated from an animal sculpture and some dolls offered to her by her mother with whom she admitted she had very little affinity. Mme Cabot refocused on the memories that mattered to her when she moved, whereas Mr Ricard needed to leave his past and his memories in place in order to start over again. I could also give the example of a woman in her thirties who moved in the context of a separation. She admitted that she usually moved house when she changed partner and that she changed bed when she moved house for the bed was the symbol of a relationship for her. As such, since the end of a relationship was far from being the end of her 'womanhood' as she put it, she preferred to change bed. A last example is that of another woman who got rid of objects associated with her father's ex-partner with whom she broke off relations. She left them behind her when she moved. She left them declaring that she hoped that somebody would burn them.

Moving becomes a means to reshuffle relationships and memories by bringing them back into consciousness, by making them explicit and for deciding which ones to reinforce, which ones to abandon or put on hold. It allows people to keep track of their relationships and memories, keep a map of these and transform this map. In other words, moving allows people to order their relations and memories. It may even become a means for reflecting on one's self-narrative as Giddens (1991) would put it, not to say for repairing the self; an occasion for people to ask themselves, as he says, 'what do I want for myself?' Can moving be considered as a therapy in the sense understood by Giddens, that of a continual self-reflexive exercise? Not exactly, although the idea that moving may become, in some cases, a process of growth just like a therapy is a seductive one. I would rather suspect that this confrontation with the self occurs especially on the occasion of disruptive events like the move. Thence, drawing upon Simmel (Frisby 1992) and Deleuze and Gattari (Allen and Pryke 1999) who emphasize how the rhythm, the speed and the pace of movement are central in the formation of subjectivity, we could say that in a context like Montreal, moving frequently even if it is over short distances becomes a means for defining oneself as a subject among the material world. It becomes a means for the people to define themselves via the transformation of the material structures in which they are intimately subjects, as Buchli and Lucas (2000) argue. In other words, moving frequently provides the opportunity to understand the fluid possibilities of relations and memories in terms of choice.

Moving towards the Essential

The empirical evidence suggests that what raises problems on the occasion of a move is less the move *per se*, with the risks of injury, the potential damage or the loss of goods, than the fact that sorting forces objects into consciousness. The apprehension of the move probably hides in many cases an apprehension about confronting things and memories. In other words, the refusal to confront one's history as accumulated in things may feed the fear of the move, not to say deter people from moving.

Some things matter because of their origin and others matter even though their origin is unknown. Things matter because they have been there 'for so long'. They have 'always been there'. People would simply never think about getting rid of them. Other things are valued because people have always dragged them with them. They are valued for having 'survived', in a sense, those changes of residence, those displacements and those multiple crises as if they could testify to it. In other words, they acquire something of a 'patina' through their displacements (McCracken 1988). Conservation, then, takes on a different meaning than the frozen, fossilized meaning of the *thésaurisation* or of hoarding. Conservation takes on its importance despite displacements. It even acquires its full sense through those displacements, *because* of them. It would be futile to start from some classification of belongings in an attempt to understand what governs the sorting out of things. It would be vain to content ourselves with thinking that what people take with them is what matters and consequently that what they don't take doesn't matter. Possessions are not simply given as mattering from the start. They come to matter *through* the sorting out. Because in itself it classifies. Put differently, a given thing is not *only* kept because it bears some value, be it economic or sentimental. It *acquires* value through the sorting process. People take with them what matters. But the things matter all the more when they are brought, once they are brought. By abandoning this thing, by getting rid of that one, a person confers more value on the objects retained. She or he confers it some importance it did not possess at the outset. The production of rarity, hence of value, is indeed the corollary of the sorting out of things.

By analogy to the acts of 'drying', 'chopping', 'cutting' and 'burning' which are involved in the building of memorials and monuments (Rowlands 1993: 144), sorting becomes a way of defining what matters. Thus, the 'essential' does not necessarily pre-exist the move. It is something to be achieved. And moving is the occasion to do so. For people get rid of things as if wanting to better remember. In a form of refurbishment of their memory.

References

Allen, J. (2000) 'Preface'. In W. Benjamin, *Je deballe ma bibliotheque*. Paris: Rivage poche.
—— and M. Pryke (1999) 'Money cultures after Georg Simmel: mobility, movement and identity'. *Environment and Planning D*. 17: 51–68.
Bahloul, J. (1996) *The Architecture of Memory: A Jewish–Muslim Household in Colonial Algeria, 1937–1962*. Cambridge: Cambridge University Press.
—— (1999) 'The memory house: time and place in Jewish immigrant culture in France'. In D. Birdwell-Pheasant and D. Lawrence-Zúñiga (eds) *House Life: Space, Place and Family in Europe*. Oxford, Berg.
Belk, R.W. (1992) 'Moving possessions: an analysis based on personal documents from the 1847–1869 Mormon migration'. *Journal of Consumer Research* 19, December: 339–61.
Benjamin, W. (1999) 'Unpacking my library: A talk about book collecting'. *Illuminations*. London: Pimlico.
Bourdieu, P. (1972) 'La maison ou le monde renversée'. In *Esquisse d'une théorie de la pratique. Précédé de trois études d'ethnologie kabyle*. Geneva: Droz.
—— (1979) *La distinction*. Paris: Les Éditions de Minuit.
Buchli, V. and G. Lucas (2000) 'Children, gender and the material culture of domestic abandonment in the late 20th Century'. In J. Sofaer-Derevenski (ed.) *Children and Material Culture*. London: Routledge.
Chevalier, S. (1994) 'Au-delà d'une apparente banalité et d'un standard: des décors domestiques particuliers'. *Archives suisses des traditions populaires* 90/2: 165–85.
—— (1995) 'Itinéraires mobiliers ouvriers'. In N. Gérôme (ed.) *Archives sensibles. Images et objets du monde industriel ouvrier*. Cachan: Les éditions de l'École normale supérieure de Cachan.
—— (1998) 'Destins de cadeaux'. *Ethnologie française* 37/4: 506–14.
Desjeux, D., A. Monjaret and S. Taponier (1998) *Quand les Français déménagent*. Paris: Presses Universitaires de France.

—— (1997) 'Âmes marchandes. Rien n'arrête les vrais pros de la vente de garage'. 23 May.

Filiod, J.P. (1999) 'L'épluchure, le matelas, la statuette. L'univers domestique à l'épreuve de la conservation'. In J.C. Beaune (ed.) *Le déchet, le rebus, le rien.* Champ Vallon: Collection mileux.

Frisby, D. (1992) 'Social space, the city and the metropolis': In D. Frisby (ed.) *Simmel and Since: Essays on Georg Simmel's Social Theory.* London: Routledge.

Giddens, A. (1991) *Modernity and Self-Identity: Self and Society in the Late Modern Age.* Cambridge: Polity Press.

Gotman, A. (1989) '"Le vase c'est ma tante". De quelques propriétés des biens hérités'. *Nouvelle revue d'ethnopsychiatrie* 14: 125–50.

Howes, D. (1996) *Cross-Cultural Consumption: Global Markets, Local Realities.* New York: Routledge.

Latour, B. (1989) *La science en action.* Paris: Éditions Gallimard.

Le Devoir (1994) 'La fête du déménagement'. 2 July.

Marcoux, J.S. (2001) 'The *'casser maison'* ritual: constructing the self by emptying the home'. *Journal of Material Culture* 6/2: 213–235.

McCracken, G. (1988) *Culture and Consumption.* Bloomington: Indiana University Press.

Mehta, R. and R.W. Belk (1991) 'Artefacts, identity and transition: favourite possessions of Indians and Indian immigrants to the United States'. *Journal of Consumer Research* 17, March: 398–411.

Miller, D. (1987) *Material Culture and Mass Consumption.* Oxford: Blackwell.

Parkin, D. (1999) 'Mementoes as transitional objects in human displacement'. *Journal of Material Culture* 4/3: 303–20.

Rautenberg, M. (1989) 'Déménagement et culture domestique'. *Terrain* 12: 54–66.

Rowlands, M. (1993) 'The role of memory in the transmission of culture'. *World Archeology* 25/2: 141–51.

Sahlins, M. (1972) *Stone Age Economics.* London: Tavistock.

Spitzer, L. (1993) 'Invisible baggage in a refuge from nazism'. *Diaspora* 2/3: 305–36.

Statistic Canada (1996) Census data.

Thomasma, M., R.C. Yeaworth and B.W. McCabe (1990) 'Moving day: relocation and anxiety in institutionalised elderly'. *Journal of Gerontological Nursing.* 16/7: 18–25.

Weiner, A.B. (1992) *Inalienable Possessions: The Paradox of Keeping-while-Giving.* Berkeley: University of California Press.

−5−

The Taste of Home
Elia Petridou[1]

In the summer of 1999 an anecdote circulated by e-mail among the members of the Hellenic Society of the University of London. It consisted of a long list of identifying characteristics of the 'CGSE', the Cool Greek Student in England. Among the incisive observations and practices which the students themselves chose for their identification, two were related to food. According to the list, to be a dedicated CGSE you should:

> Refer to all English food as being the worst in the world (without ever having tasted any), and have your *mama* [mother] or *yaya* [grandmother] send you *keftedakia* (meatballs) by post.

> Return from every holiday in the motherland with approximately 50 kg of home-made food or as much as you can possibly get through the check-in. Take the rest of your luggage inside the cabin.

Introduction

Most of the literature that focuses on home for the study of social relations has tended to identify the home with the bounded, physically defined space that we normally call 'house'. The danger that such an identification entails is that more emphasis is placed on the symbolic nature of physical structures than on the way people themselves experience and understand their environment. What is missed by focusing on the analogies between physical and symbolic structures is the dynamic way in which everyday practice makes the home meaningful to those who inhabit it.

As Mary Douglas has argued (1991), home is a 'localizable idea', it is somewhere. But the suggestion that home is 'a kind of space' is grounded on an understanding of space as a reality that is autonomous, independent of its human subjects. The concept that should be used instead and which captures the ontological

1. I wish to thank Danny Miller, Stella Galani, Cleo Gougoulis and Eleni Papagaroufali for their insightful comments on earlier versions, and also Vangelis Sachperoglou for his assistance in editing.

significance of home is 'place'. Places are 'contexts for human experience, constructed in movement, memory, encounter and association' (Tilley 1994: 15). Paraphrasing Mary Douglas, home is rather 'a kind of place', which acquires its meaning through practice; and as such, it forms part of the everyday process of the creation of the self.

In an era of increased mobility, studying the home within a defined space becomes even more problematic as it limits its use as an analytical tool and provides little conceptual weight (Rapport and Dawson 1998). According to Berger (1984), during exile, emigration, tourism and other forms of mobility, which constitute 'the quintessential experience' of our age, the concept of home can be realized in sets of practices, styles of dress and address, in memories and myths, in words and jokes (cited in Rapport and Dawson 1998: 7).

In her study on the meaning and experience of home among British under-graduate students, Kenyon (1999: 89) identified as a key element in their understandings of home the 'right to return'. The notion of return implies permanence and continuity. As Kenyon found, the enduring nature of the parental home was contrasted by the students to the constant fluctuation of their term-time accommodation. 'One of the most important factors responsible for their maintained perception of the parental space as a home was the element of continuity' (ibid.: 90).

The 'right to return' involves an understanding of home as the result of repeated practice, that of setting out and coming back. It becomes a point of reference, 'a place of origin and retreat' (Birdwell-Pheasant and Lawrence-Zúñiga 1999: 6), a starting point to which we eventually return, and which gives us a sense of history and continuity. 'Home is not a destiny of our journey but the place from which we set out and to which we return at least in spirit' (Hobsbawm 1991: 65). The journey, itself symbolic of the adventure that leads to the development of the self, is constitutive of the meaning of home. There cannot be a home without a journey as much as there cannot be a self without an 'other'.

The aim of this chapter is to study the home as practice and a combination of processes through which its inhabitants acquire a sense of history and identity. Conceptualizations of home will be explored away from the physical structures of the house but not necessarily away from its material world. The material culture of the home can be used to examine realizations of the self by focusing on the self-creation of the subject through interaction with the object in what Miller (1987) calls process of objectification. The process of self-creation of the subject through interaction with objects associated with home does not need to be geographically bounded. This is particularly important in contemporary societies that are characterized by high levels of mobility and blurring of geographical boundaries.

The material used for the evocation of home that will be the focus in this chapter is food. The advantage of studying home through food lies in the fact that food is perceived through a combination of senses, and it can, therefore, evoke the experience of home as a sensory totality. Referring to the packages of food sent abroad to emigrants by the inhabitants of the Greek island of Kalymnos, Sutton (2001) argues that food sent from home constitutes a symbolic process of restoring the fragmented world of the displaced through reconstructing the sensory totality of the world of home. Food serves as a vehicle for the recreation of this world, which is constituted of meanings and definitions as much as it is of objects. In Bahloul's words, 'the remembered house is a small scale cosmology symbolically restoring the integrity of a shattered geography' (1996: 28, cited in Sutton 2001: Chapter three). Through its link to sensual totality, food can evoke in a unique way the sensory landscape of home (Seremetakis 1994) and restore fragmentation through the 'return to the whole' (Sutton 2001). Food is, therefore, an especially useful vehicle for the study of the meaning of home.

The Greek language contains a striking parallel in the semantics of home and food, which summarizes the points I have made so far. In modern Greek, the word *nóstimos* (tasty) stems from the Homeric word *nóstos*, which means return to the homeland (*epánodhos eis tin patrídha*).[2] *Nóstimos* denotes the ability to return; it also attributes to somebody or something the quality of being pleasant, agreeable and tasty. As Seremetakis (1994:4) explains, *nóstimos* in modern Greek has come to characterize 'someone or something that has journeyed and arrived, has matured, ripened and is thus tasty'. Similarly, the Greek word *nostalghía* (nostalgia)[3] derives from the words *nóstos* (longing for return) and *álghos* (pain, labour), and 'ties painful experiences of spiritual and somatic exile to the notion of maturation and ripening' (ibid.). Tasteless, in this context, is an equivalent of meaningless. As stated in the Greek dictionary,[4] *anostiá* (lack of taste, tastelessness) also bears the meaning of *anousiótis* (lack of substance, lack of meaning).

The parallel between the semantics of food and home suggests that they both become meaningful (tasteful) through the process (journey) of maturing. In both cases, of primary importance for the creation of meaning is a sense of historical process and continuity. The importance of this semantic parallel is that it facilitates the transition from one sphere of experience to the other. The ethnography that follows will illustrate how the sense of fragmentation and discontinuity caused by displacement finds expression in judgements of food, which further extend to

2. The definitions that follow are derived from H.G. Liddle and R. Scott, A Greek–English Lexicon (Oxford: Clarendon Press, 1961).

3. See Seremetakis (1994: 4) for a difference in the meaning of *nostalghía* as used in Greece, and 'nostalgia' as used in the US. She argues that the former refers to 'the transformative impact of the past as unreconciled historical experience' whereas the latter precludes the past 'from any capacity for social transformation in the present'.

4. Dictionary of Th. Bostanjoglou (Athens, 1990 [1962]) *Antilexikón i Onomastikón tis Neoellinikís Ghlóssis, s.v. anostiá*.

judgements about the social other. In the process of making sense of the new environment and themselves within it, the displaced draw on their past experiences, constructing as they do a concept of home against which they contrast their present situation. As I intend to show, the food from home is used in this process to provide a sense of stability, as well as a sense of belonging through the experience of taste.

Upholding the Tradition of Migration: Greek Students in Britain

Migration has long permeated historic experience in Greece. During the nineteenth and twentieth centuries, significant alterations in the economic patterns of the nation directed a considerable percentage of the Greek population, especially from rural areas, towards emigration to urban centres or abroad (see Emke-Poulopoulou 1986; Buck Sutton 1983). Since the 1970s a new type of migration upholds this long tradition: that of young Greeks pursuing education abroad. 'The "New" Diaspora', as Legg and Roberts (1997: 106) called it, has been among other factors the result of restricted access to higher-educational institutions in Greece. Furthermore, high educational standards in Western Europe and North America as well as a wide choice of subjects prompt thousands of Greek students to seek better training opportunities abroad.

One of the countries that have received the biggest number of the student-migrants is the UK. Each year thousands of Greek students migrate to the UK in pursuit of higher education. In 1998/9,[5] almost thirty thousand students from Greece were studying at universities in Britain at undergraduate or postgraduate level, a 30 per cent increase in two years. The majority of the students come from the two major cities of Greece (Athens and Thessaloniki) and rely on private (usually parental) financial support.

The research was carried out among Greek students who came to London for a one-year Master's degree and were accommodated at university halls. Open-ended, unstructured interviews were conducted in two halls, one in central London which belonged to City University, and the other in south London used by three colleges for the accommodation of students of music and the arts. In 1999, in a total of 280 students in the City University hall, around seventy were of Hellenic origin.[6] In the hall in south London the number of Greek students was substantially lower.

Food from home

Food from home normally takes up a considerable amount of space and weight in the students' luggage on their return to the UK after Christmas, Easter or summer

---

5. Source: The British Council at Athens.
6. This figure was provided by one of my informants and has not been double-checked.

vacations in Greece. At the top of the list are feta cheese and olive oil. The latter, though extremely popular among the students, might sometime cause a few problems; one student still laments the five litres of pure, home-produced olive oil that was confiscated at the customs as an inflammable item; while another swore that she would not take olive oil again after the bottle she was carrying in her handbag broke by accident inside the plane. Meat, too, ranging from steaks and cutlets to meat-balls and sausages, is a common food choice for transportation, especially during phases when food scares break out such as the so-called mad cow disease. One of the students whom I interviewed admitted to having returned to London once with 16 kg of meat:

> I go to Greece almost every month because I want to see my boyfriend. Every time I carry back food. Last time I brought 16 kg of meat. Not only mine; my friend asked me to bring some for her too. I shape the meat in small portions in cellophane, freeze it and bring it over frozen. I also brought cheeses. . . I put everything in the suitcase among my things. Nobody said anything.

Greek wine and ouzo, honey, olives, pulses, cakes and chocolates, rusks (*paksimádhia*) and buns (*kouloúria*) are only few of the foods that students carry with them when they leave Greece. Home-made dishes are also popular, especially the ones that are easy to carry, such as spinach pie, cheese pie, *dolmadhákia* (stuffed vine leaves), *keftedhákia* (meat-balls) amongst others.

Food expeditions are not limited only to home visits. During the entire duration of the term, food parcels arrive by post, often on a regular basis (there are extreme cases of students who receive food parcels with home-cooked food twice a week). In the case of parcels, the nature of family relations in Greece plays a significant role.

Food is a domain where the relationship between parents (especially the mother) and children is negotiated. Feeding involves relations of dependency and power. The verb 'to eat' (*trógho*) has multiple uses in the Greek language, all of which revolve around the notion of power/strength (*dhinami*) (Potamianou and Carapanos 1984: 55); a power/strength that is offered, seized, held back, shared, lost. An example of parental pressure expressed in linguistic form is the use of the expression 'me éfaghe i mitéra mou' (my mother kept on at me, literally, 'my mother ate me' – see Seremetakis 1994: 5). A male student used this phrase in his explanation of why he ended up bringing olive oil from Greece:

> And I also brought olive oil. My mother kept on at me [*me éfaghe i mitéra mou*]: take olive oil, take olive oil. All her friends who have children abroad tell her that their children complain about not finding good olive oil here. Well, OK, the oil they have here is not the same as ours, but OK, I don't have a problem. I don't have this, I'll use the other. Nothing will happen to me.

The food parcel as a form of feeding becomes the ground on which the parent–child relationship is contested, and as such it entails a high degree of resistance by students (as evident in the example) as well as parents. In an inspiring study of the role of the lunch box (*obentōs*) that Japanese mothers prepare for their children to eat at the nursery school, Allison (1999) demonstrates how the lunch box prepared by the mother for the studying child constitutes a field where the dominant ideology can be contested, applied or resisted. Many Greek parents question expectations associated with traditional family roles, and distance themselves from the practice of food parcels. In doing so, many of them seek reassurance that their decision does not involve signs of neglect and lack of care towards their children.

It is interesting to note how one mother in particular, whose son left to study in England, resolved the problem of being a responsible, caring parent without having to send food parcels: Mrs Smirli (1999) published a book of recipes adapted to the needs of Greek students studying abroad. The book, which was dedicated to 'my son Vassilis who cooks in England', included basic instructions about food preparation, together with the recipes and urged the young novices to learn how to cook:

> The first time that you find yourself alone, student in another city or another country, away from the 'cosiness' of your family, facing the relentless question 'And now, what are we going to eat?', think, besides the fast-food, restaurants and *souvlatzidhika*,[7] of another crazy idea: to cook by yourself!!! (1999: back cover)

Even as form of resistance and cause for criticism against parental over-protection, food parcelling is an issue for consideration both by parents and students. The latter sometimes dismiss parcels as an unnecessary practice, but I personally never met a student who disliked receiving a parcel from home. Still, as will become evident in the next section, the greatest amount of home-food is brought to Britain by the students themselves. As was clearly stated in the opening anecdote, either sent or carried, food from home constitutes one of the identifying characteristics of the Cool Greek Student in England.

The Greek Taste

Maria, Thalia and Katerina[8] study music and they all stay in two adjacent buildings in a university hall in south London. Maria (aged thirty-one, brought up in Athens, postgraduate at Guildhall) had just returned from Easter vacation in Greece and had brought with her, among other things, dried mizithra cheese because, as she

---

7. Places where souvlaki (skewered meat on sticks or in pitta bread) is prepared and sold.
8. The names of all the informants have been changed.

said, she had in mind to prepare Greek dishes (*moussaká* and *pastítsio*)[9] for her friends in London. She claimed that Greek taste is only attained when the cheese is brought from Greece:

This time I brought with me dried mizithra because I had in mind to cook Greek dishes. I need to make it taste Greek. Aubergines, I don't mind, I can find them here, though still it won't be the same. But for the Greek taste [*ellinikí nostimiá*] cheese has to be brought from Greece. Cheese can't be replaced by another local equivalent. I know that the particular cheese will make the dish taste Greek.

The Greek taste is a frequently mentioned term in the students' vocabulary. Most often, reference to 'taste' (*nostimiá*) is made in opposition to the 'tastelessness' of the local 'English' food. One day, Thalia (aged twenty-four, from Athens) wanted to cook mashed potatoes (*pourés*). Maria offered her the packaged mashed-potato powder that she kept in her cupboard. Thalia asked: 'Is it Greek? [*Einai ellinikós*]' and only when Maria answered in the affirmative did she agree to use it. When I asked Maria to explain to me the difference between mashed-potato powder packaged in Greece and the same item packaged in England, she said: 'Have you ever tried the potatoes here to see how they taste?[10] What should I do? Bring raw potatoes from Greece?'

On her name day Katerina decided to cook for her non-Greek friends whom she had met in the hall. The meat and many other ingredients had been brought over from Greece. As Katerina remarked, the food was so delicious that it disappeared before she had a chance to taste it:

We always wine and dine the others [*mónima trapezónoume tous állous*]. On my name-day, I prepared chicken with potatoes in the oven, meat á la crème with mushrooms — the meat was from Greece — and rice. I had hardly put the things on the table... I wanted to treat them all first, and then I went to serve myself, and I see that there was only a few small potatoes left like the size of my nail. Nothing. From the chicken there were only some little bones left, some ribs. They went crazy because the food was very delicious. Very nice flavours. The people here are fed on sandwiches.

Here, social distinction is drawn on the concept of process, and the cooked chicken is juxtaposed to the ready-made (or easily prepared) sandwich. This is also an example of how the agency of food constructs understandings of social difference. The fact that not one bone of the cooked Greek chicken was left by

9. Pasta with minced meat and béchamel sauce baked in the oven.

10. In Maria's answer, note the use of the verb 'to see' in association with taste. Similar sensory associations in the Greek language, such as the sound of smell, are recorded both by Seremetakis (1994) and Sutton (2001), and confirm their point on the totality of sensory experience.

their guests functioned for the girls as the material confirmation that processes such as cooking, and carrying from Greece, with all the time and labour that they involve, contain value.

The triangle sandwiches sold everywhere in London were not particularly popular among the majority of the Greek students. It felt like an action of ethnic betrayal when, leaving the City University student hall one day, I entered into a corner shop to buy a sandwich. My informant who was accompanying me to the tube tried in despair to prevent me by saying 'Oh, don't tell me you are going to eat this; you'll get sick.' When her efforts to dissuade me brought no result, she said 'How can you eat that?' in a tone that sounded like saying 'you are a different creature if you can incorporate this thing'. When Thalia heard Katerina mentioning the word sandwich, she began:

> The sandwich. . . You go into the shops and you see a whole line of sandwiches. They don't eat anything else here, just sandwiches. All the students that come to the hall, they don't cook. They prepare sandwiches. They put inside cheese, ham or sausage. They boil potatoes, green peas and carrots, add a little bit of salt on top and they eat it. Now, what kind of food is that, I don't know. And when they see us cooking they make remarks, oh! that smells nice, or that looks great, etc. Once, somebody started making jokes and told us that instead of becoming musicians we should open a restaurant! It is how you learn at home. They reproduce what they see at home.

Most often the assertions students make about the 'English' way of life are projections of a limited fragmented experience comprising the hall, the university, the supermarket and the street. Out of these everyday images, the 'English' home becomes part of a narrative, disclosing no information whatsoever about English homes, but revealing a lot about the meaning of home among Greek students and the line where social boundaries are drawn. Here, the 'English' home is imagined as the epitome of social alienation brought about by the penetration of ready-made food into the domestic sphere. By juxtaposition, the Greek home is understood as the place of processes that bring people together. This is exactly what Maria is saying when she refers to the way cooking creates family bonds and is envied by other students in the hall:

> We cook a lot in the hall. We cook every evening. I come back and I know I'll find the girls and we'll have a chat. We'll join together and cook. There is a quality in the food, like a family. They tell us in the hall that we look like a family. And they envy that. They are bored to cook. They envy the quality and the process [*dhiadhikasia*].

Maria's understanding of home involves the process of cooking, food provisioning, the process of cleaning, tidying up, in one word: caring. As Maria put it, without these processes there is no 'family tradition':

Here there is no family tradition [*oikogheneiaki parádhosi*]. Everything here comes packaged from the supermarket, everything is prepared in advance. Here, the housewife (*i noikokirá*) won't care about the food [*to faghitó*][11] or the taste. Everything here is tasteless, like the weather! It is inconceivable for a woman in Greece to find ready-packaged vegetables like that in the supermarket.

It is not coincidental that Maria uses the term *noikokirá* to refer to the housewife. As a cultural term, it conveys simultaneously a set of meanings (see Salamone and Stanton 1986). When referring to a woman the term means housewife, hostess, housekeeper,[12] but also a woman who is tidy and clean, who keeps the house and the family in order. In other words, she involves herself in the process of cleaning, cooking and tidying up, according to the moral precept of *noikokirosíni*. The male equivalent of the term (*noikokíris*) denotes the master of the house as well as a man of tidy habits and a provider. These values and processes constitute Maria's understanding of home and family. Maria believes that the concept of *noikokirió* 'has lost its meaning' (*ékhei khásei to nóimá tou*) in England:

What has made an impression on me here is that all the food is ready-made. You get a portion of moussaka from the supermarket, you put it in the microwave and it's ready. The concept of *noikokirió* and cooking has lost its meaning. The concept of process [*dhiadhikasía*] has disappeared. Everything has become 'practical' (*praktikó*).[13]

One of the processes that make up the concept of *noikokirá,* which plays an important part in developing a sense of home, is the process of cleaning. Studies in anthropology have shown ways in which identity boundaries are drawn on differing perceptions of cleanliness and dirt (Okely 1983). Notions of cleanliness can be fundamental in the experience of social difference and are normally highly resistant. The issue of cleanliness brought about strong reactions among the girls:

Thalia: Cleanliness? Ah! Don't remind me!

Maria: When the weekend comes, rubbish runs out of the bags, no-one cares to clean the table and they go and leave it like this; it looks like a bomb has hit the place. In order to sit down, we need to clean up first. In general, they are a very dirty people.

Thalia: I remember one day Katerina went to wash the dishes. They have a separate tap for hot and cold water and we burn our hands. Because hands are important

11. *Faghitó* refers to food as a cooked meal.

12. D.N. Stavropoulos, *Oxford Greek–English Learner's Dictionary* Oxford: Oxford University Press, 1988.

13. Practical here means expedient. The notion of practicality and the way it relates to the argument is discussed in the last section.

for the pianists, we must be careful to avoid rheumatism and the like. And that's why we wear gloves. An English girl comes round and starts making fun of Katerina because she was washing the dishes with gloves. She said in an ironic tone: 'Are you afraid that your little hands will get dirty?' Katerina got angry and replied: 'Because you happen to have here a system that we had a hundred years ago, and you can't change it and become modernized, am I supposed to burn my hands?' The girl didn't say anything but stopped talking to us for a week.

As part of a larger habitus, in which history is turned into nature and forgotten, concepts and practices of cleanliness become uncontested 'natural' truths. This works both ways: while the Greek girls perceive the English girls as uncaring and alienated, the latter may equally perceive the former as a kind of relic of pre-feminist domestic relations, and dismiss them as such.

Appearance and Content

When we met, Liana (aged twenty-three, brought up in Athens) was pursuing her Master's degree in clinical psychology at City University. From the start of our conversation, Liana expressed the belief that English people in their majority do not cook but consume ready-made food, which she interpreted to be a sign of their superficiality. What made an impression on Liana in local supermarkets was the great variety of frozen and canned food. Although she admitted to a difference between the two categories (the former being less 'bad' than the latter), both were juxtaposed to fresh food and therefore defined as unhealthy. What Liana particularly failed to understand was why anyone would want to consume canned pasta, since it can be so easily prepared at home:

They have these long freezers. . . and the cans. I had never seen so many cans before. Canned vegetables of all kinds. What is worse are those cans that you open and eat the content like that. It is another thing to pick up a can and cook it, to process it one way or another, and another thing to open the can and eat it as it is. I don't understand the logic of ready-made pasta cans. It doesn't take more than fifteen minutes to cook it yourself. Even I know how to cook pasta, though I don't know how to cook. It's not a big deal.

Dubisch (1986) discusses the necessity of process as cultural transformation and the emphasis on the notion of 'cookedness' in relation to social boundaries. She remembers how her Greek landlady picked fresh strawberries and only served them after she had gone through the process of cleaning and sugaring. Strawberries came from 'outside' and therefore needed processing and transformation in order to become edible. In a similar way, Liana feels the need to process the content of the can in order to make it appropriate for consumption.

In the previous section, drawing on fragmented experiences of a new environment, geographically bounded between the university, the supermarket and the hall, the girls imagined the 'English' home as a reflection of an alienated society. Observing the freezing facilities in her flat, Liana pointed out the size of the freezer, and made a comparison with fridges in Greece which normally have a smaller incorporated freezer:

> Look how small the fridge is in here. Two people have to share one tiny shelf. And look at the freezer: it's double the size of the fridge. Put together they make the size of the fridge in Greece. I think this tells a lot about the people here and their eating habits. They need the freezer much more than they need the fridge.

Liana's experience of the 'English' supermarket included also a number of observations on the fruit and vegetables sections. Most comments focused on food artificiality, which was experienced as a divide between nice appearance and lack of taste. Comments, which extended from potatoes to strawberries, referred to the attractive outside colour as contrasted to the white and 'tasteless' inside. But what most students found particularly intriguing was the tomatoes. Tomatoes, Liana commented, look artificial, as if they are made from plastic:

> Tomatoes look like they are made from plastic. You look at the tomato and you wonder if you can eat it. And then you eat it with the hope that there is something nutritional left inside ... Here they put everything in plastic packaging, even the fruits, which don't get enough air. Let the fruit breathe, man! The fact that they cut vegetables and fruits, and put the slices in plastic packaging, certainly deprives the fruit of some of its nutritional qualities.

Plastic bags and cellophane are perceived to impede fruits from being in direct contact with the environment. In Liana's phrasing, the fruit cannot 'breathe'. Related to that is a comment frequently made by students on the lack of smell. The lack of smell, which they compare to the intensity of odours in Greece, contributes to their sense of alienation, which is again perceived as lack of intrinsic value in a world that puts emphasis on appearance. Natural smell, like taste, can be indicative of the intrinsic worth of food, a 'proof of material presence' (see Clossen, Howes and Synnott 1994: 205). In this line of thought, a naturally grown tomato is not expected to look symmetrically perfect or identical to other tomatoes. Perfect looks are interpreted as a sign of lack of taste. Tasty tomatoes are expected to come unpackaged, loose as in nature. Packaging is perceived as an effort to achieve a better image for the product, to make it look more appealing and to compensate for lack of inner quality.

Thalia, too, was of the opinion that there is too much effort expended on packaging and appearance at the expense of taste and nutritional quality. The emphasis on packaging, she supports, is the result of commercialization. It is interesting to observe how she uses this concept as a ground for definitions of the self:

> You go to the grocer's in Greece and you see all those fruits, loose, a combination of colours, and your heart opens. Here it's full of plastic bags. Too much packaging. All vegetables, spinach for example, it's in cellophane. Packaging seems to be everything. The foreigners [*oi ksénoi*, i.e. non-Greeks] judge the quality by the way things look [*vlépoun tin poiótita me to máti*]. They expect to see something nice in shape, one tomato should look like the others. They blame Greece for low level of exports. But often the Greek products are sent back because they don't look good. But we have quality in the taste, and that is more important.

Thalia's comment on emphasis on looks rather than content is not entirely unsupported. The shift of the power balance from manufacturers to retailers in Britain involved the introduction of products and concepts that were not encountered in Greek supermarkets. In the 1980s, food commercialization in Britain led to increased emphasis on convenience and visual appearance at the expense of flavour. Food growers were encouraged by retailers to select varieties of fruit and vegetables which look good but lack flavour and texture (Gardner and Sheppard 1989: 172). Along with preoccupation with appearance, the stress placed on convenience led to the proliferation of chilled products, cook-chill food, ready-prepared salads and dishes, and in general foods that require little or no preparation. All these have been retailer-led innovations.

It is interesting, however, to observe the easiness with which the transition from the sphere of food to the national self is effected. Among the Greek students, the experience of food as a combination of nice appearance and lack of taste/substance informed perceptions of the 'English', who were perceived to be equally 'commercialized', alienated from anything that requires time and labour, superficial and uncaring. Juxtaposed with this network of associations is the tasteful food of the Greek home, cooked and prepared by people who *care*.

Uncaring People

In order to explain her experience of music studies in London, Maria employed the notion of practicality. As she puts it, in England 'they teach you practical ways of doing things':

> The foreigners are more commercially minded in all their activities. They see things from the point of view of selling, how the appearance sells, not the quality. And in our music studies, they teach you practical ways to do things, that they don't teach you in Greece, and if you can combine what you know, then all is well.

Here, the notion of practicality becomes equivalent to that of superficiality. A 'practical' way of doing things refers to the economizing of time and labour in order to achieve results. In the context of building up knowledge, economizing is perceived as negative and contradictory to the creation of value. An emphasis on practicality involves a shift from well-built deep knowledge to the superficial sphere of technical tricks that aim to impress rather than convince. Katerina, too, experiences the difference between music studies in Greece and England as a difference of emphasis on practicality:

> In many respects, music teaching here is done *bakalistika*.[14] You are taught tricky ways as to how to do things so that they look nice. I agree that what they tell me makes things easier, but sometimes I feel that they are all tricks [*kolpatzidhika*] and they lack foundation. In Greece I would never think like that in order to develop a music technique.

The perception of surface and depth based on fragmented experiences of everyday life expands from the sphere of food and education to social relations. Like most students, Liana has her own story to tell about her contact with the local people. Starting with their English flatmate, Mat, whom she described as 'having fallen from another world', she commented on the lack of depth and true feelings in the way the 'English' express themselves:

> Here I feel annoyed with the impoliteness of the people. In the surface they are always very polite; I'm talking about an impoliteness that comes from the soul. They say 'excuse me' but what can you do with it if they don't mean it... There is an English boy living next door. In Greece, when we ask 'how are you?', we really want to know how you are. When he asks 'how are you?' he waits to hear 'fine' to disappear behind the door.

For Liana, her experience with food is projected on people: both represent a superficial world that appears to be perfect on the surface, but lacks value and meaning on the inside. Nikos (aged twenty-six, studies finance at City University) also has a story to tell about his experience with the 'English'. He focuses on the lack of care that he experiences in his new environment, a lack of care for other human beings:

> The other day, must have been in February, it was late and it was snowing. From my window I saw a man lying on the ground, still, and slightly covered by the snow. It was a very cold night. After an hour, when I came out of the building, I saw him again in the same position. I approached him and said: 'Excuse me, are you feeling well?' No answer.

---

14. *Bakalistika* means doing the work in simplified fashion using shortcuts. It derives from the word *bakális* (grocer), who would traditionally make gross calculations without attention to detail. The word 'grocer' probably comes from the word 'gross', i.e. 'in bulk', which indicates the style of trading of the traditional grocer (Blackman 1976: 149).

I touched him and his body moved in one piece as if he were frozen. The people that were passing by were all looking at me but nobody stopped. In the end, a guy approached that I would characterize as typically English: tall and thin, with his umbrella, stiff walking, his head just moving slightly, expressionless. He told me: 'Mind your own business. Probably he has his own plan. Haven't you got anything else to do?' I still can't forget the word 'plan'. The man was probably already dead. Then a Greek friend came over and we called an ambulance.

To the image of the indifferent English who do not care about a dying man, Nikos juxtaposed the image of his home and especially his father, to whom he made extended reference throughout our conversation. He spoke about his father's involvement in placing care in the processes of food production and preparation. He recalled the times that his father took him along to the oil-press to buy good olive oil, and taught him the ways to preserve it. He expressed pride in the fact that his father knew how to select exactly the right variety of grapes for wine-making and how, stung by wild bees, he became allergic in the process of making honey. Nikos emphasized these expressions of care and commitment in the process of food making, and the rejection of what is easily offered at the supermarket. The presence of a process implies for him the labour and the time required for the attainment of substance and inner value:

> My father believes in a healthy lifestyle. He takes the trouble to look into these matters deeper [*to psákhnei*][15] . . . It all started from wine. He had some friends who worked for some big names in Greek wine production. He learned many of the tricks they do inside, and he didn't like it. So he started making his own wine. Also, he used to bring big quantities of olive oil in the house and teach us how to preserve it. He wanted to have the best quality. . . . I like these hobbies, in general I like what man makes. It is not coincidental that I smoke rolled cigarettes and I don't buy the commercialized ones [*tipopoiiména,* literally standardized]. I like the process. . . thin cigarette when I don't want to smoke much; thick when I want it to last.

Nikos identifies himself with things that involve a process. When I asked him what kind of cheese he had brought from Greece, he started his answer by describing the origins of his parents. He concluded that the cheese was from a mountainous area of the Peloponnese, southern Greece, where his mother had been brought up. He said he had bought the cheese from a shop in his town (Tripoli), where he knew the owner and trusted his selections. He described him by using again the expression 'psaghménos':[16]

15. The expression derives from the verb *psákhno* (to search, to look for). Literally it means 'he looks for it'. Nikos is using an expression that refers to the action of looking deeper into things.

16. Again he is using the verb *psákhno* but in the past participle. *Psaghménos* characterizes a person who looks deep into the self, who does not go for the easy or the superficial.

I grew up in the Pelopponese; my father's lineage is from Mani. I've looked into these things [*ta ékho psáksei*]. My mother's lineage is from mountainous Kalavrita. They both come from entirely mountainous areas, the most 'hard-core'[17] [*skliropirinikoí*] people. I wonder how the lineages matched! In those areas they have very different habits. One of the good things they do over there is that they make nice cheeses. This particular cheese is from Kalavrita and it is hard and salty; they have hard cheeses up there, they can't preserve them otherwise. They make them at a household level [*se epípedho noikokirioú*], not mass production. So they are better taken care of [*pio proseghména*]. I bought the cheese from a shop I know in Tripoli. I know the guy, he likes to look deeper into things [*einai psaghménos*], he engages himself [*askholeítai*]. He doesn't look for things round the shop and that's it. He takes his van and looks for his products regardless of distance.

Nikos identifies home with a deeper search into the self; with the journey that people and things have to undertake in order to mature and become tasteful (meaningful, full of value). The cheese that was brought to London incorporated a considerable amount of personal involvement, labour and time. It was the result of a process of production by village people, of the process undertaken by the owner of the cheese shop who looked especially for the particular cheese, of Nikos's personal effort to visit the shop and of his labour to carry it with him all the way to London.

Conclusion

Food from home, as I have tried to show in this chapter, evokes a large network of associations between values and practices, such as cooking, cleanliness, family, sociability, care, all subsumed within the idea and ideal of home. In a new environment, where the displaced find themselves deprived of the meaningful familiar structures of 'home', this constructed notion is closely tied up with the constitution of the self. Food serves as a material form, which mediates, objectifies and shapes understandings of difference, and plays an active role in legitimizing action. A number of examples were used to exemplify this. The fact that cooked food, especially if the ingredients were from Greece, was highly appreciated by their 'English' friends in the hall, constituted for the three girls a confirmation that their food was 'better', that they themselves were 'better', and that they were not degraded by an alienating lifestyle objectified in tasteless food. The untidy state of the kitchen in the hall was again another confirmation for the students that the Others were leading a debased lifestyle, in that they did not care about cleaning up and could put up with the dirt. These examples demonstrate how our interpretations of the material world that surrounds us (a mundane, taken-for-granted world,

17. 'Hard-core' in the sense of conservative, difficult to change opinion.

resistant to the suspicion that our perception of it might be subject to our interpretation) can play an active role as confirmation of our beliefs about the self and the Other and as legitimation for action.

The temporary loss of historic continuity and control over a familiar environment (the students studied in this chapter had been staying in London for less than a year) was expressed by the students through a series of oppositions between surface and substance, appearance and depth. Food functioned as the material confirmation that the divide between nice appearance and lack of taste/substance was an intrinsic property of the 'English' society. Tastelessness, in a metaphoric sense, was easily projected to all spheres of social action, such as musical education, forms of greeting, social contact, care for the other.

Juxtaposed with these images of alienation were conceptualizations of home — the home that these students left behind to pursue their studies in England. Through experiences of tasteless 'English' food and uncaring people, the Greek home emerged as the centre of processes that result in the creation of meaning through care and the devotion of time and labour. Home becomes a steady point of reference in the search for meaning, a starting point for the journey of self-creation. Food serves this purpose by providing the sense of stability and continuity of the idealized home.

The relationship between what is considered deep and what is understood as superficial is by no means the same for diverse peoples and regions (see Miller 1995). People who fear that they have lost a sense of depth by leaving a place that for them contained their historical foundations and arriving in another place where they do not feel they have roots, make up for this rupture by evoking the sense of stability of home through the very mobility of food. To use Crang's (1996: 47) words, this is part of an understanding of 'a world where the geographies that matter are predominantly associated with these various forms of travel and mobility – of people, objects, ideas – rather than with static dwelling'. The students take a substance such as taste, which might be thought of as superficial, and make it more solid than the mere house in which they are expected for the duration to make their home.

References

Allison, A. (1999, 'Japanese mothers and obentōs: the lunch-box as ideological state apparatus'. In C. Counihan and P. Van Esterik (eds) *Food and Culture: A Reader*. New York and London: Routledge.

Bahloul, J. (1996) *The Architecture of Memory: A Jewish–Muslim Household in Colonial Algeria, 1937–1962*. New York: Cambridge University Press.

Berger, J. (1984) *And our Faces, my Heart, Brief as Photos*. London: Writers & Readers.

Birdwell-Pheasant, D. and D. Lawrence-Zúñiga (1999) *House Life: Space, Place and Family in Europe*. Oxford: Berg.

Blackman, J. (1976) 'The corner shop: the development of the grocery and general provisions trade'. In D. Oddy and D. Miller (eds) *The Making of the Modern British Diet*. London: Rowman & Littlefield.

Buck Sutton, S. (1983) 'Rural–urban migration in Greece'. In M. Kenny and D.I. Kertzer (eds) *Urban Life in Mediterranean Europe: Anthropological Perspectives*. Urbana, IL: University of Illinois Press.

Clossen, C., D. Howes and A. Synnott (1994) *Aroma: The Cultural History of Smell*. New York and London: Routledge.

Crang, P. (1996) 'Displacement, consumption, and identity'. In *Environment and Planning A* 28: 47–67.

Douglas, M. (1991) 'The idea of home: a kind of space'. *Social Research* 58/1: 287–307.

Dubisch, J. (1986) 'Culture enters through the kitchen: women, food, and social boundaries in rural Greece'. In J. Dubisch (ed.) *Gender and Power in Rural Greece*. Princeton: Princeton University Press.

Emke-Poulopoulou, E. (1986) *Provlimata Metanastefsis-Palinnostisis* [Problems of Migration-Repatriation]. Athens: ISMEO and EDHM.

Gardner, C. and J. Sheppard (1989) *Consuming Passion: The Rise of Retail Culture*. London, Sydney and Wellington: Unwin Hyman.

Hobsbawm, E. (1991) 'Introduction (Exile: a keynote address)'. *Social Research* 58/1: 65–8.

Kenyon, L. (1999) 'A home from home: students' transitional experience of home'. In T. Chapman and J. Hockey (eds) *Ideal Homes? Social Change and Domestic Life*. London: Routledge.

Legg, K.R. and J.M. Roberts (1997) *Modern Greece*. Boulder and Oxford: Westview Press.

Miller, D. (1987) *Material Culture and Mass Consumption*. Oxford: Blackwell.

———— (1995) 'Style and Ontology in Trinidad'. In J. Friedman (ed.) *Consumption and Identity*. London: Harwood.

Okely, J. (1983) *The Traveller-Gypsies*. Cambridge: Cambridge University Press.

Potamianou, A. and F. Carapanos (1984) 'I skhesi miteras–paidhiou stin Elladha: paraghon sti dhiamorfosi tautotitas' [The mother-child relationship: factor in the shaping of identity]. *Sinkhrona Themata* 23: 53–9.

Rapport, N. and A. Dawson (eds) (1998) *Migrants of Identity*. Oxford: Berg.

Salamone, S.D. and J.B. Stanton (1986) 'Introducing the Nikokyra: ideality and reality in social process'. In J. Dubisch (ed.) *Gender and Power in Rural Greece.* Princeton: Princeton University Press.

Seremetakis, C.N. (1994) *The Senses Still: Perception and Memory as Material Culture in Modernity.* Chicago: University of Chicago Press.

Smirli, V. (1999) *Foititis kai stin kouzina* [Student also in the kitchen]. Athens: Ellinika Grammata.

Sutton, D. (2001) *Remembrance of Repasts: An Anthropology of Food and Memory.* Oxford: Berg.

Tilley, C. (1994), *A Phenomenology of Landscape: Places, Paths and Monuments.* Oxford: Berg.

Part II
Estate Agency

—6—

Possessions
Daniel Miller

Ghosts as Estate Agents

Oscar Wilde begins his story 'The Canterville Ghost' as follows: 'When Hiram B. Otis, the American minister, bought Canterville Chase, every one told him he was doing a very foolish thing, as there was no doubt at all that the place was haunted' (1977: 193). Wilde then provides through an extended parody an outline of what may be regarded as the quintessential haunted-house story, and perhaps also much of its explanation. The two key factors I want to draw attention to are (a) that what was being purchased was an old house with its own name and history, and (b) that the purchaser was an American with little disposition to mind such things. I wish to argue, in emulation of Lévi-Strauss (1972), that the haunted house as a genre is a mythic form that constructs – at the level of myth – a resolution to a problem of social and material relations. The problem in this case is the discrepancy between the longevity of homes and the relative transience of their occupants. In consequence, feelings of alienation may arise between the occupants and both their homes and their possessions.

Within a few lines we learn that Canterville Chase was owned by Lord Canterville and last inhabited by the Dowager Duchess of Bolton. We are also shown the response of Hiram B. Otis, who proclaims that he comes from a modern country where money can reduce both ghost and furniture to a valuation, such that even ghosts can be turned into commodities to be exhibited at some museum or road show. The opposition is thus very firmly established within the first page. The first action by the new mistress is to attempt to remove (with the assistance of Pinkerton's Champion Stain Remover) the bloodstain of Lady Eleanore de Canterville, murdered there by her husband in 1575. In subsequent pages the distinguished ghost becomes horrified by the materialism of Otis and the lack of respect of his children for a pedigree such as he possesses and his many past achievements in the honourable act of haunting.

But what the ghost most desires is the final repose which is to be had at the garden of death, and it is the love of Virginia the heroine, and daughter of Otis, that may gain it for him. To cut a short story even shorter, she of course achieves just this aim, and the ghost is finally laid to rest in the garden of death. As a result she obtains a treasure-chest of jewels, clearly heirlooms, which despite her father's desire for her to give them up, she must retain. Indeed the further result is that she marries the Duke of Cheshire and joins the British aristocracy. It appears, then, that it is only possible for her to remove one form of possession – that by a ghost – if she accepts in its place another sort of possession – that is a set of objects that have comparable lineage. So the tale begins in an apparently unbridgeable gulf between the house as an abode of history and a set of occupants for whom that history has no meaning. By the end of the tale, the ghost is laid to rest, but only because there is one individual amongst the occupants who can overcome this gulf, coming to appreciate and finally become part of that historical tradition. She gives the respect that the house and its possessions are due, and thereby becomes appropriate to both take the heirlooms of the aristocracy and to marry into its scions.

The association of ghosts with stately homes is hardly an invention of Wilde. In a book called *The Stately Ghosts of England*, Norman (1963: 17) states quite simply that 'It seems that the longer the history of a place, the greater its chance of possessing a ghost. . . In Stately homes, ghost are a tradition, almost an inheritance, bequeathed from generation to generation.' What the author wishes to impress upon the reader is that such ghosts are merely (but also literally) a matter of fact. The reader is led through a hunt for ghosts at such well-known stately homes as Longleat, Woburn Abbey and Beauilieu. It is made clear that ghosts also tend to be associated with particular details of space and possessions within the home. Often particular rooms are known to be haunted or particular corridors become the route of ghosts. It is often important that the original objects are extant. In one case we are told a room would not be haunted since 'the original bed went to America, and those are most certainly not the original drapes' (ibid.: 46). But things are not always so material in their relations, rather a room gradually absorbs its own history. For example 'the room has been soaked in unhappiness so much that it has accumulated over many lifetimes and distilled into one over-powering sense of general misery' (ibid.: 57). Very commonly the ghost gives evidence for aspects of the history of the house that were otherwise unknown, for example a priest's hiding hole, or a lost hall or room (ibid.: 74–5). A ghost 'plods on blindly through walls and into passages apparently unaware of how the geography of the home has changed in the meantime'. She concludes that ghosts are the dead who cling to their old homes (or, as one might say, their old haunts).

Peter Underwood, then president of the Ghost Club, attempts in his book *No Common Task: The Autobiography of a Ghost-Hunter* (1983) to provide a fairly typical sense of the ghost phenomenon more generally. As one might expect, other older buildings such as churches are also favoured, and again certain objects become subject to the agency of the ghosts, such as bells ringing, doors being knocked upon, objects moving from their proper place. A typical example is a ghost who appears always from one deep cupboard and taps along the wall to disappear into another corner cupboard (ibid.: 96). A particularly well-known British haunting was that of Borley Rectory which was haunted through four tenancies and subject to intensive investigation by a psychic, Harry Price, and others until it burnt down in 1939 (for a sceptical account, see Dingwall, Goldney and Hall 1956). A distinction is usually made between ghosts and poltergeists, which seem lesser forms but where the materiality of their presence is more important, since it is the moving around of material objects, upsetting of furniture and the breaking of china that seems most to signify a poltergeist.

The idea of the haunted-house story as a myth in Lévi-Strauss's sense of objectifying social contradictions is given greater credence by a recent analysis by Marcus[1] (1999: 116–27) of a genre of such stories as they arose in London during the 1850s–1870s. Here again it is a contradiction of relationships that is objectified in the stories, but rather than the mere individual house it is the larger movement of housing that is of concern. The place of Otis is taken by the general rise of suburbia and the desire by Londoners to establish a sense of modernity for the metropolis. The problem was that London was evidently a historical city saturated with an older form of housing associated by these modernizers with all sorts of vices, promiscuity and disease that they saw as having flourished in conditions of overcrowding and poverty. This returned as an issue when some of these elements that modernisers saw themselves as having escaped from started to crop up again within the modern semi-detached housing. So the ghosts that featured prominently within the new genre of haunted-house stories appear 'as representatives of superceded eras and modes of thought, ghosts were seen by some as antithetical to a metropolis conceived of as a modern seat of rational enlightenment' (ibid.: 117). In short, they were both a drag on modernity but also testimony to the antiquity of London itself. To summarize then, the ghost may be said to be a partial anthropomorphism of the longer history of the house and of housing relative to its present inhabitants.

Lesser Hauntings

I too would claim to be haunted by my house, but I am afraid in a much more mundane sense than that described by Wilde. I live in an Edwardian semi-detached house, in many ways typical of north London suburbs. I am particularly fond of it, because even within the very limited claims I would make to any kind of aesthetic preference, I have a particular liking for the Arts and Crafts movement, and this house, which was built in 1906, retains most of the original features such as fireplaces and stained glass that are characteristic of the period. I gain a great deal

1. Thanks to Inge Daniels for drawing this reference to my attention.

of satisfaction from living within an aesthetic I admire, and I would wish to acknowledge that this is a rare privilege. But there are some aspects of this possession that are slightly problematic. The first is that one of the many things I lack confidence in is precisely aesthetic judgement and matters of taste.[2] I personally, at least, have great difficulty in creating any kind of decorative order or aesthetic judgements that would produce results that I find I am able to admire. It is simply a skill I do not see myself as possessing. Two things follow. Firstly I admit that the house intimidates me. It represents precisely an aesthetic ability that I might aspire to but cannot achieve. So when it comes to choosing furniture or placing decorations I feel that I am most likely to detract from the prior qualities that the house possesses by virtue of the creativity and style that went into its initial construction. Should I really have placed an artificial coal 'living flame' fire in one of the original fireplaces? This, then, is the source of one part of the fear that 'haunts' me.

The second haunting is a result of quite the opposite problem. While the house itself is to me an admirable aesthetic object, the prior owner of this house was by profession a builder. He sold us the house (yes, I admit it was a bargain) having gone bankrupt, partly because of the money he spent trying to do up the house for 'renting to the Japanese' as he saw it. Some of the results of his work I could not live with. The high metal railings placed outside with a video-phone that had turned the house into something of a fortress, simply had to go. But there is also the basic colour scheme of the house, the carpets and the paintwork. Since we have quite a few people to stay (a common result of periods of overseas fieldwork as an anthropologist combined with living in a place as central as London) our house is on the large side, and the carpeting and painting would be expensive to redo until this is required by wear and tear. So although I do not particularly like (and in some cases detest) the colour schemes, I will live with them for several more years. This poses a problem when visitors arrive. I hope I am not particularly vain but I will share my appreciation of the house as a courtesy and most visitors (especially anthropologists) are as nosy as I am and like to be shown around. As such I suppose I hope that the aesthetics of the house to some degree rebound on the self-expression of my identity and preferences. On the other hand the person being shown around will assume that the basic decorative scheme reflects our choices, and even if they share my dislike of it, they would usually be too polite to say so. I find that I am not so vain as to deliberately bring into conversation the fact that this is the result of someone else's tastes and not mine, but vain enough to care about the consequent misapprehension. I can't say that either of these matters is a haunting that exactly keeps me awake at nights, but in a minor and mundane key it brings us down to a level that most people can relate to in some degree within their own experience.

2. I speak here of course for myself alone, and not for any other members of my family.

On the one hand being intimidated and on the other hand somehow being let down by the material environment within which one presents oneself to oneself and to the world at large. In either case they show that the simple idea that one's home is a direct expression of one's taste is false.

To generalize from my own experience: in 1992 a series of excellent programmes called *Signs of the Times* was shown on BBC television. These were concerned with peoples' relationship to the material culture of their homes. Produced by Nicholas Baker (who was originally trained in anthropology) they were astonishingly remote from the speeded up 'realism' of most television documentaries. In these programmes the camera dwells lovingly and patiently on particular objects in the home and those who dwell with them while we listen to the accounts of how people established their relationships with the material culture of the home and with each other. Particular programmes focused on topics such as how couples, or parents and children, reconciled or failed to reconcile their preferences. The programmes were extremely successful as a series with a considerable following especially amongst female viewers.

One of these programmes was devoted entirely to the way in which occupants determine their relationship to the temporality of the house. One couple shown owned a stately home but felt the need at times to express the sense that it is was a living home and that they were not just curators of a museum. They therefore introduced some contemporary elements. Another couple only wanted genuine antiques, and treasured the sense that 'someone has loved it, treasured it, polished it from old. That's the difference from buying something new.' Similarly another couple wanted an old house but couldn't afford it, so they furnished the house they actually purchased with antique-looking objects to make it more similar to the house they would have bought if they had had the money. By contrast an elderly person failed to understand any of this since for her identification could only come from the longevity of the actual association an individual person had with individual objects to create 'things that matter', 'things that have lives in themselves', so that mere possession of the old through purchasing antiques was for her inauthentic.

Some occupants would buy only reproductions and others would purchase actual antiques. For the former, true antiques were seen as 'coffins' of furniture. For the buyer of antiques, the purchase of reproduction furniture is viewed as fundamentally dishonest. Those people are called 'tremendous cheats' and a betrayal of the proper search for authenticity. By contrast, for people who buy reproduction furniture it is the purchasers of antiques who are dishonest because it is reproduction furniture that is being clear about the necessary relationship of taste to the present. The debates go beyond mere purchase. Does the inglenook fireplace have to be where it would originally have been or can it be made from a conversion of a space under the stairs? Or, as with another couple, do you make the house itself with antiquated methods such as oak beams with oak pegs? What emerges from this range of views and practices is that in coming to terms with the agency expressed in the temporality of the home and the temporality of its associated material culture, one is also developing a larger cosmology of authenticity, truth, negotiation and identity that in many cases may have consequences for one's view of the world in a much wider political and moral sphere. Collecting and matching can become quite obsessive such that once again individuals are not so much choosing, but becoming increasingly possessed by what they see as the fundamental morality involved in establishing their relationship to the history of material culture.

What each of these three examples (the tradition of the English haunted house; my minor concerns with the decoration and aesthetics of my own house; and a more general concern with establishing one's relationship to the temporality of things) highlight is a major theme of this volume as a whole. If this book is part of an argument that the material culture of the home has consequences, then this particular chapter is intended to focus on the degree to which these consequences are often the result of the very materiality of things and as such they may not be an expression of our agency and they may have been unintended. So while other chapters examine the use of the home as a means of agency and the expression of social relations, my concern is to remind ourselves of the other side to this coin: that quite often we are not the agents that create the material environment that becomes the medium of representation. Furthermore there is the point that it is an intrinsic quality of materiality that makes objects transcend any such relationship to persons. In the ghost story we mythologize this problem by positing the agency as belonging to the house itself and its possessions, where these objectify those people who have previously lived within it. It is, after all, the house and its possessions that are possessed; we merely observe these ghosts and poltergeists to our terror or, as in Wilde's story, to our amusement.

Social Relations and Object Relations

The degree to which homes and their material culture may be regarded as possessing agency has been established by reference to their history, or representation of history. But it does not actually have to be limited to that case. Even where one has little interest or concern with history, the prior presence of material culture may have a constraining impact upon what one feels one can do with possessions in such a manner that they may appear to possess their own agency which must be taken into account. For example, in the face of houses built according to the ideological canons of reforming modernizers it has been their modernity rather than their history that comes to oppress their inhabitants, and the response has often been one of resistance and the reintroduction of older domestic routines and spatial orders (see Attfield 1989 and several contributions to Birdwell-Pheasant and Lawrence-Zúñiga 1999). To make this wider point I turn to the ethnographic evidence that emerged from the study of provisioning by myself and Alison Clarke. This chapter is intended thereby to complement that of Clarke's in this volume and our other publications of material from our fieldwork (Clarke 1998; Miller 1998 and 2001; Miller, Jackson, Holbrook, Thrift and Rowlands 1998).

The street where this ethnography took place was chosen partly because it lacked any outstanding features. One side is mainly occupied by council estates. Although clearly working class, they are not the most impoverished of such estates. Most of the other side of the street is owner occupied, but although more likely to be middle class it is not especially wealthy. There are many people in the area who were born in places other than Britain, but there is no single alternative place of origin that is conspicuous. In short the street is typical of north London in being cosmopolitan but manifestly ordinary. In all we have worked with seventy-six households, but as with most ethnographies there is a smaller core of households that we would claim to know much better than the others. As well as participation in shopping and other acts of provisioning, one of our techniques (which we undertook together), was to ask people stories about how objects in the living room and kitchen were obtained and came to be in the place they now occupy. This provided us with narratives not only of how people came to own these goods but the subsequent issues over how these goods should be consumed in the longer term.

I will start with the case of Judith to illustrate how social relations can de developed through the transformation of the home, and then contrast this with Berenice who demonstrates how social relations can constrain this transformation. I will end with a council estate where the impotence that people feel about changing their material environment creates a feeling of alienation which can lead to a projection of their frustration: transforming this into the agency of others in a manner analogous to the ghost story. The way that social relations can be developed through the active transformation of the home has been the subject of several previous studies (for example Attfield and Kirkham 1989; Chevalier 1998; Putnam and Newton 1990), and is considered elsewhere in this book. This chapter is intended to complement rather than contradict such work.

In Miller (1988) I argued on the basis of an analysis of kitchens on a different North London council estate that gender roles had become reconstructed as a relationship between the practice of do-it-yourself technology, which provided a male role in the house, contrasted with females who took exclusive responsibility for aesthetic decisions. Although that article did not talk about ghosts, it included examples of people who felt haunted by the sense that their apartments belonged to the council – the state – and not to themselves. The council was clearly felt by some to be an unwelcome presence objectified in the very apartment itself that haunted and depressed them. The exchange between male labour and female aesthetics had become the means by which people in transforming their environment exorcised this alien presence of the council and in effect took possession of the place in which they lived.

The relationship of Judith and her son certainly followed that generalization. They lived on the Lark estate which is an extremely dull and in many cases highly depressed block of council housing, somewhat less attractive and closer to the stereotype of the grey concrete council blocks than is the case with Sparrow Court, the estate that is discussed in Clarke's chapter in this volume. Judith's flat stands out as a clear expression of aesthetic transformation. Even from the outside, the front door and ornamentation tells the passer-by that this is a conspicuous household that has been engaged in a continual act of appropriation from the state. Plant hangers, mock-Tudor hinges and elaborate door-knockers contrast sharply with the uniform dull green doors of the surrounding neighbours. The entrance hall, panelled from floor to ceiling in dark varnished wood to match a stunning full parquet floor creates an impressive spatial transformation. When inside it is impossible to separate out the aesthetic of decoration from the multitude of actual physical changes in the layout of the rooms.

Judith is quite explicit about this schema being an expression of the relationship between herself ('I was on a pink and grey theme at the time and that's what we went for') and her son, a professional plumber. The result was that both the infrastructure and the decoration of their flat was more radically changed than any other we encountered. It had flouted all the state rules against such changes including the removal of several partitioning walls. Although Judith remarked that '99 per cent of the time we agreed', she also took pride in that one degree of their difference, in order to assert her respect for his individuality. Some further insight into this relationship is gained later on as the mother refers to the extent to which she felt she had neglected her older female children because she was working such long hours during their upbringing. It was only with this son (where circumstances had changed and allowed her to be much more involved) that she felt she had been able to develop and mature the sensitive relationship that could be observed today. Specifically she notes how much she enjoys shopping with him, and later how much she regrets that she never had time to go shopping with her daughters when they were living at home.

Judith's aesthetic as expressed in the room is a combination of many factors. She is herself confident and experienced in creating her own aesthetic order but all new objects have to be integrated into the order created by those already established. Some have a patina of affinity because of how long she has had them, or who she obtained them came from, or because of the gift relationship they expressed at that time. As McCracken (1988: 118–29) argued in his discussion of the 'Diderot Effect', it is often the consequences of one choice of object for others that renders that choice most significant: for example, the first object in a new style that suddenly makes all the objects around it look old-fashioned. The key aesthetic unit is not often a single object any more than it is a single person. Mostly it is the 'wardrobe' or the 'room' within which are found a whole configuration of objects that together constitute a relationship to taste as a social phenomenon. The interplay between these two kinds of agency becomes very clear in her statements. For example:

> Well my paintings, those were done by my father and I wouldn't part from them for all the tea in China, they been everywhere with me since I was twenty-one.

> My children bought me that last Christmas because I left that space there available in case one brought a Christmas present for me.

> It was very very artful. Actually I wanted something with the grey to match you see and John and I were shopping one day and I happened to see it and I said 'You know I quite like that', so I said 'You could tell Daniel [her ex-husband] actually, he wants to find me something for Christmas.' That's how I obtained that one. Yes I'm like that.

What Judith demonstrates is how in the right circumstance the use of the previous decorative order may move from being an alien constraint that haunts the occupant, and become instead a positive expression of the close relationships and self-sacrifice that constitute the love within families. This positive blending of social and material relations can also include the house itself, as we can see if we cross the road to the private-housing sector. Berenice and her husband would have been unable to purchase their house but for the assistance of the Friendly Society of Ancient Foresters. In gratitude the husband served as secretary for that society for twenty-five years, which in turn produced a series of ornaments given on the occasion of his retirement. Almost without exception each object we discussed had become part of her history of relationships. Some even predated the purchase of the house in 1951 as inherited furniture. A clock was inherited by her mother from an uncle and in turn passed down to her. Others, such as a lamp, represent presents from her daughter. As with Judith she has a problem accommodating the many Christmas presents she tends to receive within her decorative schema. Her close friends and relatives are conscious of this and will tend to buy objects that create such schemas around what have become known as her decorative preferences. This is why there are so many ornaments and objects with flower motifs. Or, as in another case: 'I love it very much, because it has got green in it, and I love green, it is my favourite colour, actually I adore green.' In yet another case she regrets that her daughter started to give her an array of plates that represented the seasons but lost the relationship (connected to her employment) through which she obtained the plates before the sequence had been completed.

The close association between objects and relationships creates problems of various kinds. For example with her kitchen scales 'Yes, but they are very old. I had them as a wedding present. And, it is itself just falling into pieces. But I have got a brand new set that my older daughter bought for me, and they are a kind of digital ones, and I can't get used to them [laugh], so I go back to my old ones.' While in another case 'They bought in a lovely chair, it was when he was ill, it was one of these Parker Knoll, it was a beautiful chair, but, when he died I had to get rid of it, I couldn't go in the room and look at it. So, that is a bit sad.' Even objects they had bought themselves had become socialized because of their longevity. For example when she remembers how an armchair was obtained by hire purchase over forty years earlier, and in remembering this she evokes the conditions they lived under at that time. So Judith and Berenice are not haunted, precisely because they see little separation between persons and things and they recognize the 'familiar spirits' of objects and live with them, or when these might be too intense as in the Parker Knoll chair, they get rid of them.

In both cases objects come to stand for people and relationships, they take on a fetish quality thereby. But what anthropologists once denigrated in other societies as a primitive cognitive mistake can here be recognized as a sophisticated acknowledgement of the nature of objectification. What both Marx and Mauss understood was that objects and persons have values which are interchangeable, and should possess a considerable degree of interpenetration. In their attack on materialism it was not things standing for people that was the problem. It was when a highly abstracting force such as capitalism prevented things standing for people and radically separated them off that we develop the problem of materialism (see Spyer 1998 and especially Stallybrass 1998).

There were, however, many instances within the ethnography of a more negative relationship between the order of persons and things, which prevent agency from being expressed in this way. Georgina is part of a nuclear family with a secure middle-class income and without any overt problems. Nevertheless, as in many such families there are tensions and unresolved aspects of relationships that emerge on closer acquaintance. The problem for Georgina is that her husband is a professional artist with strong views on art and many other aesthetic matters As a result, Georgina finds considerable difficulties in dealing with the aesthetics of the home, or trying to make it a medium for expressing their relationship. She is well aware that this activity of decoration could and should include far more compromise and shared forms than are likely to emerge within a sphere where his opinions are so clear and strong. She would have liked to include some romantic pictures, but she is aware that he is tending towards minimalism. As a result, there are simply no decorations on the wall at all. Instead Georgina creates decorative spaces which have much in common with Judith and Berenice in that most of the objects represent the fortuitous results of relationships such as gifts and souvenirs, which thereby speak to a different logic of inclusion. But unlike the previous two cases, this is not the kind of decorative schema that Georgina would have preferred.

She would see this kind of bric-a-brac of memory as a failure of aesthetic intervention, and Georgina feels a sense in which the house has not evolved as a mirror of the social relationships she aspired to. In other cases this often leads to a sense of recrimination and blame as the fault of their partners or their own parents (especially their mothers). For example, a woman who feels depressed and unable to even envisage a decorative order she would like, blames a man who is too lazy to do the DIY work that would transform her home, or a man who contributes very little in the home claims he could do the work but his wife doesn't come up with the new design that he could put into practice.

Another of the *Signs of the Times* programmes brought out a basic contradiction that I did not appreciate but is compatible with our ethnographic material. Quite often couples originally form on the basis of the attraction between highly genred and gendered individuals. A macho man being attracted to a conspicuously feminine woman and vice versa. When they become a couple living together the opposition which was once a source of mutual attraction may or may not be reconciled in their development of their joint home. Working-class men constantly refer to their pictures of cars, football and nudes, while their stripped-down fires and furnishing are justified as a natural and masculine functionalism. Within the middle-class male, aesthetics may be legitimated by modernist minimalism that eschews the signs of life represented by, for example, the children. Such men see the introduction of an aesthetic where sofas are covered in cushions, blinds replaced by curtains, and surfaces covered by teddy bears and family pictures as intrusive and feminizing. Women who identify themselves as conspicuously feminine may regard the same process as civilizing maturity. They may see their role as transcending the individualism of each. This may be accepted or they may find a negotiated compromise. So in one case a woman 'gets' the bedroom as her 'nest' where 'she wants an important bed (with a teddy bear in the middle) that would symbolize the act of marriage' – as long as the man can control the living room.

While decorative order may become a positive expression of relationships, or a sign of negotiation between couples, there remain many cases where differences remain unreconciled and constraints remain oppressive. The architecture of the estates was itself a sign of the alienation of the built environment from the people who lived in them. Mostly they were created according to the canons of modernism with a strong emphasis on functionalism and lack of ornament. When these estates failed as social environments, as happened with many of the 1960s tower blocks, this was seen as a failure of left-wing principles of collectivist housing. The irony was that the estates never reflected the people that had to live in them. Quite the contrary, they were designed and built by people who lived in quite different environments. Most of those who were forced to live within them had an entirely different aesthetic that positively valued ornament, and the modernism they were forced to live within was therefore largely the material expression of ideology in the Marxist sense. That is the architecture represented the dominant class but become the only form in which the dominated class were allowed to see themselves as a collective. The Lark estate was typical of such cases, and even where individuals such as Judith were allowed to alter their interiors (or did so anyway), there were still marked constraints on any alterations to the common space of the estate. It is in such circumstances that tenants became haunted by this abstract sense of power they simply call 'the council'.

In our ethnography discussions with the occupants of the Lark estate tended to be dominated by a sense of constant tension between the two main categories of occupant. One group was single mothers with children, and the other was the elderly. Each blamed the other for their dislike of the place. In many ways this represents the objective conditions they found themselves in: the failure of a housing policy that led to most other groups moving off the estate and leaving it occupied by these two highly incompatible populations. One shopkeeper on the street who served both communities put it as follows:

> there's a lot of resentment there and you have your people who wash their front doors down and their patch and they used to keep it all together all looking good all of them doing their bit. Now you get the older ones, and you get the kids sitting on their doors so you've got all that to deal with so there's a lot of resentment and sometimes I think it's a time bomb waiting to go off there really.

Another who had young children on the estate complained:

> Here everybody thinks that your business is their business. Yeah. Especially there's a lot of old people mixed in with a lot of young families so I don't think it's working. Because if the children are playing, obviously children are children. There's no grass area as such for them to play on so they'll play wherever they can. And the old people actually come out and get quite frustrated with the noise, which I can appreciate as well because they want peace and quiet. But it's not the young people's fault either. The lady opposite, any time our door opens, if she knows my son's in and if our door opens she's opening her door just to see what he's doing. So that's – she's very – it's more nosy.

An elderly resident, one of those who had lived in the flats since they were built, produced a prodigious litany of the recent crimes that she claimed had been committed by the children on the estate including direct persecution of the elderly. The elderly felt they could not leave their rooms or they would be pounced upon by the out-of-control youth. For their part the single mothers felt they would be constantly criticized by these nearly dead neighbours, who clearly gave them 'the creeps'. Arguments were particularly intense around areas of common use such as corridors or places that were supposed to be common but had in some cases been appropriated by youths for personal storage.

The situation on the council estates is one in which there is a marked tendency to feel that one is 'haunted' by one's own home. In a political climate where the stress is on the positive benefits of homeownership, people who cannot afford to own their home feel stigmatized and accept an ideology which tells them that this is a poor substitute for ownership. The 'ghost' becomes the figure of the council itself: an apparently uncaring and distant presence that possesses what the occupant cannot possess. In some circumstance this feeling can be overcome. Most often this occurs when, as in the case of Judith, the relationship between occupants develops positively through the act of appropriating the home, often through its physical transformation with home refurbishment and redecoration. But for most of the occupants, divided into incompatible populations of single parents with children as against the elderly, quite the opposite has occurred. A sense of bitterness about their own lack of agency exacerbates the sense that one is oppressed by a home that is anything but an expression of one's agency. Rather it is a constant reminded that power lies elsewhere. I do not think it is too much to claim that most of the people on this estate feel haunted, although they do not need to anthropomorphize a ghost since the figure of the council provides a clear repository for their fears and frustrations.

Conclusions

This chapter began with the evidence that the very longevity of homes and material culture may create a sense that agency lies in these things rather than in the relatively transient persons who occupy or own them. Having thereby established the idea that material culture and homes can be viewed as agents, the point was generalized using ethnographic material which highlighted the issues raised by other factors which prevent people from feeling that their homes are an expression of their own agency. At this point the argument may be broadened into a more general anthropological observation as to the nature and consequences of material culture. At least four current discussions within anthropological theory seem relevant here. The first, which has already been mentioned, is the concept of the fetish, where we are coming to recognize that the attribution of power or agency to things may be a profound appreciation of a state of affairs and not simply some kind of cognitive or category mistake (see, for example, Spyer 1998). Secondly, the evidence is quite compatible with the recent work of Latour, much of which has been concerned to transcend a simple dualism in which agency is seen as the possession of persons or society, and objects merely that which is passively worked upon. Latour (1993) has promoted instead an approach based on networks of agents that include both animate and inanimate forms. I would see this as an extension (although he would not) of approaches to objectification that arise out of dialect-ical theory (see Miller 1987). Thirdly (as also noted by Birdwell-Pheasant and

Lawrence-Zúñiga 1999: 8–9), the recent work of Gell (1998) on the agency of artworks and artifacts, which concludes on the example of the Maori house as the distributed bodies, minds and histories of the persons connected with them (251–8), provides an alternative route to this larger sense of objectification rooted in the study of material culture.

Finally I feel we are indebted to the recent book *Signs of Recognition* by Webb Keane (1997). Much of that book is concerned with the properties of material culture that make them far more than merely that which the people who employ them intend them to signify. The very durability and physicality of things make them liable to represent attributes which were not those that an individual desired them to convey: for example, that they are actually torn rather than whole, or not quite the same as the object they were supposed to replace. What he argues for exchange in eastern Indonesia is still more true for consumer culture. A culture in which the day after we have spent an exorbitant amount on a new dress, we discover to our horror that the dress is being heavily publicized as on sale at a third of the price we paid for it, and worse still it is then seen being worn by someone whose judgement we detest. Or in which fashion means that the pine kitchen has lost the positive connections we bought it for but we can't afford the pseudo-Shaker kitchen we would have had if we could now afford it. Or where we have very little choice or power to determine our material conditions, either from poverty or because of the unsatisfactory nature of the relationships we are part of: the unyielding and unappreciative demands of spouses, parents and children. In more extreme circumstance the objects around us can embody an agency that makes them oppressive and alienating and may in turn be projected in a personified form as the ghost that haunts us. In short, where we cannot possess we are in danger of becoming possessed.

References

Attfield, J. (1989) 'Inside pram town: a case study of Harlow house interiors', 1951–61'. In J. Attfield and P. Kirkham (eds) *A View from the Interior*. London: The Women's Press.

—— and P. Kirkham (eds) (1989) *A View from the Interior*. London: The Women's Press.

Birdwell-Pheasant, D. and D. Lawrence-Zúñiga (1999) 'Introduction: houses and families in Europe'. In D. Birdwell-Pheasant and D. Lawrence-Zúñiga (eds) *House Life: Space, Place and Family in Europe*. Oxford: Berg.

Chevalier, S. (1998) 'From woollen carpet to grass carpet: bridging house and garden in an English suburb'. In D. Miller (ed.) *Material Cultures: Why some Things Matter*. Chicago: University of Chicago Press.

Clarke, A. (1998) 'Window shopping at home: classifieds, catalogues and new consumer skills'. In D. Miller (ed.) *Material Cultures: Why some Things Matter*. Chicago: University of Chicago Press.

Dingwall, E., K. Goldney and T. Hall (1956) *The Haunting of Borley Rectory*. London: Duckworth.

Gell, A. (1998) *Art and Agency*. Oxford: Oxford University Press.

Keane, W. (1997) *Signs of Recognition*. Berkeley: University of California Press.

Latour, B. (1993) *We have Never Been Modern*. New York: Harvester Wheatsheaf.

Lévi-Strauss, C. (1972) *The Savage Mind*. London: Weidenfeld & Nicolson.

Marcus, S. (1999) *Apartment Stories*. Berkeley: University of California Press.

McCracken G. (1988) *Culture and Consumption*. Bloomington: Indiana University Press.

Miller, D. (1987) *Material Culture and Mass Consumption*. Oxford: Blackwell.

—— (1988) 'Appropriation of the State on the Council Estate'. *Man* 23: 353–72.

—— (1998) *A Theory of Shopping*. Cambridge: Polity Press: Ithaca: Cornell University Press.

—— (2001) *The Dialectics of Shopping*. Chicago: University of Chicago Press.

—— P. Jackson, B. Holbrook, N. Thrift and M. Rowlands (1998) *Shopping, Place and Identity*. London: Routledge.

Norman, D. (1963) *The Stately Ghosts of England*. London: Frederick Muller.

Putnam, T. and C. Newton (eds) (1990) *Household Choices*. London: Middlesex Polytechnic and Futures Publications.

Spyer, P. (ed.) 1998 *Border Fetishisms*. London: Routledge.

Stallybrass, P. (1998) 'Marx's Coat'. In P. Spyer (ed.) *Border Fetishisms*. London: Routledge.

Underwood, P. (1983) *No Common Task: The Autobiography of a Ghost-Hunter*. London: Harrap.

Wilde, O. (1977 [1891]) 'The Canterville Ghost'. In *Complete Works of Oscar Wilde*. London: Collins.

−7−

Home Sweet Home:
Tangible Memories of an Uprooted Childhood
Anat Hecht

Our house is our corner of the world. . .

Our first universe, a real cosmos in every sense of the word (Bachelard 1994: 4).

A house encompasses an array of different materials, from furniture and fixtures to ornaments and décor, collectively creating a dwelling experience that is greater than the sum of its parts. For these are more than mere 'things', they are a collection of appropriated materials, invested with meaning and memory, a material testament of who we are, where we have been, and perhaps even where we are heading. They are what transforms our house into our *home*, a private cosmos that houses our memories of bygone times, as well as our hopes for what is yet to come. They bind our past with our present and our possible futures, thereby framing and reflecting our sense of self.

To lose a home is to lose a private museum of memory, identity and creative appropriation (see Chevalier 1996, 1998). To lose a childhood home, our first secure corner of the world, is to lose a fundamental part of ourselves and our history. The memory of a childhood home thus becomes the remembrance of childhood, the remembrance of a lost part of ourselves. Remembering a bygone home-scape is then an act of reappropriation, of sowing symbolic roots into a vanished world (c.f. Steedman 1995; Bahloul 1996).

There is an extensive body of literature devoted to memory and loss; memory and narrative; memory and the senses; memory and objects; and especially memory and the home. However, the relationship between these core aspects is seldom acknowledged, let alone analysed. The following, in-depth case study aims to determine the interaction between narratives, materials and sensory manifestations, and to demonstrate their significance in the practice of history and remembrance, within a specific, domestic context. Combining several, extensive micro-studies, such as the one presented here, into a comprehensive ethnographic body of knowledge will provide an essential means to better our understanding of this multifaceted phenomenon. The following analysis is a first step towards that goal.

The paper centres upon one woman's memoirs and their material and sensory expression within her private museum of symbolic roots and beyond. Advocating a contextual, holistic approach, the review voices Nan's perception and consequent presentation of key events in her life, especially those of her childhood. Thus, Nan articulates a sensory journey from the home of her childhood past to the home of her adult present, the latter, which embodies her memoirs and self-identity as both narrator and collector, serves as a point of entry, a bridge to the past. The analysis explores the corresponding roles of material culture and oral narratives in personal reminiscences and as a means of coping with, and compensating for loss. Particular emphasis is then placed upon remembrance and the creative production of memorial-like tributes that are simultaneously personal and collective.

A World of Memory

Nan is a bright, energetic woman in her late sixties. A native of Edinburgh, as her accent occasionally reveals, she describes herself as a 'proud Scot', even though she has been a permanent resident of south-east London from the age of twelve. She is, by her own account, an amateur artist, a frustrated musician and 'a bit of a hoarderer' [sic]. But above all Nan is a storyteller; a guardian, not only of her family's legacy, but of her generation's legacy as well. For Nan's narrated memoirs and their material manifestations go beyond her personal story, telling the story of an era, the story of a generation. The following paper will demonstrate how Nan's continuous interaction with the past, as well as its preservation and presentation through various sensory means, transforms her private recollection into an almost collective, memorial-like remembrance.

I first met Nan at a 1950s reminiscing event at Lifetimes, Croydon's[1] local-history museum. Nan has been involved with the museum from its early days, lending objects (and stories) for the permanent display, participating in various events and eventually, becoming a part-time relief gallery assistant, covering for absent gallery assistants. Nan, who led the reminiscing session that day, was setting up an amazing array of 1950s materials, from ration books and Nylons, to periodical magazines, make-up cases, hair-pins, hair-nets and several dresses, not to mention healing ointments and vapour rubs, as well as coins, stamps, toys, dolls, songbooks and even a few vinyl records and an old record player. It wasn't long before the museum came to life with past-time colours, sounds and smells. The reminiscing session that followed was as lively and stimulating as the object-based presentation. Equally impressive was the fact that all of the materials on the reminiscing display

---

1. Croydon is the southern-most borough of Greater London. Croydon's Clocktower Centre was the focal point of my ethnographic research into the consumption of local-history museums, alongside present-day perceptions of past, place and identity.

were Nan's *personal* belongings, a 'mishmash of knick-knacks' to coin her phrase, that she had 'hoarded' over the years. 'You should see my house', she laughed, as we reloaded her car. 'I'd love to', I replied. And so began our shared exploration of the past and its embodiment within Nan's home.

Nan and John have been living in their current home in south-east Croydon since 1967. Much like its owners, the two-level terrace house is warm and welcoming and full of stories. Jam-packed with books, photographs, past-time ornaments and several, rather unusual collections, Nan and John's home is truly a 'cosmos' of memory, an Aladdin's Cave of reminiscence. I was privileged to spend many hours in this house, surrounded by Nan's collections and recollections, as she narrated her memoirs and shared their material and sensory manifestations with me. By doing so Nan had taken me not only into her home, but also into her world of memory and meaning.

Nan's comprehensive narration of her life history is far too extensive to be delivered in full within the boundaries of one chapter. The following life-review will therefore focus upon what Nan regards as the most significant period of her life – her childhood years in Scotland – a time that encompasses the most joyful episodes of her life, as well as the most painful and harrowing ones.

The uniqueness of Nan's autobiography lies in its twofold nature as both ordinary – in terms of portraying an experience of historical events shared by many of Nan's contemporaries – and extraordinary – in terms of Nan's individual story and her unique engagement with the past. In this sense, Nan's narration and material expositions are an embodiment of an era, simultaneously reflecting both personal and collective experiences, as well as a specific way of life that is characteristic of working-class Britain in the 1930s and 1940s.

Nan was born in Edinburgh in the summer of 1933. Until the age of seven she lived with her parents and her two younger brothers in a small, two-room flat in the Dr Begg's Buildings of Abbeyhill. The buildings' five stairs of tenements were located in the centre of what was locally known as the 'Wee World':

> It really was a wee world, virtually, because it had everything we needed – a school, shops, butchers, greengrocers, a public washhouse. There really wasn't much need to go further out. We had everything right there in our wee world – a dance hall, a cinema, the King's Park. . . and the railway of course! I can remember the old trains, the Mallard and the Green Arrow. . .

Life in the buildings was often one of hardship and poverty, though rarely one of deprivation. This is clearly reflected in the expressive memoirs of a contemporary of Nan's, Billy Hunter, who spent his childhood years in the buildings:

I was lucky because the houses in our stair had two windows that looked out into the street, so it was always very bright. These rooms though could be ice cold and the fire had to be on constantly in the winter. . . [And to get to the outside toilets at night] you had to go along the landing IN THE DARK! (1998: 14)

However, Nan's portrayal of her early childhood home minimizes these hardships. Instead it accentuates the warmth and the light, as well as the close physical proximity and family ties, within both the family home and the Wee World as a whole:

Every Sunday morning I would invariably run into the kitchen/living-room/bedroom and jump on my dad, in the bed. Mum was getting breakfast ready, in sight of us, all in the same room. I can remember that sunny room, mum cooking a full breakfast (because that was what we had in Scotland, a full breakfast) and me playing with my dad. . . Then, every Sunday afternoon, my dad would take me up on his shoulders, walking all the way down to where my grandmother lived, where the rest of his sisters had gathered with their families. . .

Nan's nostalgic portrayal coincides with the typical working-class representation in historical and fictional narratives, where the warmth, light and shininess of the interior grants it an almost magical quality, regardless of its modesty. The glowing fire illuminating the multitude of objects in the small family room, creates a sense of warm enclosure, intimacy and care (see Bachelard 1994; Steedman 1998). These notions echo nineteenth-century ideals of 'home at its best', as they were portrayed in the literary works of that era and especially in the novels of Charles Dickens, such as *Oliver Twist* (1837) and *David Copperfield* (1849). For Dickens an *ideal home* is a place of secure enclosure and love – 'a symbolic substitute for the security and union of the womb, as with David Copperfield who speaks of "My little bed in a closet within my mother's room"' (Armstrong 1990: 25). Nan's evocative depiction of her childhood promotes a corresponding sense of warmth and security:

Looking back on the whole of my life, the years I spent as a child in Edinburgh were the happiest time of my life. You had protection. You had family round you, who you knew loved you. You were safe and secure, with no responsibilities and no experience of the hardships of life. You were cocooned, at least for a little while.

Another essential feature of the *ideal home* that appears both in Nan's narration and in the written literature is the emphasis on cleanliness and order, the presence or absence of which often serves as an indicator of moral quality. This is especially evident in Nan's remarks on her mother's domestic skills and her own, consequent upbringing:

My mother was very particular. She was very clean. She had been in domestic service before she married and her mother had been in domestic service too. And when you were in service you learned how to do it, properly. And you also learned how to cope, the hard way. So we were all brought up with this sort of background. We were taught right from the beginning to look after what we had. It was a case of 'make do and mend'. If you've got a rip you sew it up, you didn't throw it out like you do now.

This typical working-class dogma of thrift and resourcefulness, of 'making do' is manifest in Nan's testimony of her childhood play as well:

We often made our own toys and invented our own games. If we found a tin or a bottle, we'd play with it. . . We played a lot of street games. There was always plenty of space to play. Each block had a front green. Well, it wasn't really a green. It was just a piece of concrete, where our parents used to hang out the washing, with poles that were permanently there. . . Looking back now, the kind of surroundings that we had were pretty grim really, so many people living in such close proximity. . . but it was all we knew. And it was all family. Many of the people in the buildings were related to one another and even those who weren't were very close. We literally lived in each other's homes. It was a very close-knit community.

The oscillation in Nan's account between the negative, physical attributes of her depicted locality and the positive, almost nostalgic qualities she ascribes to the local community, is not a contradiction in terms, but rather a term of contradiction, emphasizing the positive human dimension over the negative physical hardship. A similar notion is discussed in Bahloul's (1996) study of immigrants' memoirs. 'To have lived in Dar-Refayil becomes an adventure, a triumph. Narratives focus on the way people socialised dearth, closure and lack of privacy. They constitute themselves as a lesson in humanity. . . symbolically restoring the integrity of a shattered geography' (Bahloul 1996: 28–9).

Shattered Home

Nan's childhood home soon became a shattered one. The Second World War meant dramatic changes for many families throughout Britain, and Nan's family was no different. Her father was drafted into the army, leaving behind a pregnant wife and three young children. The climb to the top floor became a strain for Nan's mother, who then decided to move downstairs, to a ground-level flat, which meant giving up the sunlight and fresh air of their top-floor home. In many ways this physical move from sunlight to darkness is symbolic of what was yet to come. In the summer of 1941 Nan and her brother Tom were evacuated to Inverness-shire, along with twenty-five other children from the Abbeyhill district.

It was very hard. You were only allowed to take a certain amount of stuff with you. You were given a list of the things that you had to take – two pairs of trousers, two jumpers, two pair of socks, two pair of pyjamas. . . You were allowed one suitcase with all the bits in it and two toys. . . but that was it.

However, another traumatic event soon overshadowed the evacuation ordeal when, in December 1941, Nan's mother died, in Edinburgh, during childbirth:

I remember the finality of it all. The fact that, that was it, there was nobody. We were all alone, and so far away. I didn't know what was going to happen to us. I felt that I had this responsibility for my brother, Tommy. I had been told by my mum, when we were getting evacuated, to look after him. . . That's the last view I have of my mother, standing on the station, with my little brother Kenny in her arms, waving and crying. 'Look after your wee brother' those were the last words she said to me.

From this poignant key-moment onwards Nan became the custodian of what remained of her family and a guardian to the memory of what was lost. According to Daniel and Thompson (1996) the act of taking responsibility for others is characteristically part of women's socialization, and therefore undertaking such a task in childhood, although extreme, is likely to correspond with normalized expectations and an ongoing sense of identity. This may well have been the case for Nan, considering that her 'custodian responsibilities' (to keep both her family and the memory of life before the war) grow considerably over time.

Nan's father eventually returned to the UK and arranged for his children to be put in a home for widowers' children, where Nan and her brothers spent the next four years of their lives. The harsh memories of those years, of that Home still haunt Nan to this day:

As soon as daddy left, our suitcases were taken away. You never saw your own clothes again. You were given a number. You had your dignity taken away. I had quite long hair and you even had that taken away from you. Your hair was cut off as soon as you got there. . . From the time I was seven, I had nothing. Everything was left behind. You didn't have anything and you didn't have anyone. No one really cared.

In many ways, the orphanage was a kind of a Wee World as well. A carefully monitored and controlled closed system, where fear and blackmail were used as means of manipulation.

I wrote my father a letter saying 'Please daddy, come and take us away from here. . .' And of course all the letters that went out were read, and all the letters and parcels that came in were opened. Then Matron sent for me. I was scared to death of her. She said – 'If I send this letter to your daddy and he reads it, he would think that you're not happy here and that would make him unhappy. You wouldn't want your daddy to be unhappy, would you?' So I got all this moral blackmail – 'Well I think it would be a good idea if you went away and wrote again to tell him you're getting on fine and then I can post it for you.'

Thus, what started as a temporarily uprooted childhood now became a permanently lost one – a time and place Nan could dream of, long for, depict and portray, but never again go back to. All she had left were memories and an extraordinary ability to narrate and convey them.

Sensory Journeys

Recollecting one's memoirs is predominantly linked in academic literature with narration. Storytelling, and in particular the story we tell of ourselves, is often viewed as a fundamental element of human existence, deeply embedded in our psyche as a species, who Myerhoff (1978) defines as *Homo narrans*, the Storyteller. Autobiographical narration is therefore perceived as a core means of constructing, developing and maintaining a sense of identity, woven out of memories and experience (see Myerhoff 1978, 1992; Haight and Webster 1995). The process of recollecting and recounting our past, and in particular our childhood years, is consequently seen as an important agency in linking past, present and future, enabling us to order and reflect upon our experiences, as well as resolve certain conflicts and key events in our past (see Conway 1990; Rubin 1995).

Autobiographical narration is also regarded as a means of defining and articulating our notion of society and history, as they often include social and historical information about people and events that goes beyond the subjective experience of the narrator (see Gullestad, 1996). And yet, the articulation of history and memory is seldom limited to an entirely abstract, linguistic representation, even in its most formal, 'Westernized' manifestation. The combined use of a visual medium alongside a textual or oral medium has often been regarded as crucial for the precision of the conveyed message, in terms of both the actuality of the recorded event or persona and the influence they would have on later generations (c.f. Haskell 1993; Gombrich 1962, 1984). By the same token, the perception, preservation and presentation of personal histories and memories is by no means solely linguistic, given that our experience of the world, especially in early childhood days, is primarily sensual, as Nan's case study demonstrates. The academic discourse on memory tends to focus exclusively on one aspect of its manifestation at a time, often ignoring the contribution and significance of other interrelated aspects, such as the emotional dimension of memory (see Conway 1990; Rubin 1995), as well as what Merleau-Ponty (1962) has termed 'synaesthetic' – the fusion of all our senses into an overall bodily experience (see Abram 1997).

Nan's narrated reminiscences of her early life experiences in Scotland are remarkably vivid and rich in detail, perhaps because she has very few authentic materials left from that time. Her articulation of the past could therefore be viewed and analysed with an exclusively oral focus, excluding its material, emotional and sensory expressions. However, to do so would be to disregard the unique nature of Nan's recollection and her extraordinary recreation of her lost childhood world. The fusion of emotions and senses that accompany and support Nan's story enables her to recapture and convey the *sense* and *essence* of her experience, making her memories more tangible for both her audience and herself.

Our sensory journey into Nan's past begins in the present, within the private museum of her home, which houses, voices and displays the symbolic roots and embodiments of her memoirs. The first and most obvious sensory element of Nan's narration is *sound*. As she recounts her childhood memories Nan's accent becomes more and more manifest, especially while recalling key conversations and verbal exchanges, where she skilfully mimics the voices and accents of the different participants. Gradually her native Scottish lilt begins to dominate her intonation, while Scottish expressions, the jargon of her past, emerge to permeate her speech.

Bahloul (1996) describes a similar experience with her multi-lingual, immigrant informants:

> Although the principal language used in the narratives is French, because it is the language used every day by my Jewish hosts, Arabic and Judaeo-Arabic emerge at intervals in narratives, as languages of the past now abandoned. There is a narrative logic in the alternation of these languages – the code switching indicates a temporal shift. French is the language of the present (and of the future) Arabic that of the past. (Bahloul 1996: 135)

The echoes of past-times and past practices are evident in Nan's oral narration as well, especially when she gives voice to her childhood play, singing the rhymes of various ball-game routines out loud:

Right hand. Left hand. Touch your heel. Touch your toe. See you go. . .

Mary Queen of Scots got her head chopped off,
Her head chopped off, her head chopped off.
Mary Queen of Scots got her head chopped off,
On a cold and frosty morning. . .

However, the most poignant sound in Nan's childhood story is the voice of her grief and anguish over her mother's death. As she reconstructs the events of that night, she begins to mimic her own voice as a child (as well as mimicking the intonations of other people that were present, like the matron's heavy Inverness-shire accent) re-enacting, perhaps even reliving the harsh experience of her terrible loss:

> I remember being sent for, it was a cold, dark, winter's night, in December 1941. As soon as I walked into the pantry, where Matron was waiting for me, I knew it was something very bad. It was a long, narrow room and she sat at the end. And she said 'Come on in lassie, come on in. Come and sit on my knee.' And she said 'You know, your mammy's been ill.' And I started. . . I started. . . Ach. . . I'll never forget that night. 'You'll have to tell your wee brother', she said. So they got my little brother, who was five, out of bed and they brought him to me. 'Tell Tommy' they said and went away. Well, I couldn't tell him, for crying. I just couldn't get it out. 'Our mammy. . . Our mammy. . . Our mammy'. I can still see the look on his face now. He didn't know what I was talking about. He had forgotten her. It was six or seven months since we left home and he was only five years old and he had forgotten. And of course that made me want to bash him, because I got no reaction from him. He didn't cry, he just looked at me with his big blue eyes and sucked his cheeks in, like that. . .

This undoubtedly crucial moment in Nan's life was heightened by the fact that her young brother had forgotten their mother, or at least so it seemed at the time. Not only had she lost her mother and her secure past, it seemed as if she was the only one left to remember the lost world of their childhood home, the only one who could give it a voice and revive its image. This may well have been the trigger for Nan's phenomenally detailed memory and her deeply embedded need to narrate her story and recreate tangible presentations of her past.

The second, vital sensory element in Nan's reminiscence is *sight*. In her attempt to portray and preserve her vanished Wee World, Nan is forever searching for, as well as creating visual representations of her geographical roots. She has numerous books on Scottish history and geography, as well as specific books about Edinburgh, which often include maps and illustrations of the city throughout the ages, not to mention Billy Hunter's recent book on the Wee World, which she cherishes. She collects old postcards of Edinburgh in bygone days and is always on the lookout for old aerial photos of the city, especially those that include views of her local district of Abbeyhill. One of Nan's most prized possessions is an old family album, full of photographs that her aunt had taken in the 1920s and 1930s.

> Before Auntie Nan died she showed me her album. I had never seen it before. She said 'You might like to have this.' And I was absolutely amazed when I looked at it. It was incredible! She had such an eye. . . So I ended up with lots of family photographs.

Nan has her own, substantial photo collection as well. Comprising mainly landscapes, townscapes and old houses, it includes photos of the home for widowers' children, which she had gone back to visit as an adult. However, the one cityscape she truly longs for, but cannot revisit and capture with her camera, is her first childhood home in Edinburgh. The Wee World of Abbeyhill as Nan knew it, no longer exists. The old Begg's Buildings have been demolished, along with the public washhouse, the dance hall, the Regent cinema and other familiar landmarks of Nan's childhood. The only way she could preserve an image of her lost childhood world was to create it herself, and so she did, with great care and precision.

Nan's comprehensive mapping of the Abbeyhill district, as she remembers it in the 1930s (Figure 7.1), along with the meticulous layout of their 'stair' in the Begg's buildings (Figure 7.2) and the richly detailed drawing of her family's tenement flat (Figure 7.3), as well as several books and photos, accompanied all of our sessions as graphic references to her story.

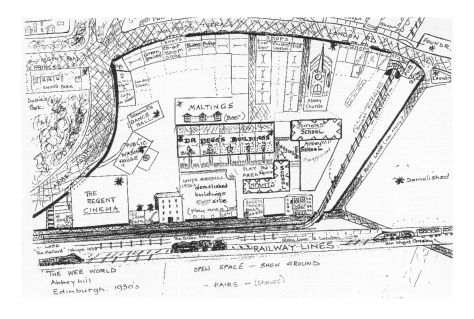

Figure 7.1. Map of Abbeyhill – Nan's Wee World (1930s)

Linking her narratives with visual illustrations enables Nan to virtually recreate her childhood landscapes, thereby appropriating and legitimizing her claim of belonging to this bygone locality (see Küchler 1993; Bender 1993). Through the carefully drawn map and floor plans, which show the layout of the tenement building, Nan can revive her Wee World, complementing her story with visual images of the meaningful landmarks and boundaries of the domestic spaces of her childhood, all of which help frame and affirm her early experiences.

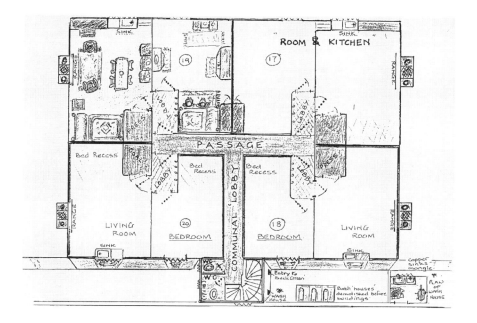

Figure 7.2. Layout of the Begg's Building – Nan's childhood home (1930s)

However, it is the drawing of the family's home that plays the most vital role, as every detail in Nan's drawing is linked with memories, stories and family practices. Thus, the memory of the home becomes in turn a home for the memories associated with it:

> I can remember my brother Tom's first steps. He learnt to walk in that room. He was sitting on that storage shelf over there, and it was just the right height for him to kinda slide his bottom off and make his first tottering steps. And I was there to see it! And I'll never forget it.

> The wireless was my dad's. He loved the wireless! We used to listen to it together. That's what started my love of music, that and the pictures.

> That little mirror there has a little shelf on it. That's where you'd keep your comb and brush, by the sink where you'd wash up and brush your hair every morning. Every home had such a mirror by the kitchen sink in those days. I've had my aunt's mirror for a while. It was very dear to me because it had been there from the early 1900s and it 'saw' and 'reflected' the lives of all the people who lived in that house – my grandparents, my mother, my aunt. . . It occurred to me, after my aunt died that it was the end of the line, the end of an era. My aunt was the last one. There was nothing left to reflect. . . I eventually gave it to a local-history museum in Edinburgh. Their researcher was looking for one and I knew she'd take good care of it.

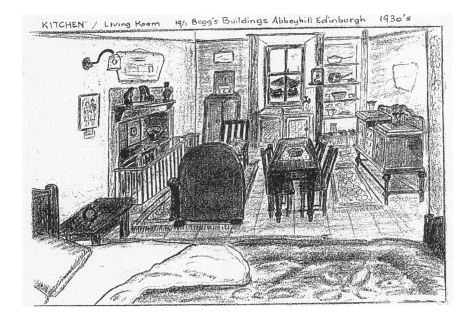

Figure 7.3. Kitchen/living room in Nan's childhood home (1930s)

Giving away her aunt's mirror was by no means easy for Nan. However, the fact that it is on display in a *local* museum, presenting a *local* past, *her past*, enables her to maintain, as well as share her personal link to her family's history and her childhood days. Nan's involvement with local-history museums, in both Edinburgh and Croydon, is a further means of preserving and presenting the narratives and materials of her past. This not only legitimizes her reminiscences, but also encourages her creative expressiveness. Nan had lent several 1950s items to the Lifetimes museum as well, and was asked if she could recall the furniture and the décor she had during that period and perhaps make a few drawings that they could include in their computer touch-screen display. This led to a series of comprehensive sketches of Nan and John's first home together after they were married, such as the sunlit kitchen (Figure 7.4) and the extremely detailed, water-colour painting of the living room (Figure 7.5).

Nan's vivid recollections are an outcome of the everyday, bodily experience of household chores, manifested in acts of cleaning and polishing, as well as in the act of decoration:

> They've asked me how do I remember it all in such detail. Well, I've cleaned it all every week didn't I. And I still have quite a few items of furniture, in use, to this day.

Figure 7.4. Kitchen in Nan's first home as an adult (1950s)

Figure 7.5. Living room in Nan's first home as an adult (1950s)

I've got the sideboard and the studio couch. They were very fashionable in the 50s. . . It was black with little bits of red and yellow on it that went well with the cherry red armchair, and the mid-brown furniture, and the rug in front of the fire that had a red, yellow and white zigzag pattern. . .

'The only thing I collect is memories'

The third and perhaps most tactile sensory aspect of Nan's memoirs is *touch*. Nan has quite literally surrounded herself with tangible representations of the past. She has an impressive range of 1940s and 1950s materials, including sets of clothes, hats, handkerchiefs, make-up cases, perfume bottles, hair-nets and hair-pins, plastic necklaces and various knick-knacks, children's books (especially nursery rhymes), as well as songbooks and vinyl records (mainly musicals and movie scores), several periodical magazines, stamps, coins, ceramic artefacts and even a 1950s bedroom suite, which is still in use today:

> It was the first thing we bought after we got married. It's quality furniture. I'm not one for throwing out things that are in prime condition, and most of my stuff is in prime condition because it gets polished every other week.

> If I like something I keep it. I'd be sorry to see it go. I'd be thinking, if it went, would other people look after it the same way I did?

The emphasis upon 'caring' for a cherished object, in terms of the investment of time, effort and care (see Drazin, this volume) can be seen as part of an overall notion of 'saving' the object (especially if it is an old or rare item that has particular sentimental value for the owner) from decay and 'extinction'. Collectors frequently view themselves as 'saviours' of lost objects and disappearing worlds, which legitimizes the time they invest in their collection (c.f. Belk 1995).

The notion of *'collecting as salvation'* is illustrated by Elsner and Cardinal (1994) in their analysis of the biblical myth of Noah's Ark. 'Here is saving in its strongest sense, conscious rescuing from extinction. In the myth of Noah as ur-collector resonate all the themes of collecting itself: desire and nostalgia, saving and loss, the urge to erect a permanent and complete system against the destructiveness of time' (1994: 1). Nan has a few older artefacts in her collection, which she regards as family heirlooms she had salvaged:

> That was my grandmother's jelly pan up there, it's brass. My grandmother used it to make jam, then Auntie Nan used it to make jam. There's two more pots along there, that belonged to my grandmother, the jam pot and butter pot. . . The letterbox there was Auntie Nan's. She probably bought it back in the 1920s when they first came out. . .

In her historical analysis of women in seventeenth- and eighteenth-century England, Vickery (1993) demonstrates how household artefacts were used to create a world of meaning and transmit a personal history. Collections tend to create meaning and metaphor in much the same way, as they often centre upon a particular theme that is in some way symbolic of the collector, be it his occupation or appearance, family history or life experiences, or even his fantasies. The collection then serves as an extension of the self, a visual representation of the collector that reflects individual perceptions and values (see Stewart 1984; Belk 1994).

A collection can also act as a means of symbolic self-completion, especially at times of bereavement. 'Freud started his collection of antiquities shortly after his father's death. . . The acquisition of these artistic and archaeological objects was almost explicitly in response to his loss, since he found them to be "a source of exceptional renewal and comfort". . . [It was also] bound up with his work. Freud's desire to be an "archaeologist of the mind" was a long standing feature of his inner life' (Forrester 1994: 226–33). Nan's extensive collection of books is one of her principal means of symbolic self-completion. The collection comprises a small proportion of fiction (mainly poetry), whilst the majority of books are non-fiction, covering a wide range of topics from history to photography, art and handicrafts, as well as cookery. While these represent Nan's impressive variety of interests, they also symbolize the most significant people in her life. Her aunt, who was a keen photographer; her mother, who was 'a brilliant cook'; and most importantly, her father, who was her hero:

> My father was a learned man, a self-educated man. He was very keen on books. . . He spoke fluent Esperanto and corresponded with people all over the world. And he was a writer, a bit of a poet. He worked as a uniformed caretaker at a very prestigious library, in Parliament Square. He was my hero for a long, long time, until I got a bit older and he re-married and we came down here and he changed. . .

Unlike the outside world of everyday, real life, the inner-world of the collection offers complete mastery and control over time, space and activity, within the 'home-made universe' of the collection. Collecting is then first and foremost an act of creative production, an experience of play with classification and aesthetics (c.f. Danet and Katriel 1994; Stewart 1984). 'Collectors create, combine, classify and curate the objects they acquire in such a way that a new product, the collection, emerges. In this process they also produce meanings' (Belk 1995: 55). One of Nan's most playful and intriguing collections is her assembled *families* of green glass bottles, which she started amassing almost unintentionally:

> We had a big party one night and of course everyone brought a bottle. . . So later on, when we were clearing up, after the all the guests had gone, I noticed all these empty

green glass bottles that were left behind. They were all different shapes and sizes and they all had that lovely green colour. John wanted to throw them away, but I didn't let him. I said 'Look, they make little families. Here's a tall thin father and his short, stubby wife. And here are their children'. John thinks I'm mad, but I think they're lovely. So now all our friends give us their empty green glass bottles. And I clean them up and sort them into little families.

Nan's bottle collection enables her not only to form symbolic 'whole families', but also analogously recreate the networks of relationships that she had lost. Furthermore, through this direct use of objects she is able to generate the same kind of imaginative, resourceful, 'make do' play she had practised as a child.

Another means of 'resurrection' and compensation for her lost childhood is a small collection of old-fashioned, mostly hand-made, dolls (some of which she has made herself):

I had a doll once, a lovely doll, whose name was Stella. Auntie Nan bought it for me. . . But then the war came and you were only allowed to take two items with you. So I took my doll. After my mother died, I left the doll with Auntie Nan and she kept it for me.

Nan's extraordinary collection of special stones and unusual pieces of wood is another playful, imaginative collection that is both aesthetically pleasing and symbolically gratifying. The pieces of wood have a special significance as they have been 'uprooted', just like Nan, and yet managed to maintain their unique 'character' or 'persona' (at least in Nan's eyes). Trees are often used as a symbol of growing, living links with mother earth, with the ground upon which they have grown, a theme that frequently emerges in Nan's narration:

Fifty-five years on, my roots are on the ground that Edinburgh is built on. It will always be. Always. When I go up there I have to get my feet on the ground, I have to walk up to the park. . .

By the same token, the stone collection can be regarded as solid, tangible, permanent, unchangeable. . . An everlasting testimony of the past. One of Nan's 'concrete stone treasures' is literally a piece of concrete. She visited the Regent cinema site after the building was demolished and picked up a piece of concrete, a 'piece of the Regent', which she keeps as a very tangible souvenir of her vanished, demolished world. Like many of the other materials Nan has collected through the years, this too is an object of memory, a bridge to the past.

I lost everything at a very young age. I lost my family, as far as parents are concerned. I lost my home, my childhood, my whole world. So I clung, I virtually clung to whatever was left of it. Maybe that's why I have all these things. . .

These 'things', as Nan refers to them, framed and fuelled our conversations, leading our shared exploration of the past. For each item in Nan's private museum is linked to countless stories, from the story of its purchase, to the past-times stories it evokes. 'You're quite a collector', I remarked, as we looked at Nan's wide-ranging array of vinyl records. 'Not really', she replied. 'The only thing I collect is memories.'

The final sensory elements in Nan's recollection – *tastes* and *smells* – are often linked to domestic spaces and practices, such as the preparation of food (see Petridou, this volume; Seremetakis 1994[2]). This was particularly manifest in our life-history sessions, as Nan was constantly preparing and serving food to either John or myself:

> The smell of Sunday morning's breakfast – that was family, all round the table in the morning. I remember the smell of the bacon and especially the smell of the freshly baked rolls. . . You could smell when they brought the rolls in, because they were still fresh. It's that smell I remember most.

Looking out at the garden, the sights and smells evoke another memory, one of lilacs in bloom and the harsher realities of life in the orphanage:

> We had nothing, we had absolutely nothing on the estate, but we had a nice teacher. And I don't know what possessed us, but we decided to go and pick some lilacs for Miss Jason. The place was awash with lilacs in spring, but we were banned you see. We weren't allowed in that area. . . So this girl and I went into a forbidden part and blow me! Along the path, walking with one of her friends was Matron! And she spotted us standing there, with three twigs of lilac in our hand. 'Get inside, now'. . . Down in the dining room there were long tables and benches. 'Right, bend over'. . .

The Custodian

In recent years Nan has been involved with various reminiscences sessions (mainly for schools and local clubs) some of which centre around memory and smell:

> I have a table covered with all sorts of smelly things and the people have to come up and have a sniff and guess what they're smelling. It might be a smell from long ago, like a pink healing ointment or Zambuck. . .

> And then I take out my special parcel. Weeks beforehand, when I know I am going to do it, I get brown paper bags and I put a few apples inside. You see, we used to get parcels from home. My mother might send a jumper or some mittens. . . but the thing

---

2. Seremetakis's account (1994) of her research in rural and urban Greece places a similar emphasis on the sensory experience of memories and material history.

that sticks in my mind most are the apples. There would be an apple for Tommy and an apple for me, and it was just that smell when you opened the parcel – amazing! So in the pack that I do for the reminiscing sessions, or for when I talk to schools, I have a parcel, wrapped up in the same way that my mother would have wrapped it, with the address and a stamp from the 1940s, sealed with red sealing wax (because my mother would have sealed it with red sealing wax) with the string and all. . .

Such symbolic representations of a beloved deceased are frequently expressed in works of art and literature. 'A successful outcome of mourning often results in a work that may itself stand as a memorial. . . James Barrie's *Peter Pan* preserved the image of Barrie's "lost" brother (who died in childhood) while yielding him up to never-never land' (Klass, Silverman and Nickman 1996: 114). Nan's reminiscence sessions have a similar quality. Reviving her mother's parcel, which signifies her love and care, is an act of remembrance through creation, which symbolically revives both the memory of her mother and the story of her lost childhood.

I always start the session with this quote from Helen Keller – 'Smell is a potent wizard that transports us across thousands of miles and all the years that we have lived. The odours of fruits waft me to my southern home, to my childhood frolics in the peach orchard. Other odours instantaneous and fleeting cause my heart to dilate joyously or contract with remembered grief. Even as I think of smells, my nose is full of scents that start to awake sweet memories of summers gone and ripening fields far away.' Isn't that lovely? So I start with that and I tell them that everybody has a story. Everybody that has a life has a story.

Alongside her Memory and Smell reminiscences sessions, Nan creates and conducts several object and story oriented sessions that focus on a particular historical era, namely the 1930s, The Second World War and the 1950s. Sharing the sensory and material embodiments of her life memoirs with others enhances Nan's self-definition, as well as her sense of purpose, responsibility and commitment, as both collector and storyteller of past-times:

I did a talk to a school up the road. The teacher asked me to talk to the children about evacuation and what it was like. So I took all my bits up with me – a gas mask box, a few toys and things that we use to play with, ropes and all that. And I made a pixie hat for them to put on and I took a doll along, and I took an old suitcase with a label to put on it, and I told them the story of what happened during the evacuation. . . One of the little girls broke down and cried and I went 'Oh, I'm so sorry.' I didn't want to upset them, but on the other hand, how can they realize what other children have to suffer elsewhere when they are taken away from their home?

As the guardian of her family history, combined with her more 'public persona' as a reminiscences narrator, Nan has an almost 'custodial duty' to create, or rather recreate, an 'inheritance' of tangible memories, an articulation of the past for the future generations:

> I've been scribbling things down for years and it came to me that it would be nice to do a few drawings to go with my stories, because all that's gone now, it's all been demolished. . . Just to give an idea of what it was like, for my grandchildren mainly. They're still young, but someday, when they're a bit older, if they're interested, I think it will be nice for them to have the drawings so they can see what it was like.

Nan's private museum of memory, as well as her public, evocative reminiscence sessions enable her to channel her bereavement and personal grief into a positive, creative act of remembrance. By doing so Nan generates a memorial-like tribute (see Rowlands 1999), where the importance of her personal loss is acknowledge, remembered, and embodied in a more collective notion of history, memory and commemoration.

Creating symbolic memorials and tangible inheritances serves a further, fundamental purpose that is closely linked to Nan's age and life-cycle stage (see Myerhoff 1978, 1992; Marcoux, this volume). 'Ordering' her life-long memoirs and various possessions enables Nan to complete the circle of her reminiscence journey, binding past, present and future.

Full Circle

Our 'journey' ends where it began, in Nan's private museum of symbolic roots – her home.

> They say a home reflects the interests of its owner, I think mine asks 'where does your interest stop?!' But I'm surrounded by all the things I love, the books, the photos, the dolls, all my favourite knick-knacks, the Scottish stuff, the tartan boxes, the bottles. . .

Nan's notion of 'feeling at home' is strongly linked with being physically surrounded by her cherished possessions. If objects play a similar role in our unconsciousness, as language does in our consciousness (see Miller 1987), then Nan's complementary use of narratives, materials and sensory manifestations, clearly articulates her life story on more than just a cognitive level. By 'housing' the material and sensory evocations of her narrated memories, Nan symbolically revives the past homes she had left behind – from the first home she and John shared as newlyweds, to her childhood home, her true place of origin and belonging. Through her remarkable attention to detail in all her articulations (be it richly

comprehensive stories, maps and drawings, or 'recreated' objects), as well as her
meticulous sense of décor, Nan is able to capture and restage the comfortable,
cosy atmosphere of her original domestic space, the *sense* and *essence* of her
childhood home. The drawing of her 1950s kitchen (Figure 7.4) emphasizes the
rays of sunlight shining through the windows and doors, thereby echoing both the
narrated description and the sketched depiction of her bright, warm, sunlit
childhood home (Figure 7.3). Nan has decorated her current living room (Figure
7.6) in a way that regenerates the warmth and closeness of her family's home, as
if creating a 'life-size depiction', or a 'lived-in set' that enables her to re-enter her
childhood's dwelling experience:

> I wanted the room to have a kind of 'back in time' feel to it, so I decided to have these
> wooden bookcases and the matching wooden frame for the fireplace.

Figure 7.6. Living room in Nan's current home (2000)

The room certainly has a 'past-time' character, with its lace covered, bottle-green
settees and quilted pillows, as well as the old-fashioned family photos. The dark-
red wallpaper and its cream-coloured leaf design creates a sensation of warm
enclosure, while the various books, ornaments and period curiosities add to the
Aladdin's Cave of reminiscence impression. Throughout the house there are
numerous 'corners of reminiscences' displaying a range of small-scale collections,
assembled together under a certain historical or aesthetic theme:

I like things that are typical of a certain era, or a specific style. It's not anything in particular, it's just something that catches my eye, because of its shape, or colour, or the memory it brings up.

One such 'reminiscences corner' can be found on a small white dresser in the spare bedroom upstairs. Like many other of Nan's collection displays, this little compilation encompasses an array of memory objects and family photos, commemorating significant people, places and periods in Nan's life. It includes Victorian jewellery boxes, pin cushion, and potpourri container, all of which were purchased by Nan in various car-boot sales, because they resemble similar items that her grandmother used to have; 1950s 'whimsies' that Nan had collected at the time; and various flower-motif ornaments, most of which she has received as gifts from the school children she has worked with over the years. With its symmetrical presentation and flowery theme (with an emphasis on roses, which are also the subject of one of her father's poems), Nan's dresser display seems like a 'memory shrine', a memorial to an array of memories, from different bygone times.

Figure 7.7. Bedroom dresser in Nan's current home (2000)

The particularity of these assembled objects, alongside the meticulous recreation of period décor in various rooms in Nan's current and previous homes, create a clear testament of material history. Her visual and oral depiction of her first home as a married woman in the 1950s, as well as her family home in the 1930s, construct a picture of a classic home, an Everyman's home of the respective era.

> One part of the chimney was covered with a lime green background with a fine black strip on top. Superimposed on that were these small, mock picture frames, they were painted to look three dimensional, inside each of the frames there was a little painting of pears and plums. . . It was a bit dazzling, but it was outlandish 1950s!

Once again, the uniqueness of Nan's depiction, be it oral, visual, or otherwise tangible, lies in its seemingly ordinariness. The typical homes that are illustrated in Nan's articulations of her personal past become material testimonies of 'the past', just as her narrated life story embodies, to some extent, the history of her generation. The objects and drawings, along with the stories they accompany become greater than themselves, as their representation goes beyond Nan's autobiography to portray an 'everyday' of a generation, of an era in British culture. In this sense, Nan becomes an ancestral figure, charged with preserving and presenting not only a personal history, but also a collective sense of past, a remembrance that is simultaneously both private and communal.

References

Abram, D. (1997) *The Spell of the Sensuous*. New York: Vintage Books.

Armstrong, F.E. (1990) *Dickens and the Concept of Home*. London: UMI Press.

Bachelard, G. (1994) *The Poetics of Space*. Boston: Beacon.

Bahloul, J. (1996) *The Architecture of Memory*. Cambridge: Cambridge University Press.

Belk, R. (1994) 'Collectors and collecting'. In S. Pearce (ed.) *Interpreting Objects and Collections*. London and New York: Routledge.

—— (1995) *Collecting in a Consumer Society*. London: Routledge.

Bender, B. (ed.) (1993) *Landscape: Politics and Perspectives*. Oxford: Berg.

Chevalier, S. (1996) 'The domestic as museum: collective and individual memory in French and British homes'. Barcelona: EASA Conference Paper (unpublished).

—— (1998) 'From woollen carpet to grass carpet'. In D. Miller (ed.) *Material Cultures: Why some Things Matter*. Chicago: University of Chicago Press.

Conway, M.A. (1990) *Autobiographical Memory: An Introduction*. Milton Keynes: Open University Press.

Danet, B. and T. Katriel (1994) 'No two alike: play and aesthetics in collecting'. In S. Pearce (ed.) *Interpreting Objects and Collections*. London and New York: Routledge.

Daniel, G. and P. Thompson (1996) 'Stepchildren's memories of love and loss: men's and women's narratives'. In S. Leydesdorff, L. Passerini and P. Thompson (eds) *Gender and Memory*. Oxford: Oxford University Press.

Drazin, A. (2001) '"Omul se va mobila" – "a man will get furnished: wood and domesticity in urban Romania"'. This volume.

Elsner, J. and R. Cardinal (1994) *The Cultures of Collecting*. London: Reaktion Books.

Forrester, J. (1994) 'Freud and collecting'. In J. Elsner and R. Cardinal (eds) *The Cultures of Collecting*. London: Reaktion Books.

Gombrich, E.H. (1962) *Art and Illusion: A Study in the Psychology of Pictorial Representation*. London: Phaidon.

—— (1984) *The Sense of Order*. London: Phaidon.

Gullestad, M. (1996) *Everyday Life Philosophers: Modernity, Morality and Autobiography in Norway*. Oslo: Scandinavian University Press.

Haight B.K. and J.D. Webster (1995) *The Art and Science of Reminiscing: Theory, Research Methods and Applications*. London: Taylor & Francis.

Haskell, F. (1993) *History and its Images*. New Haven: Yale University Press.

Hunter, B. (1998) *The Wee World – But I wouldn't like to Paint It*. Edinburgh: Hunter.

Klass, D., P.R. Silverman and S.L. Nickman (1996) *Continuing Bounds: New Understandings of Grief*. London: Taylor & Francis.

Küchler, S. (1993) 'Landscape as memory'. In B. Bender (ed.) *Landscape: Politics and Perspectives*. Oxford: Berg.

Marcoux, J.-S. (2001) 'The refurbishment of memory'. This volume.

Merleau-Ponty, M. (1962) *Phenomenology of Perception*. London: Routledge.

Miller, D. (1987) *Material Culture and Mass Consumption*. Oxford: Blackwell.

Myerhoff, B. (1978) *Number our Days*. New York: E.P. Dutton.

—— (1992) *Remembered Lives*. Ann Arbor: University of Michigan Press.

Petridou, E. (2001) 'The taste of home'. This volume.

Rowlands, M. (1999) 'Remembering to forget: sublimation as sacrifice in war memorials'. In A. Forty and S. Küchler (eds) *The Art of Forgetting*. Oxford: Berg.

Rubin, D.C. (1995) *Remembering our Past*. Cambridge: Cambridge University Press.

Seremetakis, C.N. (1994) *The Senses Still: Perception and Memory as Material Culture in Modernity*. Chicago: University of Chicago Press.

Steedman, C. (1995) *Strange Dislocations: Childhood and the Idea of Human Interiority 1780–1930*. London: Virago Press.

—— (1998) 'What a rag rug means'. *Journal of Material Culture* 3/3: 259–81.

Stewart, S. (1984) *On Longing: Narratives of the Miniature, the Gigantic, the Souvenir, the Collection*. Baltimore: Johns Hopkins University Press.

Vickery A. (1993) 'Women and the world of goods'. In J. Brewer and R. Porter (eds) *Consumption and the World of Goods*. London and New York: Routledge.

Part III
Building Relationships

8

Building Conjugal Relations: The Devotion to Houses amongst the Paiwan of Taiwan

Chang-Kwo Tan

This is an essay about building conjugal relations and building houses amongst traditional and Protestant Christian Paiwan of Taiwan. In his contribution to *About the House* (Carsten and Hugh-Jones 1995), Bloch illustrated the process of house creation and marriage of the Zafimaniry in Madagascar. Lévi-Strauss's point that the house is the 'objectification of a relationship' (Lévi-Strauss 1984: 195) (which is marriage) can apply to the Zafimaniry, in which 'marriage actually forms the core of the (marital) unit, a unit which is identified with the material house' (Bloch 1995: 71). The creation of the house and marriage are viewed as two sides of the same thing; the building and decoration of the house is bound up with the transformation of conjugal relations from fluid to thing-like, as solid and concrete as the wooden central post of a house.

Bloch's article provides a suitable comparison for my discussion of the Paiwan society, which is a good example of 'house-based society' (Lévi-Strauss 1983, 1987) as is the Zafimaniry. The married couple is the core of kinship, and is identified with the house they build together in an enduring marriage. In the thinking of the Paiwan, a successful life is based on a successful marriage settled in a material house. However, a significant difference from the Zafimaniry is that they recognize successful marriage and house building is '*pa-zangal*' (hard, difficult, expensive) (Ferrell 1982: 358), and failure is frequent if they do not '*si-zangal*' (do with great effort). Therefore, for marriage and house building they must '*pu-zangal*'. That is, to 'treasure', or, to 'love greatly'. *Pu-zangal* can be translated as 'being devoted to'. It is fair to say that the devotion to marriage and house building are amongst the core values of the traditional Paiwanese. Even though the majority of Paiwan were converted to Christianity from the 1950s, and Christianity has brought different ideas of marriage and the conjugal relationship, I will argue later that this value is preserved and even strengthened. More importantly, in both contexts the devotion to houses is the central dynamic for constructing conjugal relations.

The Paiwan are one of nine ethnic groups of aborigines of Taiwan. There were about 70,000 Paiwan inhabiting eighty villages in southern Taiwan in 1997. They are quite different from the majority Taiwanese (about 20 million) in language, culture and physical traits. They share more similarities with the Austronesian people of south-east Asia and Oceania. The history of the Paiwan is a part of the general history of Taiwanese aborigines. With the increase of Han immigrants from southeast China from the seventeen century, they gradually became minorities and were forced to retreat to the mountains. They have engaged in trade relations with the Dutch who occupied Taiwan from 1624 to 1661. They have been governed by three political regimes: Chinese Tsin Dynasty (1662–1895), Japanese colonial government (1895–1945), and Taiwanese government (after the Second World War). The introduction of a market economy and the commodification of land and labour from the 1960s in aboriginal societies has intensified their dependence on global capitalism and the cash economy (Huang 1976). Their cultural difference was suppressed by the national policy of assimilation before 1980s. The aboriginal movement which has arisen since 1983 made appeals to the restoration of land rights, multiculturalism, and self-determination. It has achieved a certain success. A national Committee of Aboriginal Affairs was established in 1996, which is active in promoting research on aboriginal traditions. Under these circumstances, discourses about traditions of aborigines and the Paiwan are involved in a cultural politics, in which academic perspectives are constantly contested.

I propose to begin with a representation of the traditional house. The term 'tradition' follows a similar word in Paiwan: '*kakudan*', which refers to 'the custom passed from ancestors'. *Kakudans* are sets of rules and taboos that should be followed by descendants as normative codes of practices. What I will present in the first section is the normative aspect of marriage and house building. Then I turn to a perspective on contemporary Christian houses, and point out the continuity and change in Christian contexts. In the latter section I will look at the particular trajectory of building conjugal relationships and houses through three case studies. This is justified on the grounds that local Christians believe God deals with them individually: everyone has unique experience of God, everyone has his/her own story of conversion and becoming 'saved'. In the same way each couple have their particular trajectory of salvation around which their house and conjugal relations are built. So while tradition is best represented as normative, Christianity is best explored through the case study.

Traditional Houses: Conjugal Relations and Reproduction

Before discussing the house, I should point out that a salient feature in traditional Paiwan society was the distinction of two social categories of hereditary rank, aristocrats and commoners. Each house of an aristocrat attracted some houses of commoners as its clients or tenants. In a settlement, there might be more than one aristocratic house, and the identities of their followers were multiple and flexible. A powerful aristocratic house would become a political, economical and ritual centre of some subordinate aristocratic houses and houses of commoners. It would be identified as a 'chiefly house'.[1]

The house (*umaq*) refers to a material building as well as a group of persons living inside. Each house has its own name, which bears rights and titles like a social person. The house was central to the constitution of kinship identity and personhood. Birth and biological parentage in itself did not have much significance in the determination of personhood in the idea of the person of the Paiwan, something characteristic of other Austronesian societies (cf Fox 1980; Astuti 1995). Social identities were fluid and multiple: a person moved among several houses from his/her birth, through growth, marriage and death, such as the house of parents, the houses of one's bilateral grandparents, and the house of one's spouse's parents (if one is married). All these houses could be called one's *tjumaq* (original house). All of them had an inclusive (even predatory) tendency to extend the realm of their membership by providing substance of life and by giving blessings of prosperity. The inevitable result of the combination of the multiple affiliation of a person and the inclusive tendency of one's *tjumaq*s is the constant oscillation of one's identity among different *tjumaq*s (see Bloch 1995) .

The house built by oneself and one's spouse in the process of marriage has special meaning and functions to provide a stable anchor in this fluid social world (Bloch 1995). A new house was created when a couple got married.[2] In marriage exchange, the bridewealth provided by the *tjumaq* of the bridegroom was the central concern in marriage negotiation. The new house was built with support from the couple's *tjumaq*s. When it was finished, there was an inauguration ceremony held by the couple, during which the house was given a name through negotiation between the couple's *tjumaq*s. Meanwhile *tjumaq*s of the couple divided a portion of their possessions to give to the new house (Hsu 1994: 211). The new house was established only after being given a name and some possessions from *tjumaq*s. Then the couple gain their membership in the exchange network of houses, in which they were entitled to get a portion of meat and wine in public rituals and feasts.

Figure 8.1 is a traditional house which was quite typical among commoners' houses.[3] The house in Figure 8.2 belonged to the paramount chief, which will be

1. Due to the prominence of chiefly houses in social structure and cultural representations, the Paiwan was regarded as a 'hierarchical society' for decades, and much of the literature on the Paiwan has focused on relations and representations of hierarchy (Shih 1971; Matsuzawa 1979; Chiang 1983, 1993). Recently there has been a growing tendency to see the Paiwan as a 'house-based society' (for example Tan 1992; Chiang 1993; 1995).

2. It is the case when both bride and bridegroom are not the first born. If one of them is the first born, she/he will stay at home after marriage, and his/her spouse will move in. If both are the first born, they will take charge of two houses and take turns in residence.

3. Recently, researchers of the built environment and anthropologists in Taiwan have co-operated in projects to reconstruct the traditional houses of aborigines. The co-work of Li Chin-yea, a graduate

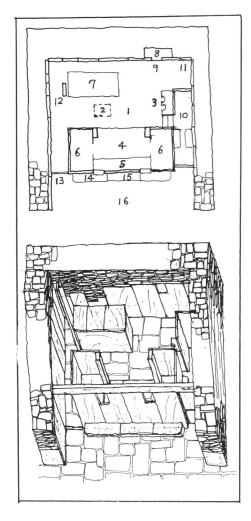

1. The living room
2. *luvang*: The cave where corpses were placed
3. The hearth
4. The bedroom
5. The long stone slate for sitting
6. The bed
7. The granary of millet
8. *tavi*: the altar for offerings
9. *puzayazayan*: the passage way in front of the *tavi*.
10. The toilet and pigpen
11. The place for burying the placenta and umbilical cord
12. *tsukes*: the central post
13. The door
14. The window
15. The long stone slate
16. The courtyard

Figure 8.1. Traditional Paiwan commoners' house

taken as an example of the original house. The two houses were located in the old settlement of Tjalagavus village. This village was resettled in 1953, and now villagers perceived houses in the old settlement as 'traditional', in contrast to those

student in architecture, and Chiang Bien, an anthropologist specializing in Paiwan culture, is a typical example. The material on traditional houses comes from Li's MA thesis (1994) and Chiang's (1995) paper.

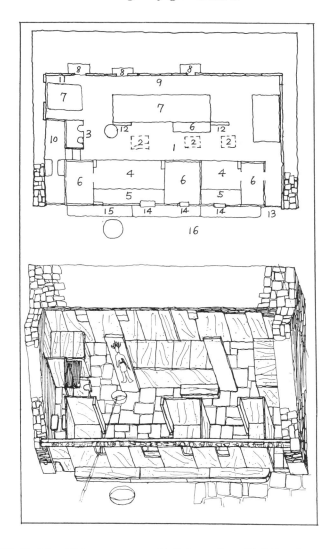

Figure 8.2. Traditional Paiwan paramount chief's house (From Li 1994: A-21, 22, 29, 30)

built after resettlement. A major difference is the material: houses in the old settlement were built with stone slates and wood beams, whereas later ones were built mainly of concrete. The architectural features and the organization of space are also quite different from later 'modernized' houses.

Alongside ethnographies of traditional ideas and values (Tan 1992; Hsu 1994; Chiang 1993, 1995), these data can be interpreted as follows. First, the house provided a space to keep the couple together and contributed to their unity. The traditional ideal was that they could 'adapt to each other, become one body, one soul, one person' (Tan 1992: 136). The couple owned a fixed bed where they could have sex and sleep together; they ate together around the hearth (c.f. Janowski 1995; Carsten 1995). The granary stored the millet, yams, and potatoes which were the result of the couple's co-work. Second, the house was the central site of daily mutual caring between the couple. The wife cared for the husband through female activities such as cooking (on the hearth), sewing (on the stone chair) and feeding pigs; the husband cared for the wife through the male activity of hunting. He should also protect his wife.[4] In many ways the couple needed to be complementary in order to keep themselves alive and maintain the viable condition of the house. Third, the house was the dwelling place of the guardian spirit, *umaq-an*, which was a personified spirit of the house (Hu 1998: 19). It protected its inhabitants from attacks of evil spirits. On the other hand, it punished those who did not pay respect to it by violating taboos and polluting it (for example by smoke or urine). The spirit could be anywhere in the house, but the *tavi* (or *tsukes*, see Hu 1998: 13) was the main place to place offerings to it. The *umaq-an* came into existence during the inauguration ceremony. A sacrifice must be given to ancestors in order to create it. Like a human body, it was an organism composed of different parts of the house, and interconnected through the 'living power' (*luqem*). This living power was shared by possessions and persons. So the granary, the hearth and the couple were integral parts of the guardian spirit, and all of them shared its reproductive duty (cf. Waterson 1990: 115–37).

For traditional Paiwan, the aim of marriage was to serve 'the mission of reproduction'. Without this vision the marital relation was transient and fragile, like the occasional sexual relationship between immature boys and girls. The house played an essential role in this mission because it brought the couple together through one bed, one hearth, and enhanced their unity (one body, one soul) which was the necessary condition of their fertility. The house played the role of protecting, keeping, and fostering fertility, through the power of the guardian spirit (*umaq-an*) and the materiality of the house, in particular, the heat of the hearth (see Carsten 1997: 58–9). The house was also an agent of reproduction, like the womb of a woman. Chiang (1995: 189–90) pointed out that the whole of house building was designed in the image of the womb, a dark, warm container that was capable of keeping the life-giving power of the sun. In addition, the life-giving power of millet, game (caught by the husband), and pigs (raised by the wife) could contribute to the fertility of the couple.

---

4. Chiang (1995: 184) points out that on the stone walls near the door and the living room there always hung some weapons for the male to defend the inhabitants of the house from attacks by enemies.

The imagination of the house as a womb reached its climax when the labour of the wife began. Only the wife and midwives stayed in the house (on the bed, or in the living room in front of the central post), and all other relatives and friends, including the husband, had to avoid coming into the house. They were kept outdoors to wait. If there was difficulty in the labour, the husband would invite female shamans to pray, and meanwhile he would try to help the delivery by 'destroying an end of stone walls, uncovering a part of the roof, shaking the central post' (Chiang 1995: 189–90). After the birth, the placenta and the umbilical cord could not be thrown outside. They must be kept in the house, buried in the corner near the hearth, or put in a bamboo tube and hung on the beam above the central post.[5] If the wife should unfortunately die from difficult labour, she would be buried in a special graveyard outside the village. Her corpse would be treated as 'rubbish' rather than receiving a proper burial, because people thought that death from a difficult labour was the worst kind of death (Hsu 1994: 122–3). It was seen as the most serious failure of the couple and the house, which was punished by being abandoned, and the site became taboo. The husband would be punished throughout his life. He was not allowed to take part in the event of childbirth or ritual events for children, and it would be difficult for him to remarry. Chiang argues that such severe punishment was due to the failure of the 'mission of reproduction' of the couple and the house, because '. . . the essential mission of the house – like the womb – is to procreate life, deliver life. The failure in this mission is equivalent to negating the meaning of the house's existence, and to announcing the death of the house' (1995: 201).

The couple would survive if they were successful in having their first baby born. The relationship would be much more settled, and they would receive rewards: the families of their *tjumaq* would give the mother gifts to comfort her and hold a series of life-cycle rituals to celebrate. The first born was called *vusam* (meaning the 'millet seed'), the key symbol of reproduction. He (or she) was the heir of the house and its possessions soon after the birth, while the couple became caretakers of the *vusam*. They were like guardians of the house, and acted more and more like the *umaq-an*. The addition of a person to the house meant an increasing demand for food and resources, which often drove the couple to seek help from their *tjumaq*. They also asked the blessings of ancestors from elders in *tjumaq* to foster the growth of the baby, meanwhile *tjumaq* would ask the baby to feed them in return

---

5. This was meant to protect the new-born baby who was very vulnerable to the influence of its environment and attacks of evil spirits. Similar practices can be seen in south Sulawesi. See Errington (1989: 38–9).

6. One ritual made this point clear, in which the couple brought the baby (normally one month old) to visit the natal houses of the couple. The grandparents of the baby would feed it with a spoon in the house, meaning that the baby could come here to eat in the future. Then the grandparents would make offerings to ancestors to ask blessings and protection for the baby (Tan 1992: 124).

when it grew big enough.[6] At this stage the significance of the house as a ritual construct related to ancestors became more and more salient. Many life-cycle rituals were held in the house of the couple or their *tjumaq*s, which normally took place in front of the central post.

When the child was reaching the age of marriage, the couple had the duty to accumulate possessions for the coming marriage exchange. These possessions, including iron tools, metal woks, and valuables such as ancient beads, pottery, could be acquired by exchange of millet, pigs and game. Besides, the fame of the house was significant in marriage negotiation. As 'symbolic capital' (Bourdieu 1984), the fame could lift the status of the house in public evaluation (see Munn 1986), and became a powerful counter in marriage negotiations. If the couple could accumulate enough possessions and fame, they could make a good marriage negotiation for the *vusam*, who stayed at home rather than being married out. By contrast, other children would get married out. If this happened, and the couple had grandchildren, then the couple would be called *vuvu* by their grandchildren. *Vuvu* was also an intimate term for 'ancestors'. Actually they were more and more like living ancestors, the benevolent guardians of the descendents. The house of the couple, now passed on to their *vusam*, would be called *tjumaq* by their children being married out, who would bring their babies back to ask blessings from the (founding) couple in front of the central post. And the (founding) couple won the devotion of their descendents in return, who took charge of the duty to feed and to care for the (founding) couple, their *vuvu*, and to ensure the viable continuity of the house of the (founding) couple, their *tjumaq*.

The devotion to *tjumaq*s (original houses) was a central value for traditional Paiwanese (Hsu 1994: 163–5). They thought that from birth through to death a person was always cared for by *tjumaq*, materially and spiritually. They return to *tjumaq* to seek refuge and delivery when facing troubles and difficulty in their life, and *tjumaq*, as the representative agent of ancestors, must act as a benevolent guardian of its descendents. This relationship was represented by traditional Paiwan in the organic metaphor of origin and offspring (see McKinnon 1991). The origin was the source of the life-giving power of the offspring, which issued from the origin and was dependent on the protection of the origin. The offspring, correspondingly, was obliged to return the debt of long-term caring to the origin. The same idea could extend to the devotion to the chiefly house, which was perceived as 'tj-tjumaq' (the true origin house) of the community.

An appealing way to express this devotion was to offer the body of oneself to the tomb cave of one's *tjumaq* after one died (see Chiang 1995: 202). However, there was a condition to be met in order to be buried in the house, that is it only applied to those who died a 'good death'. They would be worshipped as ancestors after funerals, and people believed the presence of their corpse in the tomb cave would bring fertility to the house. The more corpses the house possessed, the more fruitful and prosperous the house would be. So to be buried in one's *tjumaq* was an honour for the deceased. It was to return the debt to the house of origin. Moreover, it was a statement that one's *tjumaq* and oneself were inalienable from birth to death, and one's body was the 'inalienable' possession of one's original house.

This inalienable relationship was expressed explicitly in the idiom of siblingship, in which siblings shared 'the same womb, the same tomb'. So there was a norm among traditional Paiwan that they should return to their *tjumaq* to be buried together with their siblings, where they had always kept their placenta and umbilical cords and their tomb since they were born (Chiang 1995: 202).

Hence we can imagine that when the couple reached the edge of death, the issue of where they should be buried created a dilemma for themselves and their descendents. To be buried in the house they constructed was a solemn expression of the couple's devotion to the continuing reproduction of the house, to the long-term fortune and prosperity of their descendents, who tended to keep their corpses in the house that the couple constructed rather than the *tjumaq* of the couple. However, it would decrease the value of holiness of the *tjumaq*, which would demand vehemently the returning burial. Hsu (1994: 164) pointed out that in previous times there often occurred a struggle for corpses between *tjumaq*s of the couple and the house they created. Sometimes *tjumaq*s agreed to let the couple be buried in the house they constructed. Eventually the devotion of the couple to the house transformed them into the 'inalienable' possession of the house they constructed and the descendents they created.

However, the struggle between devotion to the *tjumaq* and devotion to the house the couple constructed was an unresolved dilemma for traditional Paiwanese. In times when the idea that the *tjumaq* possessed the power of fertility, the devotion to the *tjumaq* was a practice with longer term consideration for reproduction. Besides, the devotion to the *tjumaq* was the ideological basis of the devotion to the chiefly house, the *tjumaq* of all *tjumaqs*. So when the authority of chiefly houses was dominant in social life, devotion to the *tjumaq* was more legitimate than the devotion to the couple's own house. Within this ideology of reproduction, marriage was a means rather than an end. The conjugal relationship itself was not regarded as the central agent in reproduction, but has always been downplayed. The relationships with the first-born sibling and the first-born child were more sanctified. This hierarchical order of relationships is altered in Christian contexts. To what extent did Christianity transform traditional houses, conjugal relationships and reproduction? It is to this question that I now turn.

Christian Houses: Conjugal Relationship and Marital Love

Walking along the main road of Laliba, we will see many shining and colorful two-storeyed concrete houses. Each differs in the design of roof or windows.

Between their high walls there are some small and old houses of wood and bamboo. One-storeyed concrete houses with brick roofs and wooden doors and windows, built around the 1970s, are in the majority.

Laliba is a Paiwan community in south-east Taiwan. It was a small settlement with 116 households. The majority of the residents (70–80 per cent) are Protestants of Presbyterian denomination. The history of conversion began with a Chinese pastor who launched missionary activities in 1950. The first church was constructed in 1964, when an indigenous pastor settled here. A two-storey Presbyterian church dedicated in 1993 is now the centre of community life. So far, over the course of half a century's evangelization, this village has produced three pastors. Since the late 1970s, more and more villagers have left the village to find their livelihood in cities because of the decline of local agriculture. Most of them became construction workers, and many gathered in Taichung city through kinship and friendship ties. Some of them lived in the settlement called 'Little Laliba'. My fieldwork in Laliba, a part of my PhD research project, was conducted from October 1997 to February 1998. I also stayed in 'Little Liliba' for three weeks in August 1998.

For Laliba Christians, the mission of reproduction is still the major reason for marriage, and the house is still central to fulfilling this mission. They are very interested in exploring how to appropriate Christianity to realize their wishes for success and fruitfulness, such as having desirable babies, finding suitable partners, and building satisfying houses. In those practices their motivations and aims are not so different from people who are devoted to ancestors and adhere to traditional rituals. What makes Christians different is that they recognize their subjects of devotion as 'God' (*KaCemasan*) and 'Jesus Christ' (Yisu Kilistu), and they use the method of prayer (rather than killing pigs) to ask for blessings. The centre of each Christian house (usually the centre of the wall facing the door) is the place for the cross and a board with words like 'Christ is the Lord of this House'. On the side walls there could hang tapestries with biblical images of 'Jesus is a Good Shepherd' or 'The Last Supper'. In every room they place at least a cross on the wall. Jesus for them is like a guardian god of the house to protect their lives and possessions and give them peace. He is supposed to be more powerful and benevolent than ancestors or the guardian spirit, because he is 'the only Son of God Almighty', 'the King of kings'.

The second aspect of appropriation is incorporating the church into the project of reproduction. In general the church has replaced the status of the *tjumaq* and the chiefly house in believers' eyes and become the holiest place ('the Temple of God') where they seek blessings and life-giving power. They ask help from staff of the church at the events of life-cycle rituals, particularly weddings and funerals. Correspondingly, the church demands a return from each Christian house through regular services and constant offerings, which contribute to maintaining and expanding the church in ministries and resources. The result is that the church, surpassing chiefly houses, has become the greatest and most glorious building in the village.

The church is a two-storey hall with massive stone walls in light green and arched windows in white frames. There is a white cross on the top of the bell tower, which can be seen from a distance. The appearance of the church is high and bright. The interior is spacious and orderly. On the centre of the rear wall is a big cross of light-brown pine, in front of which is an altar decorated with flowers. Under the altar are lines of chairs of light-brown pine for the congregation. The decoration is harmonious, and the surface of the furniture, the wall and the ground always remain clean and bright. Overall it is the highest quality building and decoration believers can manage. They have transferred their former devotion to glorifying and beautifying their *tjumaq* and chiefly house to the church. Even though they still carry out kinship duties to their *tjumaq*s, and still pay certain respect to the chiefly house, they no longer regard the *tjumaq* and the chiefly house as higher than themselves in terms of the hierarchical order of holiness. In short, these institutions do not deserve their devotion.

Closely connected to these projects is the reformulation of marital relationships through Christian values. Christian ideas of marriage are different from traditional ones in two aspects. First, it is stressed that marriage is primarily a 'mission of love' rather than a 'mission of reproduction'. In this mission the couple are demanded according to God's law to keep a covenant of love throughout their lives. Second, it follows that for Christians the conjugal relationship should be 'inalienable' in that only death can break it. No other human relationship on earth is more sanctified than the conjugal relationship, which is joined together by God. Traditional belief in ancestors has sanctified the siblingship which was imagined as 'inalienable' even after death. The conjugal relationship could be 'inalienable' only if the couple were successful in their mission of reproduction. But both these conceptualizations are rejected by Christians, for whom only the relationship between God and humankind is a genuine 'inalienable relationship' which can transcend death.

The traditional devotion to the house the couple constructs, however, continues to be the norm of marriage, and Christian ideas of marriage as a holy institution and the conjugal relationship as inalienable throughout lifetime has justified and strengthened this devotional practice. Two perspectives should illuminate this point. First, the house still plays the central role in reproduction of Christians. Christian doctrine does not make reproduction the concern of marriage, but it does encourage the married couple to 'bear fruits', to build up a Christianized family, and to glorify the Kingdom of God, which for local Christians means to build a house, to have children, and to nurture them in Christian disciplines. The more children they can raise in a Christian way, the more glories they will bring to God. Second, as local Christians have found, the house is central to the mission of love. The house is a medium to express feelings and love; it is a concrete sign of the inalienability of the conjugal relationship; and its materiality is an agent in the execution of affection and love. In short, the house is the objectification of the conjugal relationship as loving and inalienable. The devotion to the house is the commitment to this ideal relationship. The Christian couple, therefore, tries to combine the mission of love and the mission of reproduction together as its life-long project. The enduring devotion to the house they construct is the way they can fulfil both missions.

I have illustrated the connection of traditional houses and reproduction in the last section, and pointed out some continuity and changes in Christian contexts. In the following I want to focus on the connection of houses and love for Christian couples. I must firstly clarify local Christian ideas of love (*kilivak*), which cannot be separated from the idea of marriage. The teaching on love is very salient in the New Testament, which is the source of sermons on conjugal relationships in the wedding service, and the source of authority for advice given by elders to the newlywed. These teachings, however, are rather abstract. The couple may come to know what love is and how to love only through their lived experience, through the process of mutual adaptation, through trial and error. I propose to understand local practices of love through three case studies. My aims are twofold: to illustrate the uniqueness of the trajectory of marital love, and to find underlying principles of the building process of conjugal relations and houses.

Compassion Through Home Decoration

Lerem and Baubu are a young migrant couple. They live in the settlement of 'Little Laliba', which was located in a late-developed suburb area of Taichung, the greatest city in central Taiwan. This temporary dwelling for aboriginal migrant workers was surrounded by spacious wet rice farms of Han-Taiwanese. Two blocks, the major living space, were inhabited by eleven couples with their children (Figure 8.3). There were also three single males in their twenties. I lived in a room next to the living room of Lerem and Baubu; Lerem, aged twenty-four, a devoted wife and mother, was my key informant.

Lerem met Baubu in a hospital where she looked after her sick aunt. She had wandered on the streets of Taichung in order to escape her family in her village before she came to the hospital. But she was deserted by her aunt's families and nobody cared for her. Baubu, having worked in Taichung for several years, came to visit her aunt who was also his relative. He took pity on Lerem, and gave her money and food. Later he invited her to live with him. They soon got married, then moved into a flat in 'Little Laliba'. One year afterwards Yaen, their only son, was born. Due to mistakes by doctors, he suffered from long-term brain damage one week after birth. He was nearly deaf, and had great difficulty in learning. Looking after this child was distressing for Lerem, who began to hate her husband

Figure 8.3. Habitations in 'Little Laliba', Taichung

in her agony. She became easily angered and violent. Through the persistent care of an evangelist from her home church and Christian relatives who shared her grief and tears with her, she was converted, and gradually changed her attitude toward Baubu. She realized that she would live in misery if Baubu had no pity on her. At least he had provided her a secure and stable environment. She also felt sympathy for him, because he came from an uncaring family like hers. She felt thankful to him and she was determined to give him love in return.

Before conversion she did not care about the place they lived, and she often broke things and destroyed the furniture in her rage. With her change she redecorated the bedroom with great zeal. She replaced the old bed with a king-sized bed. In the tiny room, this bed became the dominant furniture. It was made of pine, with crimson sheets, duvet cover and pillowcases in rose pink. She then decorated two windows with curtains in rose pink and a floral pattern similar to the duvet cover. The same colour and pattern extended further to the wallpaper, which gave this room a warm and relaxed atmosphere. In the corner was a chest of drawers, and this was followed by a wardrobe near the door. All furniture was in the same pine effect which made them harmonious with the overall feel of the room. There was a bottle of dry flowers on the dressing table; the fragrance made this room smell good, and distinguished it from other parts of the domestic space, particularly the kitchen which was the abode of bad smells.

The harmony and fragrance of the bedroom represented those qualities Lerem wished to create for a place of rest. Sharing the same feelings with other housewives who lived here, she had much pity on her husband who worked and stayed outdoors for at least eight hours in every working day. She felt obliged to let him have a good rest, physically and psychologically. Even though for them the main reason for staying here was to save money, Lerem still spent a lot of money on home decoration. This spending on the interior decoration of the home was in opposition to the ideal of thrift, which dominated domestic consumption for most working-class families living here. Lerem, however, did not regard thrift as central to the matter of home decoration. For her, home is where the heart is (*izua varung, izua tjumaq*). Home was somewhere her heart could be settled and satisfied; home was somewhere her heart could devote itself to, and she could love and be loved. In practical terms this meant for her that home was a place where her husband and son could satisfy their needs, and a place where she would love them. Home decoration was a channel to express her compassion for the husband.

The kitchen was another place to express her love. Separated by some distance from the flat, it was located in a shelter covered by a massive roof. Lerem's family used a chamber 5 m long, 2 m wide, 2 m high. Rats were often seen, because it is difficult to keep the ground clean. Overall the kitchen was ill equipped, rough and dirty. Lerem said she needed much patience to work in such poor conditions, but she still spent at least two hours here everyday. She used the kitchen as a place of caring, and showed her love by being patient with an unpleasant working environment.

In the same way Baubu shared the idea of 'home is where the heart is' with his wife, and he was devoted to their home through his commitment to a tough and risky job. He was an industrious and trustworthy worker with the virtue of perseverance. He had followed his boss for seven years through the highs and lows of the construction industry. Such a stable relationship was rare among aboriginal workers. In his leisure time, the car was a medium through which he made specific contributions to their home. The car provided a space to create the sense of intimacy and togetherness which is the essence of home. It was also a vehicle to connect them with their *tjumaq* in their home village. The car was an integral part of home, and was capable of creating a mobile home transcending the constraints of a fixed home. Thus he treasured the car, for which he built a tent to protect it. He also enjoyed caring for it by washing and polishing it making it shine in a dull housing environment.

From this example we can see home and home decoration can be an objectification of the conjugal relationship (Gullestad 1992). It is obvious that domestic space like the bedroom and kitchen are mainly the medium of female love, such as compassion and patience. Male love was implicated mainly in the working environment outside home, or the mobile domestic space, which transcends the fixed home in the care of the car. But above all home comes to accord with the Christian ideal of home to which they devoted themselves to carrying out the mission of love.

Forgiveness Through Giving Possessions

In Laliba there are more and more cases of family disorder in which the husband's addiction to alcohol upsets marital relationship, whilst the wife suffers from the consequence of a damaged marriage. The story of Piya (husband, in mid-forties) and Savan (wife, in late thirties) is a case in point. They have raised three children, and live in a one-storey concrete house which is quite typical of the village. Their house is much improved compared with the flat of the young couple. The kitchen and shower room are an integral part of the house, the main bedroom is enlarged, and the number of bedrooms has increased with more children. The greatest difference is the addition of the living room inside and the courtyard outside. Materially and spatially it is already a complete house.

Piya was a retired sergeant. He worked overseas for two years, during which he saved enough money to buy the present house. Savan was a nurse and worked in the local hospital. They enjoyed a glamorous life when Piya was a local MP for eight years. After stepping down from his office, however, he could not cope with an ordinary life with routine duties. He kept up a habit of lavish consumption, and became addicted to alcohol. He lost the will to work, his health deteriorated. His lack of devotion made Savan an exhausted wife. She often made complaints in front of his drinking friends to humiliate him.

Her attitude, however, was dramatically changed by one event. The cousin of her husband was afflicted by evil spirits and returned to the village for healing. All of her Christian families and friends united together to pray for her. Eventually she was cured and converted to a Protestantism (from Catholicism). Savan was amazed and determined to revive her devotional life. She found several Christians who shared the same wish, and they formed a prayer group conducting morning prayer each day. I was invited to participate in this group because Savan was my close friend and key informant. A couple of weeks later one member of this small prayer group proposed to build a Holy Mountain on his own land. Ideally, it is a place where they can concentrate on meditation and prayer.

Savan saw this project as a chance to restore her marital relationship. She offered her labour to clear the forest, food to feed co-workers, and money for its future development. More persons were healed on the Holy Mountain, and she regained the 'baptism of the Holy Spirit'. This charismatic experience gave her much hope for the transformation of herself and her husband. She came to consider that his failure was also her failure, and she should bear the burden of her husband to overcome his sins (*pasalisaliw*). If she kept her self-pride, and was unable to forgive her husband, then she would have committed a sin, and God would not forgive. She felt that to give away her possessions could break her selfishness and open the channel of forgiveness. Although their financial situation was difficult, she still extended her giving (of money and food) to neighbours and the poor in community. She also offered her home as a place of praise and prayer, and kept the door open for Christians or non-Christians.

This case reveals three interesting points. First, the Christian practice of forgiveness (*pazekat*) is very different from the traditional pattern. In a traditional context, 'forgiveness' meant to accept the explanation or apology from the offending party. For example, in the case of a spouse who has committed adultery and asked the forgiveness of the offended spouse, the former should take the initiative and bring some gifts for compensation. The latter always played a passive but superior role in deciding to accept or reject these. By contrast, for Christians the virtue of forgiveness inverts these actions. It is the offended party that takes the initiative. Hence, it is Savan who took initiative in this case. Second, Christian doctrines demand women play a submissive role in domestic sphere (see Jolly and Macintyre 1989); and in cases of marital disorder, wives are asked to remain tolerant and perseverant. In traditional circumstances, by contrast, the wife was given more autonomy in initiating divorce.

Third, the practice of giving away the possessions of the house in order to be forgiven or forgive reveals the particular character of local Christianity. An implicit local understanding is that the possessions given away are like carriers of the sins of the house. To give them away from the house can remove sins. This is quite close to traditional practices of sacrifice which seeks to remove sins by offering pigs. But local Christians reject this analogy and claim they follow Christian rather than traditional norms. Perhaps we can say this is another manifestation of the appropriation of Christianity.

Restoring the Conjugal Relationship Through House Building

There are many wives like Savan. Their husbands have the problem of excessive drinking, and they hope sincerely that there will come a moment when their husband will be transformed. In some cases the husband does not change, and the couple ends up divorced, whereas in some cases the transformation did happen. I will cite the story of Buka and Lanau as an example.

Buka is a pastor in a neighbouring church. Lanau, in her early forties, is a housewife and a assistant to her husband's ministry. They have three children, and the first-born daughter was married out and had children. They are now the most respected couple in the village, particularly among Christians who adore them as a model of conjugal relationships. Their relationship, however, was not always so good. They had confronted similar problems of alcoholism during the pastor's early thirties. At that time he was the evangelist of Laliba church. He was extremely successful, but he became proud of himself and indulged in self-seeking activities, such as singing contests and drinking parties. Lanau persevered throughout, even though she was heavily beaten. She did not give up hope, and put her trust in God.

Her perseverance was rewarded eventually. Buka was shocked by the violent death of a drinking companion. To him it was like a judgement of God, a sign of his future if he did not repent. He renounced drinking, then went to seek the forgiveness of his wife. She was overjoyed. She encouraged him to receive advanced training, while she devoted herself to taking care of the family. Buka often tells people: 'I really thank my wife, because she never turned away from me. She is always the pair of hands praying behind me. So today we can be successful like this.'

They began to build their own house soon after they had saved enough money for purchasing the site and acquiring the loan. Since then they devoted their spare time to construction work. I lived in the house next to them, and sometimes visited them. Once, Lanau commented that the process was *pazangal*, difficult and expensive:

> Building the house is much harder than delivering babies. I have delivered three babies in four years, but the pastor and I have built this house for five years. . . Sometimes believers came to visit us, and found out we were so poor. They offer us some meat and some money, so we can buy materials and finish as soon as possible. . . When we were short of money and could not continue, we prayed; when we could not find workers, we prayed. Very often we must stop for months. Problems were always solved somehow, and we could carry on. Thanks be to God! Thanks be to God! I cannot believe my eyes, it is nearly finished now.

The new house is two storeys, standing on the highest open ground of village. The overall appearance is bright: walls in cream-yellow, roof in brown and a balcony in white, which makes the house shine in the background of green mountains and blue sky. Four long arched windows in white frames are the same as those on church's walls (Figure 8.4). There is a light always kept on throughout every night. It is the landmark of the village, which people can see from a distance. The courtyard is the centre of the village and the most used collective space. In the Christians' view, this is the model of an ideal house after the model of the church, with qualities of brightness, spaciousness, cleanness and order.

These qualities continue to permeate through the living room, study room and kitchen (Figure 8.5). In the living room, a huge rectangular board inscribed with 'The Faithful Servant of Christ' is placed on the upper centre of the wall facing the door. Under the board is a pine cross. Below it there is an open Bible of white clay inscribed with 'Christ is the Lord of this House'. On each side of the cross there is a display unit with photos and souvenirs remembering important events in the pastor's career. In all these photos the pastor is the central focus with his wife in a complementary place. Around the living room, the walls are white, the floor is paved in cream porcelain tiles, and the ceiling is white. All these, along with four windows, make the living room bright and spacious. In the pastor's study room, a big desk occupies the centre. On the desk there is a verse, 'Nothing is

Figure 8.4. The house of Buka and Lanau

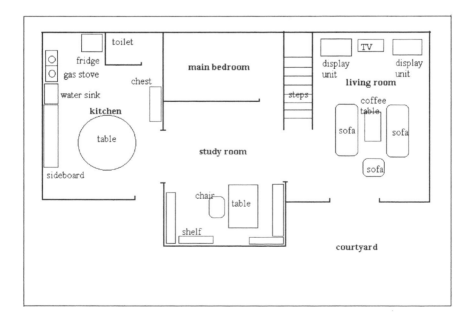

Figure 8.5. Plan of Buka and Lanau's house

Impossible for God', inscribed on a marble stone. This verse is the pastor's favourite. In the spacious kitchen, a big round dining table dominates the space. Along the wall are inbuilt sideboard, chests and shelves. The gas stove is on a platform covered by white porcelain tiles. On top of it there is a smoke extractor fan. The floor is paved with porcelain tiles, which give an extra sense of cleanness and coolness. A piece of white paper is pasted on the door of the fridge with four eye-catching red Chinese words meaning 'Jesus Loves You.'

It is obvious that the couple attempt to present themselves as a model couple through the exterior design and interior decoration of the new house. The whole house is full of religious inscriptions and symbols, including the living room, the study room and the kitchen. The couple want to communicate that this house is a holy temple, and that their relationship to God is intimate and inalienable. Moreover, what makes this house special is its consistent pattern of aesthetics. Brightness, cleanness, straightness and smoothness are highlighted, resembling the aesthetics of the church, and evoking the imagination of holiness. These aesthetic values are associated with Christian virtues, such as 'the light of the world' (Luke 5: 14), 'a clean life', 'making straight paths for the Lord'. The aesthetics evoke the Christian virtues that the couple hope they can emulate. As Comaroff and Comaroff put it, Christians take it for granted that the '. . . houses, and the routines they inscribed, construct their inhabitants' (1997: 277). For the couple the house is not only a daily reminder of their moral expectations, but also has the power to construct and protect qualities of their marital relationships.

The same idea can be seen in other places. In the living room the couple present the pastor as a faithful servant of Christ, and the wife as a helper playing a complementary role. They stressed their unity by displaying large photos in which they held hands. This unitary and complementary relationship is materialized in the study room and kitchen. The study room is a personalized space in which the pastor works. Through the devotion to his work he makes a contribution to the viable continuity of the house. In the same way the kitchen is his wife's specific place of devotion. In addition, the study room and kitchen are close to each other. They can see and talk to each other if the door is open. The ground and walls of the two spaces share the same material and aesthetic quality. The aesthetics of closeness and sameness materialize the couple's expectation of their intimacy. On the other hand, there is a significant difference between the study room and kitchen. The study room is close to the living room and belonged to the main building. It occupies the place with the best view in the ground floor. The kitchen is an extension of the main building and placed behind it. This location hides the kitchen from visitors' sight. Overall this design is an objectification of the ideal pattern of the Christian conjugal relationship in which the husband is the head and the wife is submissive. Through building this house, the couple wish to materialize an ideal marital relationship in which they are united as one flesh through mutual love for each other and common devotion to the house while the husband is recognized as the head.

Above all, for the couple, this house is a glorious monument of victory in the struggle throughout their marital life. For the Paiwan, including traditional Paiwan and Christians, marriage and house building are things *pazangal* (difficult, expensive) to which they must be devoted. But if they are successful, they will be *mapu-zangal* (joyful). In the inauguration ceremony of the new house, there was a dancing party led by the couple, who dressed themselves in traditional costumes. Shining and glamorous, they were like a victorious chiefly couple. All guests gathered around them in a circle to celebrate their success, which has brought glory to God and fame to their *tjumaqs*. And above all, glory and fame will go to their own house. It has fulfilled most of the mission of love and the mission of reproduction.

Conclusion

I have shown that the Paiwan is a 'house-based society', in which social and cultural reproduction are bound up with the reproduction of houses. For traditional Paiwan, the goal of marriage is the mission of reproduction, and the ideal conjugal relationship is the one in which the couple share a common devotion to the reproduction of the house they created. For Christian Paiwan, a mission of love is integrated with the mission of reproduction for the purpose of marriage. An ideal couple should love each other and bear 'fruits' from their love, that is the reproduction of Christian houses. It has been illustrated how through building houses to realize these missions, the conjugal relationship is transformed from ideal to concrete. Moreover, I have argued that the house and its possessions are active agents of making conjugal relations concrete in both cases.

I would like to make some concluding reflections on where the power of the house and its possessions come from. In traditional contexts, the devotion to the house is a demand of ancestral custom which sees the devotion to *tjumaqs* (original houses) and chiefly houses as the necessary condition of social and cultural reproduction. The house is the central site of the operation of this ideological and material power which force the couple to devote themselves to original houses (cf. Waterson 1995). On the other hand, there is a kind of power coming from inside the house the couple created. Through building a house and turning it into an object of devotion, the couple build themselves as ancestors, the subject of devotion (cf. Bloch 1995: 79–83; see Miller 1998: 114–23). In this dialectical process the conjugal relationship is built metaphorically and materially by the hearth, the bed, the granary, the central post and the tomb. The ideal of 'one body' becomes concrete through the process of objectification (Miller 1987) in which the couple objectify themselves in these material possessions. The house is essential for this process through the operation of its 'keeping' power. Materially, it holds the couple and its possessions together and keeps them away from the destruction caused by material or spiritual forces; metaphorically it is a powerful symbol of reproduction that binds the couple together and elicits their devotional practices.

Christianity has strengthened the power inside the house by turning the focus of marriage on the mutual love of the couple which emanates from the interior. No matter whether it be a flat of rough appearance or a fully furnished house, a home is an anchorage in a transient world for the couple, and a place where their hearts can be settled through its 'keeping' power. Some possessions are capable of not only 'keeping' the couple together, but also 'giving' them the power to have compassion, such as the bed and the car in the first case study. Some possessions, when given away, empower the capacity of forgiveness, as in the second case study. Similar to traditional contexts, mutual love of the couple unfolds through the process of objectification, in which the husband/wife objectifies himself/herself as a service or a material form of possession as a gift for the wife/husband, who appropriates the gift as a part of herself/himself. Then the process reverses. This process can be described as the dialectics of dispossessing and repossessing, in which each spouse gives a part of himself/herself in an objectified form to the other, then receives a part. In this process the couple are transformed, joined together, and become inalienable through the mediating and transforming power of possessions. In addition, the keeping power of the house contributes to making marital love continue to flow, and to overcoming events which would break the house and separate the couple.

Moreover, the house has a power of 'cosmological authentication' and legitimates 'an authority that transcends present social and political action' (Weiner 1992: 4). Under traditional circumstances, the authority of chiefs was legitimated by their ownership of a house with a carved central post, altars for annual ceremonies, and precious inherited possessions which authenticate their linkage with founding ancestors. In a similar way, the authority of the original houses was legitimated by possessing heirlooms, titles, tombs of ancestors. Hence, the house is a form of 'inalienable possession' through which prestigious origins and authority connected to the past are authenticated. Above all, the house, like inalienable possessions, is the material expression of 'keeping', which is 'to bring a vision of permanence into a social world that is always in the process of change' (Weiner 1992: 8).

Protestant Christianity in Laliba denied the authority of chiefly houses and original houses by rejecting the authority connected to the past and to ancestors. But in Christianity the house has a kind of power to authenticate change from the past, and the present relationship with the divine. As the third case study reveals, the pastor and his wife's house authenticates their claim that they have been genuinely transformed and their faith is authentic so that they have already been saved and blessed by God. Besides, they have found more favour in God's eyes than have others, because they are more successful in marriage and house building than others. This authentication gives the couple an authority that is not based on traditional grounds but on 'charismatic grounds', which is 'resting on devotion to the exceptional sanctity, heroism, or exemplary character of an individual person, and of the normative patterns or order revealed or ordained by him' (Weber 1968: 215). The couple exactly exemplifies the character of the local Christian community, and they are seen as extraordinary in spiritual gifts and divine grace. Their behaviour is regarded as the normative pattern, which is also objectified in their house, as I have illustrated and analysed it. Through the display of exterior design and interior decoration, the house becomes an 'exemplary centre' (Geertz 1980) of normative Christian values. In this sense the power of the house is not about coercion and domination, but about its capacity of inviting and attracting followers and transforming their hearts. The power of the house, therefore, lies not only in 'keeping' but also in 'transforming'. Through keeping and transforming conjugal relationships, the house itself is kept and transformed, and becomes an inalienable partner of the couple.

References

Astuti, R. (1995) '"The Vezo are not a kind of people": identity, difference, and "ethnicity" among a fishing people of western Madagascar'. *American Ethnologist* 22/3: 464–82.

Bloch, M. (1995) 'The resurrection of the house amongst the Zafimaniry of Madagasar'. In J. Carsten and S. Hugh-Jones (eds) *About the House: Lévi-Strauss and Beyond*. Cambridge: Cambridge University Press.

Bourdieu, P. (1984) *Distinction: A Social Critique of the Judgement of Taste*. London: Routledge & Kegan Paul.

Carsten, J. (1995) 'The substance of kinship and the heat of hearth: feeding, personhood, and relatedness among Malays in Pulau Langkawi'. *American Ethnologist* 22/2: 223–41.

—— (1997) *The Heat of Hearth: The Process of Kinship in a Malay Fishing Community*. Oxford: Oxford University Press.

—— and Hugh-Jones, S. (eds) (1995) *About the House: Lévi-Strauss and Beyond*. Cambridge: Cambridge University Press.

Chiang, Bien (1983) 'A new approach to the aristocratic system of the Paiwan'. *Bulletin of the Institute of Ethnology* 55: 1–48. Taipei: Institute of Ethnology, Academia Sinica.

—— (1993) 'House and Social Hierarchy of the Paiwan'. PhD thesis, University of Pennsylvania.

—— (1995) 'The spatial structure and meaning of the house of northern Paiwan'. In Huang Ying-kuei (ed.) *Space, Power and Society*. Taipei: Institute of Ethnology, Academic Sinca (in Chinese).

Comaroff, John L. and Jean Comaroff (1997) 'Mansions of the Lord'. In Jean Comaroff and John L. Comaroff, *Of Revelation and Revolution*, Chicago: University of Chicago.

Errington, S. (1989) *Meaning and Power in a Southeast Asian Realm*. Princeton: Princeton University Press.

Ferrell, R. (1982) *Paiwan Dictionary*. Pacific Linguistic Series 73. Canberra: Australian National University.

Fox, J. (ed.) (1980) *The Flow of Life*. Cambridge: Harvard University Press.

Geertz, C. (1980) *Negara: The Theater State in Nineteenth-Century Bali*. Princeton: Princeton University Press.

Gullestad, M. (1992) 'Home decoration as popular culture: constructing homes, gender and classes in Norway'. In M. Gullestad, *The Art of Social Relations: Essays on Culture, Social Action and Everyday Life in Modern Norway*, Oslo: Scandinavian University Press.

Hsu, Gong-ming (1994) *The Ritual and Culture of the Kulalau Village of Paiwan*. Taipei: Dau Shiang Press (in Chinese).

Hu, Tai-li (1998) 'New perspective of ritual and image study: the inspiration from vitalizing ritual texts among the Paiwan, Kulalau'. Paper presented in the Conference of 'New Perspectives of Fieldwork'. Taipei: Institute of Ethnology, Academia Sinica (in Chinese).

Huang, Ying-kuei (1976) 'The economic changes of Taiwanese aborigines after 1945'. *Bulletin of the Institute of Ethnology* 40: 85–95. Taipei: Institute of Ethnology, Academia Sinica (in Chinese).

Janowski, M. (1995) 'The hearth-group, the conjugal couple and the symbolism of the rice meal among the Kalabit of Sarawak'. In J. Carsten and S. Hugh-Jones (eds) *About the House: Lévi-Strauss and Beyond*. Cambridge: Cambridge University Press.

Jolly, M. and M. Macintyre (eds) (1989) *Family and Gender in the Pacific: Domestic Contradictions and the Colonial Impact*. Cambridge: Cambridge University Press.

Lévi-Strauss. C. (1983) *The Way of the Masks*. Trans. S. Modelski. London: Jonathan Cape.

—— (1984) *Paroles données*. Paris: Plon.

—— (1987) *Anthropology and Myth*. Oxford: Blackwell.

Li, Chin-yea (1994) *The Reconstruction and Interpretation of the House of the Village of Tjakaluvas, Paiwan*. MA thesis, Dung Hei University, (in Chinese).

Matsuzawa, Kazuko (1979) 'The chiefly house of the Paiwan, Taiwan: its relationship with the chieftain system'. *Social Science* 26: 1–40. Doshisha University: Institute of Humanities (in Japanese).

McKinnon, S. (1991) From a Shattered Sun: Hierarchy, Gender, and Alliance in the Tanimbar Islands. Madison: University of Wisconsin Press.

Miller, D. (1987) *Material Culture and Mass Consumption*. Oxford: Blackwell.

—— (1998) *A Theory of Shopping*. Cambridge: Polity Press.

Munn, N. (1986) *The Fame of Gawa*. Cambridge: Cambridge University Press.

Shih, Lei (1971) *Su-paiwan: Ethnographic Fieldwork Report of a Paiwan Village*. Ethnographic Fieldwork Report 21. Taipei: Institute of Ethnology Academia Sinica (in Chinese).

Tan, Chang-kwo (1992) *House, Hierarchy and the Idea of Person in the Taiban Village of Eastern Paiwan*. MA thesis. Taipei: National Taiwan University. (In Chinese).

Waterson, R. (1990) *The Living House: An Anthropology of Architecture in Southeast Asia*. Kuala Lumper: Oxford University Press.

—— (1995) 'Houses and hierarchy in island southeast Asia'. In J. Carsten and S. Hugh-Jones (eds) *About the House: Lévi-Strauss and Beyond*. Cambridge: Cambridge University Press.

Weber, M. (1968) *Economy and Society*. Trans. and ed. G. Roth and C. Wittich. New York: Bedminster Press.

Weiner, A. (1992) *Inalienable Possessions*. Berkeley: University of California Press.

9

A Man *will* get Furnished: Wood and Domesticity in Urban Romania[1]

Adam Drazin

'My opinion is, in Romania at least, because of the taste of the market, of the psychology of the population, willy nilly [mort copt], in any situation, at any effort and sacrifice, a man will get furnished [Omul se va mobila].

(Marketing officer in the furniture factory, Suceava, Romania)

This chapter is about being Romanian. Being Romanian means, among other things, being domestic, warm, caring, hospitable, open-minded and respectful of others. Being 'Romanian' in this sense, however, is a norm to work towards, a norm that may not always and in every case be achieved. The chapter investigates knowledges and practices which surround wood in urban Romania, and in particular its role in making manifest the primary qualities of domesticity and care. The above quotation illustrates how wooden furniture may be not so much a necessity as a compulsion. As previous chapters in this book have shown, the environment where people experience such compulsions, the household, should be seen not as a self-evident and 'natural' institution, but rather as a process, being continually formed through practices (Marcoux, Clarke, Miller, this volume; see also Weismantel 1989). Unlike in some other investigations in this book, most people whom I encountered in Romania would present their home first of all as existing in a world replete with difficulties, before considering its potential as a locus for self-fulfilment, and this leads to particular conclusions. Wood lends physical permanence to domesticity and caring in Romania's changing social environment, and is perhaps compulsive because, in changing times, it helps people to reinterpret their own Romanianness.[2]

Conversations about furniture in Suceava, a town in north-east Romania, reveal how domesticity, worries and caring, are bound up with one another. The domestic

1. Fieldwork for this paper was conducted with the assistance of a grant from the Research Support Scheme of the Soros Foundation.

2. Others have looked at Romanianness in the context of a longer historical perspective: see, for example, Verdery (1983). *Romanian Review* (e.g. 1995) is an accessible resource for Romanian authors on the subject.

space appears as an area carved out of a world of emotions and difficulties. Dragos, an eighteen year old, told me of his family's experience in the 1980s:

> I want to say that you asked me whether my family at that time bought furniture, because at that time you could buy that kind of thing. Okay, I want to say that we didn't buy furniture because of the fact that my father was the kind of man who, if he had the opportunity, used to try and take something from the house and sell it. . . so he wasn't a person who liked family, who liked to create something for the family, who liked to create the place, the dwelling *locuinta*, and to buy goods.

Dragos' father was alcoholic, and has since left home, while Dragos' mother died of cancer, which makes the family very different from the norm in Suceava. As head of the household, responsible for his three younger brothers and sisters and his disabled aunt, Dragos is gradually 'creating the place' through furniture. The irony is that nowadays it seems more difficult than ever to buy furniture. The socialist system gave a job and a wage to his father, in spite of his alcoholism, and furniture was purchasable, but nowadays money and jobs seem more scarce. At the time of our talk, Dragos' latest project was a rack by the door for their limitless pile of boots and shoes. He could not buy one, so he got the wood to make one when he found the time. Wood is often the standard substance for such tokens of care.

Care is at once a daily burden and a luxury. In many cases, when one person is cared for in luxury, it is another person who is carrying the care on their own shoulders. Care is shared, often unequally, and means an unequal emotional burden. I would like to use the word 'caring' as a catch-all term for a mixed bunch of different ideas and activities – some positive, some negative – which in my opinion share some characteristics, and merit being looked at as part of the same social processes. Many forms of care are talked about, while others are revealed in the material world, especially in the home. The simplest word for 'care' in Romanian is *grija*. As with its English equivalent, it has a variety of uses, but the situations in which it is used are sometimes different. The two main possible meanings to distinguish for *grija* are firstly to care for, to have responsibility for, and secondly care in the sense of worry. The expression for the former is the phrasal verb *a avea grija de* – 'to have care of' – or the verb *a ingriji* – 'to take care of' – or *ingrijire* – 'caring'. Almost anything one does can be described using this verb. If one does something in a social context, one is taking care of it. The term generalizes one's actions, making them an ongoing event. Childcare, cooking, cleaning are typical examples, yet the phrase can also be used to express a one-off responsibility.

When used in this positive sense, *grija* asserts the way that exchanges are a contribution to the household group. The aim of such care is at least twofold. On the one hand, there is the economic aim, the necessity of the survival of household members. On the other hand, there is the creation of an atmosphere of caring, that is generally in Romania a domestic atmosphere. Caring contains the seeds of its own *raison d'être* in this sense, especially in a domestic context, because caring is itself a creator of domesticity and care.

When *grija* is used not in a verbal phrase, but as a noun, it usually has a more negative, more bitter sense. It has more of the emotional connotations of caring 'about' something rather than caring 'for'. *Griji* – 'cares' – are talked about interchangeably with 'problems' (*probleme*) or 'worries' (*ingrijorari*), but are less specific. The word is one that in many ways expresses the current climate in Romania. The press makes use of phrases such as 'every Romanian with his problems' ('fiecare roman cu problemele lui'), or in the advice column of one paper 'every Romanian with his pain' ('fiecare roman cu durerea lui'). In such phrases, the course of current national history is linked with the pain of an unfulfilled caring felt in every heart.

When caring and domesticity are woven together in furniture, in Romania they form a package which establishes emotional norms. This is not necessarily the case in other contexts, although in many countries, material objects mediate norms and difference in times of change. Michael Rowlands' (1994) work in Cameroon, for example, looks at parlour furniture as a projector of ideals of success:

> The modernist fantasy in Bamenda is organised around the house and in particular around the reproduction of the extended family. The emphasis is on children, health, collective well-being, and is lived in the parlour which contains all the signs that project a desired future. (Rowlands 1994: 164)

Furniture in Cameroon acts to capture a sense of certainty about future success and reproduction of the household. At the same time, however, this success is Western and exteriorized, and the aspiration for *outside* resources involves a feeling of distinction in furniture which transcends, but is couched in, the local. By contrast, Gullestad (1984) highlights some of the contradictions of class, power and taste that furniture mediates in some working-class households in Norway:

> The ideal living room gives off an impression of luxury and comfort . . . There is more or less a continuous interest in home decoration. Young couples look at advertisements and coloured pictures in brochures from local furniture stores and discuss what they fancy themselves and what couch ensemble, cupboard and bedroom set their different friends and acquaintances have bought. . . They usually buy, if not the least expensive items, then the next cheapest items in the selection. (Gullestad 1984: 90–1)

The initial aspirational, individual quality of furniture for these people is inevitably transformed into sameness in the process of buying (although Garvey, this volume, notes the infinite capacity for exploration within this sameness). Romania, like Cameroon, is awash with the oft-frustrated drive to be a success. Yet furniture is often not portrayed as a marker of difference, but is avowedly local and bought by simple convenience. Examining the context of wood in Suceava, its consumption and the industry surrounding it, will illustrate the way wood has played a part in the materialization of domesticity and caring in Suceava.

The Anthropology of Wood

The Romanian is a very house-based person, very 'nailed down' [batut in cuie], very established, and lends a lot of importance to the home in the first place.

(Marketing officer in the furniture factory, Suceava, Romania)

Recent studies of wood in anthropological contexts have developed the idea that trees, being another form of life in the human landscape, lend themselves in many cultures to the role of symbols relating to Life and Being (Rival 1998). In many cultures, the 'social life of trees', however, includes being cut down, processed, packaged, manufactured and consumed, and this aspect of trees, not as a 'natural' form but a mass-manufactured and consumed form, has received little attention. In Suceava, the way in which wood is used to create domesticity is evident within the context of the wider landscape. In a public world of grey concrete, one is struck by the wooden fittings whenever one enters a home. The closed doors of Suceava flats epitomize Miller's (this volume) assertion that the domestic world is relatively unexplored by social scientists. Representations of Romania (just like Japanese homes – see Daniels, this volume) have often been influenced by dominant sets of ideas rather than observation. The images of factories and other institutions, such as hospitals or orphanages, which can be commonly encountered in the international media, deceptively suggest that life in the country is epitomized by the hitherto dominant public domain, rather than the warm, hidden private realm.

The way to an apartment in most Romanian towns lies across a boring and grey public landscape. The ground between the blocks is often muddy and lacks tarmac. Where there is tarmac, it has been pitted and humped into extraordinary shapes by the constant freezing and thawing of deep winter ice. In older areas, from the 1960s or 1970s, green trees may have grown, but rarely with any sense of order. A doorway presents itself as a rectangular opening in the side of a block. In better-off areas, the paint beside the doorway may have survived, and it is possible to check the block number and staircase number. Inside is an unlit and unfurnished concrete hall. There is probably a battered electrical fusebox hanging off the wall, and somewhere is the Residents Association's humiliating glass display case, listing each family's still unpaid bills for gas and water. If there is a lightbulb, this list can be used to check for family names, and verify that this is the correct doorway. To avoid this whole process, most people arrange to meet guests at the local landmark and escort them to the flat.

Entering an apartment from the dim staircase is overwhelming. The temperature may jump tens of degrees, and the grey concrete of the stair is replaced by brown or beige wood, and colourful paints. Grained wooden doors are increasingly replacing the original painted doors of the apartments. In the past, the individuality of these doors used to conflict with the communal idea of the blocks as originally built; painted doors are uniform, whereas wooden doors must be distinctive and expensive, and installing one might have been a source of debate, although for a consideration the authorities might turn a blind eye. One staircase resolved this dilemma by having all their doors painted to look like wood, with identical beige and black wood grain. In a similar vein, when neighbours agree to have their

Figure 9.1. Wooden and painted 'wood' doors

staircase redecorated, dull grey is often the colour they choose, helping each family to ensure their own private space stands in contrast to the public one.

Shedding shoes and coats on the wooden coat rack, guests are ushered into the living room (*sufrageria*), often dominated by wood. The big bookcase/display case (*biblioteca*)[3] is often the first piece of furniture a married couple buys,[4] and it dominates one wall, providing a wooden background for the living room and for the marriage – it is supposed to last their entire married life. Its shelves may be bare in the home of a young or less well-off couple, who have spent their wedding money on it, but in more established homes the shelves fill and then overfill with books, ornaments, photographs, handicrafts, painted eggs and mementoes. It has many compartments, glass-fronted display areas, drawers and cupboards, and is a store for all kinds of possessions and stashes of money.

The bookcase will often be positioned opposite the sofa, unavoidably creating from the space available a display for visitors and household members. This is especially the case for more 'modern' households, who maximize the sense of space by keeping the centre of the room clear, or use a small off-centre coffee table. In the homes of pensioners, or those following rural styles, the focal point is the room's centre: a large shiny wooden dinner table surrounded by chairs stands ready for any visitors who might pop in to sit and be offered food or drink.

In living rooms, bedrooms and halls, the floor is wooden. A parquet floor overlays the concrete of the block. The style of this parquet has changed over the years, from 1960s beechwood tiles at right angles to the walls, to herringbone patterns later on. During the sparse 1980s, new residents were promised opulent oak tiles, but often instead found themselves with imitation-wood linoleum. The wood is almost always made evident – even when a family can afford fitted carpets a wide margin will be left at the walls so the wood is visible. This visibility of wood also distinguishes the urban homes from the trend of rural farmsteads, where home-made rag rugs cover the floor completely, wall to wall, making the floor invisible. The many wooden surfaces of the urban home are therefore partially on display, partially covered. The ubiquitous mats, cloths and hangings are a little smaller than the surface they cover, and are placed cross-wise so the corners dangle and the wood is clearly seen. On the doors of the bookcase, small pieces of crochet, toys or Christmas decorations may dangle. In some homes, traditionally embroidered towels (*prosoape*), tightly bound in the middle to make a double-fan shape, frame traditional carvings or icons. The role of wood as a base surface for the apartment is thus heightened. Wood may frame embroideries, carpets and mats, and also be

---

3. The particular evolution of this piece of furniture has occurred in parallel with Soviet design. In Russia, the word for *biblioteca* is *steanca* – see Buchli (1999).

4. As an article in *Capital* magazine on the furniture industry said, furniture is 'an investment for life' – 'o investitie pentru o viata' (*Capital* January 1996).

framed by them. It is a substance that fulfils an 'embracing' role, a role that McCracken notes creates 'homeyness' in America (McCracken 1989: 171).

Standing in a living room, we may forget we are surrounded by the grey, gritty concrete skeleton of the block; we may suspend our disbelief and see wood as the essential fabric of the home, because the home displays itself as wooden. Domesticity is wooden. Yet feeling happy with wooden surfaces, and keeping them imbued with caring and domesticity, means work. Cleaning surfaces, carpets and coverings is difficult and labour intensive, especially for older tastes. The old large, central dining tables require a hard, shiny polish to look their best, as do the finely lacquered dark furniture with gold trim of the 1970s and 1980s, much of it made for the Russian market. This dark furniture shows up dirt easily and is far from childproof. Newer furniture, made using new polishing technology, and with Western European markets in mind, requires less care. It is neither dark nor light, and the wood grain is very visible.[5]

The creation of domesticity in the home in this way is not simply a matter of taste and of buying furniture as required, but a long-term aim and investment. Parents often start buying household goods for their children many years before they marry. Old furniture, washing machines, carpets and cookers can be found standing idle in the corners of apartments, waiting for one of the children to marry. As a woman who works in the marketing department of the local furniture factory comments,

> Here [la noi], I don't know, here for example parents are very – are very preoccupied even if the children are of a young age. There are people who have children of – I don't know – the fifth class [i.e. around age eleven], who are still at school, and they prepare them for the future, and eventually buy them furniture.

From a young age wooden furniture can furnish the expectation in children, not simply of marrying or getting an apartment, but of developing domesticity for its own sake for the future. Just like caring, domesticity is its own motivation and is situated in time. Looking at rural homes in France, especially their furniture, Chevalier (1999) argues it has a role in establishing continuity for the home, by acting as an inalienable reification of its past. The transition from rural homes to the Paris suburbs, urbanization and alienation, did not mean a fundamental shift in the nature of material consumption for these people. Rowlands (1994) looks at the 'modernist fantasy' in furniture, which involves incorporating an idea of the West into the home by merging local and adopted styles. In Romania, there is certainly the possibility to express modernity in the arrangement of furniture, and

---

5. Forty (1995) discusses the history of similar themes in the design of furnishings, namely the conflict between cleanliness and plushness.

yet the substance of wood itself stands in contrast to the modernity of the concrete public realm. The specifics of the history of wood in Suceava may throw some light on the archaeology of domesticity and care in Romania.

Domesticity and the Wood Industry: 'The Motor of Suceava'[6]

Many accounts of the history of domesticity in Romania might relate that an uncaring socialist state engaged itself in the destruction of domesticity (see Mihailescu 1995; Verdery 1996). Ceausescu's infamous 'house of the people' in Bucharest stands as a monument to folly, built on the ruins of Romanian homes and lives. Such a state might lose any claim to legitimately call itself Romanian. Historical accounts of furnishings in socialist countries testify to their destructive power (e.g. Buchli 1997; Groys 1988). Yet retrospectively, a more positive interpretation of power can emerge, through which Romanianness, domesticity and caring have always been fostered in Romanian homes (see Buchli 1999). The history of wood and furniture in Suceava has always been bound up with a self-legitimizing state, but the ideas of power that it contains may be read either as a negative force from above or a positive force that 'comes from below' (Foucault 1998: 94), always recreating Romanianness domestically.

The great forests of Suceava county have long been established as a valuable Romanian patrimony, and a resource to be exploited. A quarter of Romania's surface is forest, and half of Suceava county. In previous centuries, the Princes of Moldavia, who for a time located their Royal Court at Suceava, granted the Orthodox Church the right to administer these forests for its benefit. Yet everyone used wood, notably to build their houses – wood is usually still the material of preference. Communism arrived, and the forests and their administration were appropriated by the state.[7] In the early communist years, this profitable forestry industry was engaged in paying war reparations to Russia. To the indignation and shame of many Romanians, a railway line on the Russian gauge was established, devoted to the full-time transportation of timber and furniture into the Soviet Union.

It was the frighteningly organized early communist government that set about transforming Suceava into a town which would be the local centre of the wood industry and one of the main population centres in north-east Romania. The transformation of Suceava town on socialist principles changed in nature over the decades, but always proceeded relentlessly, ideologically and physically. As physical fact and as emblem, the wood industry thereby helped to shape the landscape, the house and the home in Suceava. The *casa de cultura*, built as an ideological centre for party rallies, is of concrete shaped to look like traditional

---

6. The local paper's description of Suceava's wood industry (*Monitorul* 6 February 1998).
7. The administration was modelled on the French system – Giurgia (1995) gives details.

Figure 9.2. Wood factories dominate Suceava's industrial zone

local wood carving. Propagandistic tourist guides of the 1960s eulogized the two key industrial conglomerates in the centre as 'the industrial heart of Suceava with powerful beats' (Sidorovici 1964), and compared them to giant metallic birds (Zidarita 1967). The plan for the town located the Wood Processing Conglomerate and the Paper and Cellulose Conglomerate as the centre of Suceava; the old town and the villages of Itcan and Burdujeni were meanwhile designated to become suburbs of this supposedly productive centre. Houses were to be demolished and concrete blocks of flats built to house the multitudes of workers required by the wood factories. By 1989, the population of Suceava town was nearly 120,000, compared with 17,000 at the beginning of the century.

The building of blocks was one of the main means for the transformation of Suceava into a model socialist society. Whereas in the Soviet Union the state attacked both house and household, through communal kitchens and shared spaces (Boym 1994), the Romanian state preserved the idea of individual households. Yet the attack on the house, as a real thing and as a concept, became emblematic of persecution. Homes and property were forcibly taken and levelled for building, in preference to new land. Young in-migrant couples might appreciate their new flats with central heating and piped water, but at the expense of others' sorrow at the total annihilation of their established homes.

Wood is not the only mainstay of the Suceavan economy, which has diversified – especially since the 1970s. Nonetheless, its exploitation has been central in the building of a problematized urban landscape. Modernistic concrete dwellings lined with wood swept away traditional dwellings built using wood. Within the space of a generation there was a marked, forced shift in the way wood was consumed to create domesticity, and in the way a domestic space founded on wood was located within the urban environment.

While the state was the vehicle of alienation, it simultaneously provided the means of establishing a sense of domesticity through consumption. For its very legitimacy as Romanian, the state had to provide wooden furniture (see Verdery 1996), but there were other arms of the state in Suceava. Apart from the factories, other bureaucracies grew: banks, a power station, water and other utilities. In the areas designed for workers' homes, shops, distribution and other facilities were built. All of these state institutions, developing unevenly and imperfectly but with some modicum of agreement and communication between them, meant that the consumption of wood products was experienced at this time as a more unified process.

Furniture is expensive. Before 1989 it would often be bought on credit. The loan of money might come from one's employer, it might be from the co-operative bank (the CEC – the only savings bank), or it might be from the furniture firm; the CEC, knowing that a person worked at a certain enterprise, would provide a certificate of guarantee to be presented at the furniture shop. Furniture would then be paid for by instalments deducted directly from one's monthly salary, requiring no further effort. Even though salaries might be small, because employment was compulsory this system placed the purchase of furniture within the reach of many families, even those without large savings. This system existed intact from the 1960s right up to 1990, and became a part of the normal life expectation of people in Suceava. Of course, the system was open to manipulation, and was pervaded by friends and contacts, but the unofficial worked within the official channels. Having a place of employment, getting married, obtaining an apartment, and the progressive gaining of furniture and other goods all became a part of the same, achievable process.

A woman comments, with the benefit of hindsight, on how her experience of buying furniture was relatively easy under the communist government:

> It wasn't difficult at all before to buy. That is – that is the reality. It was much easier than now, for us at least, for ordinary people [oameni de rind]. Because they were paid, they had jobs, it was certain, that. . . The majority of things in the house, I bought them in instalments, in instalments. I paid in instalments monthly. I had a secure job, they knew I could, for ages [*un an de zile* – literally 'a year of days', pay instalments, to the state. And I bought things which I needed, necessities.

Thus in the midst of a problematic public realm, and in spite of an economy that is famous for lack of attention to consumers, there was at least some means to try to create a sense of domesticity in apartments and houses (cf. Miller 1988).

What happened in the late 1990s to eat away and threaten to destroy the Suceava wood and furniture industry? Although some workshops and timber yards seem to be thriving, people are very pessimistic, especially when it comes to jobs and the central Wood and Paper Conglomerate. A legion of economic problems are cited, too numerous and complex to explore in detail here, but including such examples as overmanning; rising energy costs; high running costs because the state factories are so huge; sudden rises in the cost of raw materials, especially wood; illegal wood export; liberalization of wood export in 1997–8 so more went abroad; corruption in forestry; corruption in management; basic apathy; the dramatic falling away of factory export orders in 1997 as the weighing scales of market forces suddenly swung from competitive to uncompetitive; competition from new factories in countries closer to Western Europe; the distance and cost of transport to Western Europe; a decline in the Romanian and Suceavan market since few homes have been built since the 1980s and people have less money; a decline in the German market in its post-reunification malaise; a decline in the Russian market since the break-up of the Soviet Union; overdependence on sales abroad and in Suceava, half of its domestic sales being in the town; poor marketing, a function that used to be conducted on a massive national scale by the Government; or the simple lack of a brand.

We should note two main themes that arise. One is the pervasive sense of corruption, described by the local paper as a 'wood mafia'. Wood is felled and exported illegally by many people, from their own small plots or the state's vast forests. Secondly, there is the threat to household incomes and employment. The local newspaper reported in 1998 that 37 per cent of the county's industrial income came from wood, and that 40 per cent of industrial employees worked with wood (*Monitorul de Suceavu*, 6 February 1998). At that time, the liberalization of the wood industry was seen as potentially delivering the *coup de grâce* to the furniture factories. The union of wood workers (the UJSL) staged demonstrations in Suceava – 2,000 people on 28 February 1998 – and the local union leader lamented 'the transformation of our country into a colony' of Europe.

Figure 9.3. New furniture in a private firm's showroom

The issues of corruption and economic failure are inextricably interconnected, and become important to the household because they threaten the household morally and economically. Someone expecting a relative to lose his or her job at any moment comments on this:

> The owner of the factory, who has bought them the majority pack of shares. . . He takes all the machines that used to be in the factory, and belong to the state, so to say, you know, and sells them to other little factories – which by pure fortune are led by people who are in the higher hierarchy of the factory, you know, bosses, second manager or something like this you know. And they suppose that even the union leader is having one factory. I mean which, they only take one machine away, which produces bags or paper bags, you know, and they put it in another place, and have another company, and they just only follow their interests, not the interests of the people. So this is what really happens.

Judged in terms of its caring role, and fostering of a capacity to create domesticity, the post-communist public sphere may seen to be just like its predecessor. Many people have been able to buy their own homes, it is true, but ownership does not equate with the capacity to create an environment of domesticity and care. In simple terms, the adage is cited that 'we used to have money, but the shelves were empty. Now the shelves are full, but we have no money.' Prices have risen radically, while the threat of losing one's job has become much more real. The combination of inflation and lack of economic stability has meant that the system of credit and of buying in instalments has virtually collapsed during the 1990s, with some false starts at local and national level. In 1997, the main furniture factory resurrected the system of credits with Bank Co-op, but the scheme was short lived, and it resorted to a potentially very selective credit scheme of its own, as an official at the factory comments:

> People right now don't have any money to allow them to pay, not at all. At least through Bank Co-op they were – it was that the installments were very large. So, the interest rates were very high, and they came to almost double the price of the product. If you buy from [our] system, so we make an offer that you can do that, with the approval of a director here, but only when the person in question has a secure job, works with a firm, let's say at the police, at, I don't know, the financial control office [garda financiara], at a stronger firm – so as to receive, so to have assurance that they will pay instalments without interruption. And that's something not everyone can do.

A credit scheme that was once intended to offer opportunity to all has thus become a mechanism of privilege. This official does not even seem sure about who can apply – that is for directors to decide. If this quote is read in association with the quotation above, it is easy to see how from 'the outside', the situation feeds accusations of corruption. And yet given its situation, it is hard to see what the factory can do except acknowledge that nowadays, unlike in the past, some customers can pay their instalments and some cannot.

With the decline of buying in instalments, the only way for many people to buy furniture is to pay in cash on the spot. Money can be mobilized through family, by borrowing or by getting married (although even getting married no longer guarantees getting a place to live, because flats are not being built). Parents still have an active role in obtaining furniture, with or without the assistance of state and banks. Their significance in taking care of furniture and domesticity, it could be argued, has been heightened by the collapse of the state system, and at the same time rendered more difficult. The paradox of the challenge to achieving a norm of domesticity is that perhaps the norm can no longer be seen as normal, but a privilege.

By contrast with the woman quoted above, who bought furniture during the 1980s, a woman who married in 1994 faced a more uphill struggle. Although from a relatively well-off family, high inflation made prices unpredictable. In buying two bookcase pieces, she made the most of factory rejects, of pieces that still bore the old price, and of a low-inflation 'window' in 1996:

Figure 9.4. The main furniture shop

For example, last Summer I bought that with three hundred and something thousand, and exactly – and it was the last, but it had a defect, you know, and we repaired it; but, exactly the same immediately after, at several hundred, maybe a million? – at seven hundred and something thousand, so double, we found one someplace. So, the price had stayed the same from some while back, you see. . . And the corner piece was last year, a million two hundred thousand, now it's two million, that too. And we paid in instalments, you know. It was when the instalments, when the interest rate was low. . . last year, yes. Three months when the interest rate fell to something very small, something per cent, the interest rate from the banks, and their interest rate fell too, so we made three instalments at one time to shorten the time, you see.

Obtaining furniture is often reported in very unspecific terms. There is no need to specify where, because there is a single shop. The shop is referred to not by name – it has always been just the furniture shop – but by the name of the area, Georg Enescu. Of course, in some households taste is important – the colour, the size, the polish. Yet taste is often played down, and people even deny their interest in such aspects. The most common portrayal of obtaining furniture is: it was in the shop, at the right price, and they bought it. Cristi, a newly married man in his twenties, comments on what they looked for when buying their bookcase:

It's not a mentality of that, of – of freedom. Here what matters in the first place is quality, you know. . . Because you can't just get a piece of furniture for a really short period, because it's very expensive. A salary, so, like my salary is, as an engineer, doesn't allow me even to buy a table, you understand? A big table for example for two-plus people, only the table, without chairs. So I'd need three months' salary to buy it, you understand? And so you look for something, even if it's expensive, you look for something of good quality, you understand? So it doesn't matter, the colour, or the 'modernism'.

Cristi's furniture is capable of evoking themes for him, themes of liberty and employment alongside material properties of quality, colour and style. His apparently blasé denial of taste might seem strange given the overwhelming importance of wooden furniture to the home, and of the home to Cristi. Faced with a foreign researcher, he feels the need to put several issues straight: post-communist Romania is not a realm of upwardly mobile style-seeking consumers, although people have now bought their own homes (cf. Dolan 1999), although having capital is legitimate, and although many shop shelves are full. Wherever one turns, institutions and elites appear as obstacles. It appears as though an elite minority have stable jobs themselves, have control over the employment of others, and are able to furnish their homes, having money and access to credit schemes. In addition, furniture is made with foreign, not domestic tastes in mind. This is the negative side to the meaningfulness of furniture. On the positive side, buying furniture evokes a sense of security, and achieving some form of stability for the future.

The older generation in many cases goes to amazing lengths to shoulder the burden of assisting their children with their home and furnishings. When Cristi refutes that buying furniture involves 'liberty', he is partly asserting how Romanian domesticity values the household group above individual liberty. The household persists across generations, and in a 'traditional' context, we might compare this household group directly with the house-based society which Tan (this volume) discusses. By contrast with Tan, however, the Suceava household is the vehicle of relationships with both, on the one hand, community and the older generation and on the other, perhaps more importantly, with public organizations. The normative properties of furniture should thus be seen in historical context. They are neither the simple result of a traditional 'signification' of wood in Romanian 'house' culture, nor of the communist/post-communist context. The history of furniture feeds into an ongoing construction of home, in interaction with the diverse experiences of the people in those households (see also Attfield 1989).

Having been built up over history, the experience of wood is not uniform, but polysemic and contrasting. Buchli (1999) points out how furniture can materialize, incorporate and partially reconcile the accretion of contrasting meanings over time. I have considered in my historical overview in particular the material world of the home and the material landscape which surrounds it. Upon this contrast we can examine a set of binary oppositions, not as a deterministic schema, but as a set of issues explored in wood:

Romanianness	
Private	*Public*
Home	*Landscape*
Grija *as caring*	Griji *as cares*
Wood consumption	*Wood industry*
Romanian normativity	*Negotiable values*
Downplaying of taste/choice	*Imposition of foreign tastes*

What this set of dualistic perceptions suggests is a development of domesticity against the background of a public realm that is both Romanian and international. There are polyphonic, and often discordant, ideals that relate to the household, but in general the household is elevated emotionally and in terms of its certainty, compared with other institutions such as 'state' and 'market'. This posits a way of organizing similarity and difference that is not so much based on Romanian as against foreign, or past and future, but on domestic and what is not domestic. It is important to emphasize the emotional contrast of this distinction, and the domestic location of care in Suceava.

Some Suceava Homes: Creating a Norm of Domesticity

This paper has so far tried to illustrate, firstly, how wood, domesticity and caring are bound up with one another in Suceava and, secondly, how even a brief look at the historical background of economics and power surrounding wood challenges and problematizes this set of associations. Several examples of households in Suceava illustrate how these themes are bound up together and embedded in material form in the home. The experience of obtaining, fitting and using wooden furniture coalesces into one and the same experience of domestic care. Wood provides an emotional as well as economic resource, helping to bridge the different senses of care, and determinedly carving caring out of an uncaring world.

Coping with Cares

The Pavel family comprises three people. Mr Pavel works at a construction firm, and Mrs Pavel as an attendant at the Cellulose and Paper Conglomerate. They live in a small two-room apartment, which, as their son Dan reminds me, is *nedecomandate*. In other words, there is no hall or passage – getting to the back room means walking through the living room. This kind of apartment can also be referred to as 'reduced comfort' (*confort redus*). Mr and Mrs Pavel sleep in the living room, Dan in the other room. Entering the apartment gives an immediate impression of a carefully adorned home. From the ceiling above the doorways in the small entryway hang short red drapes. Embroidered cloths are draped over the mirror and on the coat rack. I am reminded by Dan that I must not forget to take my shoes off, since his mother is very particular about the living room.

The living room is also carefully arranged. A large table stands near to the centre of the room, surrounded by chairs and surmounted by a crochet table cloth and vase of flowers. The mid-section of the table is a very pale colour compared with the two ends, and the story of this section of the table illustrates the way a table such as this plays a central function to households and household formation, through hospitality.

> It's a custom to have a table in the living room, you know, to have guests on a Sunday or Saturday, or when it's your birthday, you have them put at the table, lay the table, and serve all kinds of stuff and so on – so they bought a table. The story, it is fine because – you know why? – this table was borrowed, some people some years ago, like twenty, or fifteen years ago, I don't know. It was for a wedding, yes, they lent the table, they borrowed the table, in order to have something at the wedding, but when they

Figure 9.5. Wood gives the home its character

returned the table, they'd given – when they got it back it was a 'mixed table' because it had pieces from another table, so this table is still a mixture of two tables.

This multicoloured table, in the centre of the room, emphasizes the room's potential for hospitality, as do the surrounding pieces of furniture displaying ornaments. The *biblioteca* and wardrobe also used to be a light colour, as the table, but two years ago they sold their original set because it was starting to look dated, and they updated the place with a new set of darker furniture. The original set, twenty years ago, was bought in instalments – according to Mrs Pavel, most things in the home were bought in instalments. The newer set was bought for cash, partly raised by selling the old set to an acquaintance in the country. The furniture acts as a display area for a number of items, gifts and souvenirs. At the centre of the biblioteca is a clock standing on a small crocheted mat (*mileu*) made by Mrs Pavel. This is 'the first clock my husband bought when we were married', she says.

Since 1989, the family has bought things in cash, rather than instalments. This makes good sense in many ways, because inflation is unpredictable and consumer durables are a good way to invest money so that it keeps at least some of its value. The way they bought the television illustrates this, and Mrs Pavel told the story with a somewhat bitter humour:

> The money for the television is our life savings, which I put in the savings bank certificates [CEC] for five thousand, which used to have some value then. . . They had the revolution, money lost its value, and – 'how much do I have? what shall I get? Hey, let's get a TV, invest something.' Hey, my husband got really angry then. For me to hand over his life savings – and a good thing I got it, because now we could buy absolutely nothing with that kind of money, with sixty thousand, we couldn't get anything, absolutely, what, a TV which is two million and something now.

The TV is on a wooden stand in the corner, on a crocheted tablecloth that Mrs Pavel made when she was pregnant with Dan, and they bought it on Christmas Day 1992. Everyone wanted a colour TV at that time, although there was only one channel to watch. There were no colour TVs at the old state shop in the centre (since replaced by a private shop with pretensions to taste), but someone in the shop said they had heard of some colour TVs in another area. So they went there, and there was one in the window but none for sale. They put their name down on a waiting list, and on Christmas Day morning got a call saying the televisions had just come in. Who knows why someone was working there on the 25 December, but they were. They liked the TV and brought it home, wrapped up in a blanket on a sledge.

Mrs Pavel is increasingly worried about her job because prospects are bad at her factory, although there have been no serious redundancies so far. In the summer of 1997, the news has been focusing on which enterprises in the country are going to be closed, spurred on by the requirements of the IMF's infamous representative Paul Thomson, and there is no back-up plan for employees in these cases. Closures are not accompanied by investment in other areas, either by the government or from abroad, and she has no confidence in the management.

The Pavels have careful preferences, especially governed by Mrs Pavel. The way in which their taste has developed and modernized, however, depends heavily on having the right furniture to form the basis for the home. The many individual items visible against this background are there more for personal reasons than because of any reference to 'taste'. However, at the same time modernizing their taste meant updating, not searching around: like everyone else, they went to the single well-known furniture shop in Suceava. The most important aspect of the furniture is the way it assists in creating a caring domestic environment, so as to be caring inside when faced with cares from outside. The stresses of loss of earnings, of life savings and potentially of employment altogether are compounded by incidents that might otherwise seem minor. Arguments with neighbours over noise levels blow up inexplicably into threatening to take court action. Dan splits up with his girlfriend. Mrs Pavel becomes concerned about the various evils (*rei*) which had afflicted the house – turning to religion to avert the problems, she hangs an icon and sprig of basil (*busuioc*) above the door of the back room. Her care of the household and sense of responsibility extends not only to its furnishings, its hospitality, but also to its feeling of well-being. In many ways, the Pavels offer us a normative perspective on households in Suceava. Norms, however, often exist in the way they differ from the actual situation. Looking at a couple of other households provides some comparison on how their own norms, practices and material environments are formed.

Leaves Burned into Wood

The Olars are a family who illustrate how wood and furniture creates and recreates domesticity in a situation of divorce. They live in a top-floor flat with a fine view over Suceava, which catches the sun through a large window in one corner of the living room. As I sat on the sofa in this room visiting at Christmas time, I noticed that the large bookcase opposite me had the dark shapes of leaves burned by the sun into the wood in a couple of places. Asking about these shapes in the furniture evoked the divorce and their domesticity.

Mrs and Mr Olar were married in 1970. Like many couples, they came from villages to go to high school and for work and met and married in the town. They got local jobs in the textile factories and they settled in a three-room apartment nearby, obtained through the factory. They bought locally made furniture in instalments. It was contemporary, dark and highly polished, made of laminated chipboard covered with stained oak panels. The *biblioteca* was placed against the one free wall in the living room. Each of the other three walls contained either a door or a window. Opposite the *biblioteca* stood the sofa-bed (*pat*) and a small table at its head. They had two children, Ionel and Claudia, who used to spend long holidays with relatives in the country: Mr Olar's father was a forester, and left the children with memories of fishing, and collecting wild strawberries and mushrooms in the forest.

In the early 1990s, when the two children were at university, problems within the marriage resulted in a divorce, perhaps related to the post-1989 climate, perhaps not. The process of divorce was sticky, took several years, and had a major impact on everyone in the family. Not only did Mr Olar move out, meaning that the family only had one salary, but there were also problems at the factories, and a string of redundancies, threatening both their jobs. Divorce also reflects badly on a family in Romania morally, and the Olars lost friends; a couple of friends of Ionel's were discouraged by their families from seeing him, now that his parents were no longer together.

Ionel suspended his university studies and began to trade in Suceava's bazaar in order to help support the three of them, buying and selling any goods he could possibly obtain through contacts in Hungary and Istanbul. It was an exciting time for him, as it was for many people in the bazaar, where much of the business consists in seeking out loopholes in the laws and ways to import goods without paying duty. At one time, he was detained by the police, probably due to rival stallholders, and he lost most of the stock of leather jackets he had at the time. Mrs Olar felt at the time that it was a house full of troubles and misfortune (*necazuri*).

At around this time, Mrs Olar made several changes to the home's layout, which I envisage as emotionally therapeutic in the same fashion as Garvey (this volume) investigates in Norway. The family dismantled a large table, which formed the centrepiece of the room, and moved out six chairs. They moved a small coffee table away from the wall. The result was a lighter (*mai luminos*) room, and a more 'modern' one. The bookcase was moved across the room, away from the window. It had been standing in the well-lit corner for twenty years, and from the keys to its three cupboards had hung small traditional crocheted vine leaves made by Mrs Olar in the country when she was young. The shape of the small vine leaves was preserved as a dark shape in the wood of the bookcase, although now it stood in a dark and shaded corner. In addition, a priest was asked to bless the house. He conducted a service, and blessed every room. On the wooden lintel above each door, he traced a cross using incense (*mir*). The crosses are still visible when seen from the right angle, shining in the light even now. Mrs Olar also keeps a small icon in every room: on display in the kitchen and bedrooms, but unseen in the living room, tucked away on top of the bookcase. In many ways, therefore, the innocuous layout of the home contains a host of reminders of the hidden scars borne by the family, and the way the effort to create a caring home is unending.

The family's domestic situation has eventually improved, helped among other things by their grandfather, the forester. He sends economic help in the form of money, vegetables and other produce. Country relatives also provide moral help, being living examples of how to be domestic – truly Romanian, warm, and hospitable. Since the Olars switched the room around, they have to carry the big table up from the cellar for guests; yet if I were to go to their country relatives, I would see how things are really done. A Romanian, Mrs Olar says, has to keep the whole house entirely clean. If the rest of the house is not clean, you usher guests into the living room and shut the door while you smarten the place up.

Figure 9.6. Shadow of a crochet leaf on a cupboard

The Olar household illustrates the way in which the furniture of the home is not only an item transacted when a couple marries, but a way of constituting a home through its life. It is by no means a simple matter to keep a household together, especially when times change and peoples' situations feel more vulnerable. When difficulties arose, the Olars' wooden furniture and fittings became the focus for reinvigorating the home, and family contacts with forestry provided support. Good and bad memories can be woven around wood, even in the urban situation of a concrete block of flats.

Building for the Future

The Colac family has found itself more able than most to cope with the difficulties of setting up and maintaining a household. Everyone has friends who help them, but while other couples seem to have had help in getting old or damaged furniture, the Colacs seem to have been able to get everything new. Their home is furnished with great care using an assortment of modern wooden furniture and fittings, which one senses celebrate their ability to achieve and maybe transcend the expected norm.

Ruxandra and Petru married as students in the 1980s, and have a daughter. At first they lived in a bedsit, but in 1991 were lucky in finding a large apartment in a newly built block near to the town centre. A combination of new legislation on the purchase of apartments for private property, high inflation, and non-obstructive officials meant they paid very little for the four-room flat – 400,000 lei at a time when most apartments already cost over a million. They also got perhaps a third of their furniture on credit, including of course the big main bookcase, and paid off the instalments over the following year or two.

The setting up of the Colacs' household coincided with the acceleration of social change post-1989. Petru briefly tried to become one of the entrepreneurs making a fortune in Poland. For several days, he stood among the crowds at the station, surrounded by bags of salami, cognac and tinned food, trying in vain to board one of the crammed carriages and cattle trucks to Warsaw. Eventually, having drunk the cognac and eaten the food, he gave up and went home. Over the years, though, his aspirations to become a success bore more fruit, and he got a good managerial job in a large local company. Ruxandra meanwhile works as a secretary.

Ruxandra made very considered calculations when devising their home. The sofa, carpet and walls in the living room all match, which took a great deal of searching. When the workmen were mixing the plaster (*var*) for the walls, the shade of blue was too bright ('ghastly'), and Ruxandra mixed the plaster herself. The carpet, unusually, is fitted carpet, also of the matching shade. It is not fitted wall-to-wall, but leaves a couple of feet of wooden floor visible at the edges. She says it would have been too expensive to get a complete wall-to-wall carpet, and they saved a lot of money in that uncovered (and generally unused) area of floor. She does have some regrets about this room – buying ready-made furniture, for example, means it never quite fits the room exactly. What she would really like to do is to get furniture specially made, as in the kitchen: the kitchen is a modern, fitted kitchen, the cupboards made in a nearby factory. When a ventilator and grill was placed above the cooker – a kind of fitting not commonly manufactured in Romania – Petru made a special visit to the factory for her. He knows some of the managers, and had the piece made specially.

There is a sense of taste and style about the Colacs' home which marks it out; it is notable that it has been put together with a whole schema in mind. Ruxandra's taste is partly responsible – her sister describes her as sophisticated (*finuta*) compared with other members of the family. She also has sources of inspiration, such as the dog-eared 1980s Neckermans catalogue that a friend brought from Germany ten years before. Any frustrations that they encountered in furnishing the home – financially or in finding furniture – seem not to have been insurmountable. Ruxandra is exclusively and undeniably in charge of furnishings and fittings such as this, but Petru will go to great lengths to fulfil her vision of what she wants. Yet it appears that the creation of this caring domestic environment in families such as the Colacs' may be built upon the very kind of activities outside the home that are open to the accusations of being uncaring. There are many managers in Suceava, people with positions of responsibility in factories and shops and the civil service and schools and in every institution; and like everybody, their salaries do not match their status. In other words, there is money and influence in the town. Obtaining furniture can mean exercising this money and influence, such that creating domesticity becomes exclusive, and can involve making moral compromises.

Conclusions: The Emotional Landscape

This chapter began with the compulsion to buy furniture, suggesting that wood and furniture relate to being Romanian. Romanianness is a norm that incorporates domesticity and care. I could have investigated this household 'norm' as a traditional phenomenon. As people have uprooted and moved to the town, the wooden surfaces of the home might be seen to anchor identity in time and in space, in harmony with traditional Romanian culture. To show this, I might have explored the many traditional meanings of wood in festivals, weddings and funerals (cf. Vulcanescu 1972) – not least the placing of a branch atop any newly built house for its success. Tan (this volume) investigates the traditional aspects of household, and how material objects play a part in its changing nature, more successfully. But I have considered industrially mass-processed wood, which has had a distinctive historical part to play in Suceava. While Tan considers the Paiwanese house, both traditionally and more recently in Christian families, as a dominant and largely unchallenged social institution, in Romania in recent history many traditional houses were actively destroyed by the state. Only recently, and in certain circumstances, is it re-emerging as dominant, rather than resistant.

Wood in Suceava is therefore a powerful substance, which can be interpreted in at least two ways, depending on how we view power in Romania. The reason it is rendered powerful is that Romanianness is not an unchallenged concept. To be Romanian in Romania should mean, almost by definition, to be legitimate – but where do we find the springs of legitimacy[8] in contemporary Romania, living after communism? After looking at power and the negotiation of legitimacy, we can proceed to looking at how it relates to Romanianness, domesticity and caring.

One interpretation of the power in Romanian furniture runs like this. The Romanian state has always made use of wood and furniture in the way it rules, partly because, as a resource, wood was important in establishing its legitimacy

---

8. I employ the term legitimacy to capture the sense of a local ideal which is the aim of much social action. As an anthropologist, I consider that legitimacy is rarely unchallenged, and therefore difficult to actually achieve, in any culture or society.

and its claim to Romanianness. It appealed to the principles of domesticity and caring, building dwellings and supposedly caring for the populace. And yet at the same time, the state destroyed domesticity. It flattened houses and nourished seemingly uncaring bureaucracies. One of the many paradoxes was that the Romanian state appeared to be un-Romanian. When, during the 1990s, the state gradually changed, its legitimacy was still an issue, because in many ways its Romanianness was judged by the standards of the previous regime. The legitimizing lynchpins established during socialism have withered. Although people are allowed to buy and own their own homes, unlike under socialism, it is difficult to furnish that home. The goalposts have moved. The post-socialist state, elected though it is, lacks legitimacy and appears non-Romanian inasmuch as it fails to help many Romanians create domesticity and caring through wood.

A second interpretation of the power in Romanian furniture sees power as not oppressive and negative, but a positive force that 'comes from below' (Foucault 1998: 94). People may say that their work to create domesticity and care is a fight. Their liberty (an idea that Romanians famously celebrated in the early 1990s and to some extent since) seems endlessly to be confounded by local, national and international elites. Yet in this, people are laying claim to true Romanianness. In their own hands lies the recreation of what it means to be Romanian; and there can be no doubt that domesticity and care are thriving in homes in Suceava, in the face of problems. Even in the face of rising unemployment, rising divorce rates,[9] rising alcoholism, and at the expense of moral compromise, at any effort and sacrifice, a household will get furnished. A simple bookcase, however it is acquired, standing solid and silent, testifies to legitimacy, domesticity, care and warmth in a household, in spite of expressions of oppressiveness. At the same time, wood focuses these issues at the domestic level rather than the individual one, and can be seen to exacerbate issues of personal liberty. The Romanian idea of domesticity asserts the household group; this is by contrast with, for example, the US. DeVault (1991: 85) makes the point that the household group in America is created out of care for individuals, not the group in common.

It is in this context that the general assertion of a 'norm', and downplaying of individual 'taste' can be seen. The norm can be seen, paradoxically, as both liberating and oppressive. Georg Simmel was one of the first social commentators to observe how the issue of fashion, either its assertion or its denial, 'signalizes the lack of personal freedom' by highlighting social expectations, and is consequently especially marked in groups or classes experiencing a clash of subjugation and liberation (Simmel 1957: 541). Commenting cynically on the superficiality of fashion, he adds 'man requires an ephemeral tyrant the moment he has rid himself of the absolute and permanent one' (ibid.: 556). Many other writers have built on

---

9. As shown by county statistics – see Directia Judeteana de Statistica Suceava (1997).

Simmel's themes, which resurface in writings about post-socialist countries. Post-socialist taste is often portrayed as superficial, experimental to the point of ineptitude, and plagued by corruption and by frustration (see Sampson 1994; Humphrey 1995). In Suceava, we can detect the issue of a 'lack of personal freedom' in the very terms that are important: Romanianness, domesticity and care. And yet we should be careful to contextualize and not trivialize the issues.

Caring practices not only assert domesticity, but act to embody the issues surrounding liberty. Caring comprises both emotion and action, and it is this unity that makes it relevant to both one person's experience and to historical change. It is not possible to sit back as a spectator while events go by and at the same time claim to be caring. Caring is participatory, and this renders the material qualities of a substance such as wood important. In what sense does a person, or a family, experience caring, freedom or subjugation? Is it possible to feel it on your skin or inside you, in the same way as it is possible to feel the grain of a table or a bookcase under your fingers? Garvey (this volume) presents a strong case for self-exploration through ordinary physical acts of moving furniture around. It is important to note the role of wood as a physical embodiment of caring emotions (see also Rosaldo 1984; Lutz and White 1986). Emotions may not simply be considered as a phenomenon internal to the person, but by their very nature participatory. Emotions of caring should neither be seen as arising inside and imposed on the outside world, nor as external and outside of the person's control, but arising in the sensitivity of interaction. There are many moments of emotional self-introspection using furniture, such as in the Olar household; but by comparison with Garvey, I would indicate how the unknown and the problematic can be represented as external to the home, not only interiorized in the person. The historical role of the state in Romania, by contrast with Norway, is significant in this.

The landscape of which wood is a part in Suceava, especially domestically, can thus be seen as an emotional landscape in many ways, in which cares and caring are embodied. I refer not to an overarching format imposed on the post-socialist landscape, as others have discussed, especially in a spiritual context (Humphrey 1993; Anderson 1998; Bridger and Pine 1998). Rather, I wish to highlight the way in which people participate in their environment through wood and imbue their environment with emotionality. It needs to be emphasized how people in Suceava are active but not completely free in this. People are active emotional agents but, to paraphrase Marx, 'not under conditions of their own choosing'.

References

Anderson, D. (1998) 'Living in a subterranean landscape: identity politics in post-Soviet Khakassia'. In S. Bridger and F. Pine (eds) *Surviving Post-Socialism: Local Strategies and Regional Repression in Eastern Europe and the Former Soviet Union*. London: Routledge.

Attfield, J. (1989) 'Inside Pram Town: a case study of Harlow house interiors, 1951–61'. In J. Attfield and P. Kirkham (eds) *A View from the Interior: Women and Design*. London: The Women's Press.

Boym, S. (1994) *Common Places: Mythologies of Everyday Life in Russia*. London: Harvard University Press.

Bridger, S. and F. Pine (eds) (1998) *Surviving Post-Socialism: Local Strategies and Regional Repression in Eastern Europe and the Former Soviet-Union*. London: Routledge.

Buchli, V. (1997) 'Khrushchev, modernism, and the fight against petit-bourgeois consciousness in the soviet home'. *Journal of Design History* 10/2: 161–7.

—— (1999) *An Archaeology of Socialism*. Oxford: Berg.

Chevalier, S. (1999) 'The French two-home project: materialization of family identity'. In I. Cieraad (ed.) *At Home: An Anthropology of Domestic Space*. Syracuse: Syracuse University Press.

DeVault, M. (1991) *Feeding the Family: The Social Organisation of Caring as Gendered Work*. Chicago: University of Chicago Press.

Directia Judeteana de Statistica Suceava (1997) *Judetul Suceava in Cifre (1990–1996)*. Suceava: Directia Judeteana de Statistica Suceava.

Dolan, J. (1999) '"I have always fancied to have me own lion": ideological motivations in external house decoration by recent home owners'. In I. Cieraad (ed.) *At Home: An Anthropology of Domestic Space*. New York: Syracuse University Press.

Forty, A. (1995) *Objects of Desire*. London: Thames & Hudson.

Foucault, M. (1998 [1978]) *The Will to Knowledge*. Harmondsworth: Penguin.

Giurgia, V. (ed.) (1995) *Protejarea si Desvoltarea Durabila a Padurilor Romaniei*. Bucharest: Arta Grafica.

Groys, B. (1988) *The Total Art of Stalinism: Avant-Garde, Aesthetic Dictatorship and Beyond*. Princeton: Princeton University Press.

Gullestad, M. (1984) *Kitchen Table Society: A Case Study of the Family Life and Friendships of Young Working-Class Mothers in Urban Norway*. Oslo: University of Scandinavia Press.

Humphrey, C. (1993) 'Avgai Khad: theft and social trust in post-communist Mongolia'. In *Anthropology Today* 9/6: 13–16.

—— (1995) 'Creating a culture of disillusionment'. In D. Miller (ed.) *Worlds Apart: Modernity Through the Prism of the Local*. London: Routledge.

Lutz, C. and G. White (1986) 'The anthropology of emotions'. *Annual Review of Anthropology* 15: 405–36.

McCracken, G. (1989) '"Homeyness": a cultural account of one constellation of consumer goods and meanings'. In E. Hirschman (ed.) *Interpretive Consumer Research*. Provo, UT: Association for Consumer Research.

Mihailescu, V. (1995) 'Le Bloc 311'. *Ethnologie Française* 25/3: 484–95.

Miller, D. (1988) 'Appropriating the State on the council estate'. *Man* 23/2: 353–72.

Monitorul de Suceava, assorted articles, Jan.–Mar. (1998). Iasi: Nord-Est Press.

Netting, R. McC., R.R. Wilk and E.J. Arnould (eds) (1984) *Households: Comparative Studies of the Domestic Group,* California: University of California Press.

Rival, L. (ed.) (1998) *The Social Life of Trees: Anthropological Perspectives on Tree Symbolism.* Oxford: Berg.

Rosaldo, M. (1984) 'Toward an anthropology of self and feeling'. In R. Shweder and R. LeVine (eds) *Culture Theory: Essays on Mind, Self and Emotion.* Cambridge: Cambridge University Press.

Rowlands, M. (1994) 'The material culture of success: ideals and life cycles in Cameroon'. In J. Friedman (ed.) *Consumption and Identity.* Chur, Switzerland: Harwood Academic Publishers.

Sampson, S. (1994) 'Money without culture, culture without money: Eastern Europe's nouveaux riches'. *Post-Communist Transition* 3/1: 7–30.

Sidorovici, G. (1964) *Suceava – Indreptar Turistic.* Suceava: Sfatul Popular al Regianii.

Simmel, G. (1957 [1904]) 'Fashion'. *American Journal of Sociology* 62/6: 541–58.

Verdery, K. (1983) *Transylvanian Villagers.* Berkeley: University of California Press.

—— (1996) *What Was Socialism and What Comes Next?* Princeton: Princeton University Press.

Vulcanescu, R. (1972) *Coloana Cerului (The Column of the Sky).* Bucharest: Editura Academiei.

Weismantel, M. (1989) 'Making breakfast and raising babies: the Zumbagua household as constituted process'. In R. Wilk (ed.) *The Household Economy.* Boulder: Westview Press.

Wilk, R. (Ed. 1989) *The Household Economy,* Boulder: Westview Press

Zidarita, S. (1967) *Suceava: Ghid Turistic al Regiunii.* Bucharest: Editura Meridiane.

–10–

The 'Untidy' Japanese House
Inge Maria Daniels

Although the television set is becoming an ubiquitous presence many houses are devoid of the myriad decorative possessions that fill Western interiors . . . Usually the Japanese interior is restrained and orderly, and in the way that it recalls the calm and peacefulness of the past. (Slesin, Stafford and Rozensztroch 1987: 61)

The above quotation praising the simplistic, minimalist interior of the Japanese house was extracted from a classic among the huge English-language literature on Japanese style. In the design/architecture section of any major bookshop in London one can find a myriad of similar books with titles such as *A Japanese Touch for your Home* (Yagi 1982), *Japanese Accents in Western Interiors* (Rao and Mahony 1988) or *The Japanese Home Stylebook* (Goodman 1992). These kinds of works built on a romantic ideal of the Japanese house that strongly appeals to audiences in Europe and North America.[1] I too, long before actually going to Japan, was fascinated by the Japanese house as it has been 'exoticised and rarefied behind glass walls in museums and in glossy prints of picture books' (Fawcett 1980: 9).[2] However, in Japan, I have looked in vain for the stylish houses, 'restrained and orderly', void of decorations. Or perhaps I did see them: the reassembled houses from the Tokugawa period (1600–1868) in an outdoor museum, a deserted tea house on the grounds of a temple complex or minimalist buildings designed by modern Japanese architects such as Tadao Ando. Time and time again I was astonished by the sheer amount of things people actually keep in their homes. This intriguing disparity has motivated my article.

1. I will use the terms 'West' and 'Westerners' to refer to a diversity of people living in Europe and northern America. However, I am aware of the danger involved in using 'Westerners' as a single racial category opposed to 'Orientals' or 'Japanese'. Moeran and Skov, for example, call it an example of counter-orientalism (Moeran and Skov 1997).

2. Fawcett (1980) is an architect who raises questions about images of the Japanese house that are void of any reference to the home culture. Bognar (1989), another architect, rightly argues that the modernist movement was responsible for introducing the myth of the Japanese house in the West and in Japan. Unfortunately, both authors focus their discussion of the contemporary dwelling on empty minimalist houses built by Japanese avant-garde designers.

Inge Maria Daniels

The Elegant House: Harmony in Aesthetics and Social Relations

The continuous popularity of a fragmented and decontextualized image of the Japanese house is fuelled by strong underlying ideas of orientalism. During the second half of the nineteenth century Western artists, architects, designers and so on turned to Japanese aesthetics for inspiration (Japanism).[3] *Japanese Homes and their Surroundings* written in 1886 by Edward Morse, a celebrated American Japanophile, was the first account in English about the domestic architecture of the middle-class Japanese dwelling. Although Morse mentions the inconveniences of Japanese houses, on the whole, as the following text demonstrates, his discussion was laudatory:

> Absolute cleanliness and refinement, with very few objects in sight upon which the eye may rest contentedly, are the main features in household adornment which the Japanese strive after, and which they attain with a simplicity and effectiveness that we can never hope to reach. Our rooms seem to them like a curiosity shop, and 'stuffy' to the last degree. (Morse 1886: 309)

Morse's book became an authoritative source of information for the Modern Movement, which treasured the simplicity and austerity of Japanese architecture.[4] The World Fairs at the end of the nineteenth century offered a broad public the opportunity to experience the curious Japanese buildings first hand. The following abstract from *Impressions of Japanese Architecture* by the architect Ralph Cram, published in 1905 after his visit to Japan in 1898, characterizes the appraisal of the perfect beauty and harmony of the empty Japanese house[5] at the turn of the century. It also hints at parallels drawn between the simplicity of the Japanese house and the life of its inhabitants, a point I will return to later.

> For the courtesy and simplicity of Japanese home life, the domestic architecture forms a faultless setting. It is absolutely frank and straightforward in construction, perfectly simple in its forms, and reserved and refined in its decorations; all the ornament is rigidly constructional, while the furnishings are of the simplest quality and only such

---

3. A famous example of this is the influence of Japanese woodblock prints (*ukiyo-e*) on Western painting, especially Impressionism.

4. The influence of minimalist Japanese aesthetics was most profound in Frank Lloyd Wright's work (Nute 1993). In Kurokawa's view, minimalist aesthetics have been overgeneralized by the Modernists. He argues that in Japan, traditionally, the simple and the undecorated go together with the bold and the colourful (Kurokawa 1988: 54).

5. Three ideological concepts often cited in relation to traditional Japanese aesthetics are *wabi* (simple quietude), *sabi* (elegant simplicity) and *shibui* (refined austerity). They suggest a modest beauty close to nature exemplified in the tea ceremony.

as the nature of the life demands. There is no ornament for the sake of ornament, no woodwork or carving not demanded by the exigencies of construction, no striving for picturesque effect through fantastic irregularity, no overloading of unnecessary decoration, no confusion of furnishings, no litter of trivial and embarrassing accessories. (Cram 1982: 139)

These observations may not have been that off-beat at the end of the nineteenth century. As Hanley has shown, pre-modern Japanese did not possess an excess of consumer goods as in the West, but a few items designed in accordance with a Japanese lifestyle that did not waste scarce resources (Hanley 1997: 74–5). This is in sharp contrast with 'the aesthetics of abundance' that characterized American consumer culture during the same period (Orvell 1989: 42–9). However, Cram's work is problematic because he came to the conclusion in 1905 that 'the period of good architecture is over in Japan' (Cram 1982: 72). This purist attitude towards Japanese architecture is also paramount in later works by foreign commentators, such as in Bruno Taut's *Houses and People of Japan* from 1937.[6] Throughout this work Taut expresses his disdain for what he calls 'ugly things, many "modern" things and much trash' (Taut 1958: 53). The following quote illustrates his belief that they were contaminating the pure Japanese aesthetics:

There were new cheap ornaments in cut-out boards above the cardboard sliding-doors, all the cheap and senseless things that are merely a light and quick satisfaction to eyes that do not see any more the fine proportion and calm effect of material. (Taut 1958: 67–8)

Recurring expressions of disappointment about a lost sensibility among the Japanese allude to the possibility that the majority of the Japanese probably never lived in elegant houses. This point will be taken up again in my discussion of the historical development of a minimalist aesthetic ideal in Japan.

A factor which I believe has contributed to the circulation of a distorted, ahistorical view of the Japanese house in the West is the growing interest in Zen aestheticism since the 1960s. Zen basic religious–philosophical principles of order

---

6. I observed a contemporary example of Westerners exoticizing Japanese architecture while living in Kyoto during the period 1996–7. Kyoto is a 1,200-years-old former capital city, famous for its cultural and historical assets. The whole city is a UNESCO cultural heritage site with strict building regulations. In recent years old wooden houses that fall outside the heritage regulations – that most Japanese deem unpractical and dirty – have been torn down in rapid succession to make room for modern concrete condominiums and prefab model homes. Kyoto is home to a big foreign population, many of them living in the more traditional Japanese houses. It is telling that it was among this group of foreign residents that the first official protests against the destruction of 'traditional' houses was launched.

were frequently clarified referring to the tea ceremony held in the austere tea hut, as the following text below demonstrates:

> In the absence of decorative distractions, one must concentrate on his own mind and the minds of others present. Host and guest find their focus on one another has been deliberately enhanced, breaking down the barriers of separateness and individual identity. (Hoover 1988: 144).

The discourse of the elegant Japanese house void of decorations, seen as representative for Japanese architecture in general, became perceived as the embodiment of Zen harmony, in turn considered the canon of Japanese social organization. Engel's celebrated volume about the Japanese house (1964), for example, explicitly draws a link between the aesthetical order of the home and the family who lives in it. He indicates that

> the Japanese house is characterized by a strong interdependence of the order of family and the physical order of house. In fact, the Japanese house is but the materialized order of family. (Engel 1964: 435)

This brings us to another discourse, rooted in Japanese and Western scholarship, which celebrates the harmony of the family unit as well as Japanese social relations in general. The Japanese term for dwelling, *ie*, encompasses the household, the whole family clan, the ancestor lineage, the family wealth and territory (*Daikangorin* 1992: 886). The house and its property were indivisible and the *ie* can be described as an economic, political and religious unit of continuity from one generation to the next based on a system of primogeniture. The social function of the individual depended on his/her position in the family unit.

A number of studies that focus on the *ie* have contributed to a better understanding of traditional kinship structures. However, this body of literature is also highly problematic because it has created some kind of idealized form of Japanese family life that ignores radical changes in the composition of the household in contemporary Japan.[7] An associated idea is the holistic theory of groupism that holds that the Japanese value the group above the individual and that they, therefore, strive for harmony and consensus. With the imaginary of a harmonious family group living in an orderly, minimalist house we have come full circle.

---

7. See Ochiai's view that 'the post-war family has been understood within the following basic framework: the Western family is typically a nuclear family consisting of husband, wife, and children, while the Japanese family was originally a unique social system, the *ie*, produced by a unique culture, and the *ie* has been transformed into the nuclear family through the process of social change known as modernisation' (Ochiai 1997: ix–x).

This article challenges common typifications of the Japanese house – the building and its inhabitants. Through an ethnographic investigation of the material culture of everyday life of two households, the tension between the aesthetic and social ideal of harmony and contemporary home aesthetics and family life will be explored. The anthropologist Brian Moeran's ethnography of a pottery community in southern Japan provides another example of the discrepancy between social and aesthetic ideals of harmony and more individual social and aesthetic practices (Moeran 1997: 207). I will deal with domestic consumption and the production of social relations (Silverstone and Hirsch 1992; Jackson and Moores 1995). My study provides evidence for one of the significant claims made in this volume, namely, that the material culture of the home is expressive of the changing social relationships of its inhabitants. The particular contribution of my research lies in the fact that it highlights the complexities, conflicts and compromises involved in creating a home

This chapter moves away from traditional approaches that stress the uniqueness of Japanese culture towards a more comprehensive understanding of Japanese modernity within the global context of consumption.[8] Consumption located in the concreteness of everyday life has become the major means of self-expression in Japan. In Clammer's view Japanese class-consciousness is principally constructed around consumption, which is 'seen as a process, a continuous activity of self-construction, of relationship maintenance and symbolic competition' (Clammer 1997: 101). His concept of class as practice is similar to Miller's idea that class differentiation is no longer based on occupations but that 'elements of consumption such as shopping increase in importance as central instruments within a continual process of class construction' (Miller, Jackson, Thrift, Holbrook and Rowlands 1998: 137). Skov and Moeran have argued that because a deep-rooted ideology of homogeneity that pictures Japan as a middle-class society has a strong bearing on the consumer market, 'gender and age have become to be the real playgrounds for market differentiation and segmentation' (Skov and Moeran 1995: 55). The home is an important site of consumption and this chapter aims to uncover different lifestyle choices in a consumer market highly segregated according to gender and age.

Differentiations are established through consumption activities and this finds its expression in the material culture of the home. Rosenberger (1992) argues, in one of the scarce articles concerned with contemporary Japanese home decoration, that the aesthetics of the Japanese home reflect an underlying disparity in society. The homes of the aspiring classes are modelled after the American family and characterized by a redundancy of Western items of material culture. The wealthy

8. Elsewhere, I have given a detailed overview of recent works about Japanese consumerism (Daniels 1999).

identify with European culture while they continue to appreciate the simplistic beauty of the Japanese style (Rosenberger 1992). Rosenberger studied the production of images in magazines without paying much attention to their reception in everyday life. My research will show that differences created through home decoration are subtler. Through an ethnographic study of the material culture of two contemporary households I hope to reveal what contemporary Japanese deem attractive.[9] I draw on previous ethnographic research that has explicitly linked domestic aesthetic experiences with the objectification of family values (Forrest 1988; Halle 1993; Gullestad 1993).

The romantic notion of the elegant Japanese house, discussed above, is not merely a Western construct. Japanese scholarship, rooted in the *nihonjinron* ideology that stresses the uniqueness of Japanese culture, has actively promoted the fragmented, decontextualized image of the house abroad and at home. Many of the classics idealizing the Japanese home – but also the tea ceremony, the kimono, the bonsai tree and so forth and so on – are adapted translations of Japanese books, often introduced to Western readers by Japanese publishers.[10] A contemporary Japanese example of the ahistorical depiction of the Japanese house can, for instance, be found in *Katei Gaho*, a magazine for upper-class urban women. In his analysis of this magazine, Moeran (1995) has shown how the empty Japanese houses devoid of people is a major element in creating an ideal world in which housewives in kimono live alone the dream of Japaneseness. One advertisement depicts

> a woman in kimono kneeling on the veranda of a beautiful old wooden house, set against a background of a spacious wooded garden. Nearby are a vase of flowers, with displays of food on a long wooden table, a glass statue in one corner of the room, and a scroll hanging on the dried mud wall beside it. The house looks very Japanese, very beautiful, very special, very different from anything lived in by ordinary readers. (Moeran 1995: 136)

Before turning to my ethnographic analysis, it will be necessary to trace the historical roots of the minimalist aesthetic ideal in Japan and rethink its position within the development of the post-war middle-class dwelling.

9. The data presented in this paper were gathered during spring 1999 when I spent one month each in the home of two families in the Kansai region. I knew these informants for a long time prior to this research because I have lived in this region for five years from 1992–7. In order to protect the anonymity of my informants, all names have been changed.

10. *The Elegant Japanese House* (Ito 1969), for example, appeared originally in 1961 as *Nihon no sumai* (The Japanese Dwelling). It is also noteworthy that Cram's volume discussed above (Cram 1982) was based on a second edition that appeared in 1930 without updating the contents. The publishers of both editions were Japanese.

Contextualizing the Japanese House: 'Japanese Style' and 'Western Style'

What is today regarded as the prototypical minimal Japanese house has its roots in the Tokugawa (1600–1868)[11] residence of the elite built in the *sukiya* style. The *sukiya* residence combined the elegance of the previous *shoin*-style with the rustic teahouse developed by Zen monks (Bognar 1989: 188). It is an open space, light architecture that focuses on the formal meeting space and displays closeness between house and garden. These houses were scarcely decorated and *tatami* mats placed on the floor were used to sit and sleep on. Only a small upper-class elite lived in these kinds of dwellings where they practised the aesthetics of simplicity and social harmony inspired by Zen Buddhism.[12] Tokugawa society was highly segregated with four official status strata consisting of samurai, peasants, artisans and merchants. People not only had to obey a strict code of social behaviour but they were also subjected to multiple regulations concerning the aesthetics of everyday life such as restrictions on type of dress, food and housing. The material culture of everyday life reflected given, framed identities. For the majority of the population social and aesthetical order was imposed on them and all too often austerity was an expression of real poverty.

At the end of the nineteenth century the feudal system was abolished. The modern Meiji State idealized the gendered division of home and work, rooted in the old samurai family ideology but also evident in Western middle-class ideas of domesticity. Industrialization and urbanization in the first half of this century saw the growth of a 'new urban middle class'.[13] The lifestyle of these Japanese was characterized by a Japanese–Western hybridity.[14] New building styles were diffused slowly. There were two trends. Firstly, the application of modern materials in the housing style of the elite, for example the use of glass instead of paper windows. Secondly, a diffusion of innovations from the houses of the former Tokugawa elite to the dwellings of the commoners, such as the use of *tatami* mats[15] (Hanley 1997:

11. The basis for the Japanese modernist project can be traced back to Tokugawa Japan. At the end of the seventeenth century continuous political stability under the military rulers led to an enormous growth of the Japanese economy and an urban consumer culture expanded (Hanley 1997: 15–19). Seventeenth-century Edo (contemporary Tokyo), for example, was the biggest city in the world with a population of over one million people.

12. The houses of the Puritan settlers in New England in the seventeenth century provide us with another example of how spiritual principles of order seen as underlying social order can be materialized in the austerity of the dwelling (Wright 1981: 1–17).

13. As opposed to the old middle class of artisans and merchants.

14. In her research about the development of a modern culinary tradition in Japan, Cwiertka clearly demonstrates how a hybrid Japanese–Western style became associated with this new middle class (Cwiertka 1999: 73).

15. Jeremy and Robinson (1989: 165) discuss the main features of *tatami* mats.

157–8). I will return to the *tatami* room later, but here it will suffice to stress that *tatami* mats only became widespread in the houses of the common people during the Taisho period (1918–26). Most rented urban accommodations were not fitted with *tatami* until after the Second World War (Koizumi 1980: 61).

The post-war middle-class Japanese family surrounded itself with electrical appliances.[16] Washing machine, fridge and a TV, also called the three sacred containers, became widespread. During the period of high economic growth of the 1960s differences in income narrowed, education became more democratic and the mass media increased the accessibility of information and knowledge. A 'new-middle-class mass culture' developed.[17] It idealized

> the construct of an affluent household surrounded by electrical appliances, which possesses its own car, a piano,[18] etc, with the husband working extremely hard for his family and the wife regulating the household as a place for relaxation. (Sōgō josei rekisi kenkyūkai 1992: 250)

Since the eighteenth century two trends in residential housing have coexisted in Japan. Firstly, private residences of high quality with a garden built by skilful artisans. The second type of accommodation was cheap standard rental housing made by contract workers without *tatami* or fittings (Yoshino 1994: 117–18). The sharp distinction between these types of accommodation continues to this day (Clammer 1997: 28). High land prices linked with space shortage causes people to live in small rented accommodation far into the suburbs of cities. The majority of tenants consider this a temporary stage in their lives and aspire to move as soon as they can afford better housing. In Britain, for example, we see a similar ranking of house types according to owned or rented accommodation linked with social status (Parker Pearson and Richards 1994: 9). The following text summarizes how the ideal dwelling should look like for contemporary Japanese:

16. After the Second World War, *danchi*, government substituted high-rise complexes, became the typical accommodation for middle-class families in suburban centres. The layout of these apartments was standardized. They consisted of a dining room–kitchen, where sitting on chairs replaced the lifestyle of sitting on the floor, a six- and/or a four-and-a-half-mat Japanese-style room, a bath and a Western-style toilet.

17. All my informants called themselves middle class. According to Taira, a similar view is expressed by 90 per cent of Japanese (Taira 1993: 169)

18. The most desired object for the home, apart from electrical appliances, was the piano. A survey conducted in 1971 shows that 35 per cent of elementary schoolchildren had a piano in their home. In 1976, 45 per cent of Japanese elementary schoolgirls were taking piano lessons, followed by violin and ballet (Sōgō josei rekishi kenkyūkai 1993: 246). Löfgren has called the piano 'a key symbol of civilized manners'. In eighteenth-century Britain, for example, the piano was a key item in the rivalry between the economic and cultural elite (Löfgren 1994: 49).

Today whether built by the owner on his or her own property or by a developer, the two-story detached house with a tiled roof, a small (sometimes tiny) ornamental garden enclosed by a high stone wall or hedge, and garage space for the family automobile remains the ideal for the majority of Japanese. (*Japan, an Illustrated Encyclopaedia* 1993: 572)

A survey conducted by the Japanese economic planning agency in 1988 shows that 62.3 per cent of the population owned a detached two-storeyed house. It is common practice for people who plan to acquire their own property to visit a housing park with ready-made 'model houses'. There one chooses a house that one likes, subscribes to a mortgage scheme and has the whole package reassembled at the desired location. These model houses are what Yoshino calls 'eclectic prefabs' that express 'an individual style not based on traditional Japanese aesthetics but on pragmatism' (Yoshino 1994: 123). Inside these ideal homes the stress is on living a comfortable live. The interior is in Western style with a dining-room–kitchen area, bedrooms with Western furniture and carpeted, tiled or wooden floors.

The families discussed in my case studies below own their two-storey detached houses.[19] They are wealthy families, although both consider themselves to belong to the middle-class mass. The Miyada family lives in the countryside in their more than one 100-years-old family house, while the Mori's built their own eclectic model house in an suburban area with easy access to Osaka and Kobe. The exterior features of both houses are standardized. The Miyada's house is a 'traditional prefab' built around a wooden frame. An approximately 2 m-high grey stone wall with a roofed entrance gate and latticed wooden sliding doors surrounds the structure. The Mori's live in an 'eclectic prefab' with a steel frame covered with grey prefab segments in a brick pattern. The whole structure is enclosed by a low see-through fence and a latticed black iron gate with a buzzer. The only personal detail on the outside of both houses is a plaque with the family's name hanging on the entrance gate.[20]

The layout of the interior is also standard. The central living space is a dining–kitchen area mostly with an adjoining Japanese-style room. The rest of the space is divided in bathroom and toilets and a variable number of Western-style bedrooms. Wallpapers, floors, doors and windows are prefabricated elements with minor differences. The interior is filled with a standard range of electrical equipment associated with modern living. The standardization of the exterior and major parts

19. I was unable to study the homes of people living in rented accommodation. The data presented here is, therefore, only representative of those Japanese who are house owners.

20. The Miyadas have a wooden name plaque and the Moris a plastic one that lights up in the evening. During my fieldwork in spring 1999, colourful plaques with message such as 'welcome' or personal names written on them decorated the doors of some dwellings in urban areas.

of the interior of the dwelling restricts expressions of creativity. This article aims to demonstrate how two contemporary Japanese families employ material culture to create an identity for their home.

I am aware that my choice to discuss two geographical different families may lead some readers to conclude that they merely exemplify the contrast between rural and urban family life in Japan. In this interpretation the countryside is depicted as a traditional place where the ideal notion of the extended paternal family (*ie*) continues to exist, while urban life is characterized by the pursuit of a more individualistic, Western lifestyle. In my view, the divide between everyday life in the rural and urban Japan is rather blurred. On an island in Hiroshima prefecture, where I have conducted extensive fieldwork, for example, many houses are inscribed with long family histories, but several young couples built model homes without Japanese-style rooms. Old family houses are also found in urban areas. Moreover, although deserted mountain villages do exist, in recent years a growing number of urbanites chooses to live in rural areas such as those who return to their rural family home after retirement from an urban job. The anthropologist John Knight has recently studied Japanese 'rural resettlers' (Knight 1997). In short, a nationwide media and transportation network has made the same information and goods available anywhere in Japan. New trends are diffused from urban centres to the countryside, but rural areas are part of the same consumer society.

According to the Kodansha illustrated encyclopaedia of Japan, 90 per cent of all new homes in Japan have at least one token Japanese-style or *tatami* room with a decorative alcove, *tokonoma*,[21] inside (1993: 572). Ninety per cent might be a bit overestimated, but my fieldwork data as well as advertisements for model homes indicate that a Japanese-style room is incorporated in many Japanese dwellings. This raises issues about the relationship between tradition and modernity. In Japan the discussion about modernity frequently takes the form of a Western versus Japanese dichotomy. The terms 'Japanese style' (*washiki*) and 'Western style' (*yoshiki*), which feature regularly in my discussion of the home, should be seen as part of this native cultural classification. For those readers not familiar with the Japanese case, it will be necessary to clarify this notion. Goldstein-Gidoni's recent work about contemporary Japanese weddings provides us with some excellent explanations. Her research sheds light on the relationship between the production of Japanese weddings and brides and the ongoing construction and invention of a Japanese cultural identity around Western and traditional Japanese traits. In her

---

21. *Tokonoma* referred originally to the entire room with an alcove in it, but these days the decorative alcove is a niche approximately 1 m deep. The prototype of the *tokonoma* developed during the Muromachi period (1338–1573) when it became practice in upper-class homes to hang a Buddhist picture scroll on the wall and place a thin, low table set with a flower vase and incense burner in front of it (Nishi and Hozumi 1985: 134).

view, the ambiguous mixture of Western and traditional Japanese elements in wedding ceremonies should be understood as a matter of styles and differences because from a 'consumerist perspective, the Western and the traditional Japanese both contribute to the sense of Japaneseness' (Goldstein-Gidoni 1997: 9). Thus, returning to the house, the terms 'Western' and 'Japanese' need to be interpreted as two styles among many others that have been decontextualized before they are mixed indefinitely and adopted as different consumer choices.

The Japanese-style room and *tokonoma*, decorative alcove, inside are of special importance for my discussion of the material culture of the home because both feature in the contemporary rhetoric praising the Japanese house. I will return later to aesthetic practices inside the *tokonoma* and the Japanese-style room of both families studied. First, I will focus on how both families mediate between an ideal notion of family and the fluidity of social relations in their home.

The Miyada Family: A Home in Transition

The Miyada family has lived for more than 200 years on a small island in Hiroshima prefecture. At the beginning of the nineteenth century the Miyada family business which produces and distributes kitchen utensils was founded. Mr Miyada, sixty-six years old, is the fifth successive Miyada president of the company. Thirty-seven years ago he married Yoshiko, now sixty-two years old, who is originally from Hiroshima city. Mr and Mrs Miyada and their two adult daughters, Kaori, thirty-six, and Naoko, thirty-four years old, live in a detached two-storey family house. Their son Ken, who is thirty, has been living in the USA for three years. The main house was built approximately 100 years ago, but after the birth of their three children an adjunct house was turned into an annex. Mr and Mrs Miyada repeatedly apologized to me because their house was old (*furui*) and inconvenient (*fuben*). Mrs Miyada expressed two major complaints about the house. Firstly, it is sunless. Indeed, the first floor of the house has just a few small windows, high up the walls with thick opaque glazing. Secondly, she would have liked to make the second floor nicer, but because of the high costs involved they did not proceed with that plan.

The dining kitchen area is the central space in the house. It consists of a white 'open American kitchen' – as Mrs. Miyada calls it – and a sitting area with a veneer dining table and four chairs. The kitchen used to be much smaller and was separated from the dining area, but because Mrs Miyada felt isolated a separating wall was removed and a cork floor was laid down. All members of the family eat at different times while watching the big TV placed close to the kitchen table. The home life of the Miyada family evolves around the TV. The family rarely has visitors. Mrs Miyada told me she sometimes chats with friends at the kitchen table but claims that it is difficult to let people who are reserved into the kitchen. Guests are guided directly from the hallway into a formal guestroom.

This mostly unused Western-style room, widespread in affluent homes in rural areas, is the main private/public space in the house (Chevalier 1998: 49). It functions as a display area to impress guests and bears resemblance to the parlour or front room common in working-class houses in inter-war London (Attfield 1994: 217–18). The Miyadas' guestroom is decorated in the typical style with carpets, bookcases, an armchair set with flora pattern around a low coffee table, a piano and a TV. The Miyada couple acquired all items, apart from the TV, more than thirty years ago. In this room the achievements of their children are proudly displayed. Three of youngest daughter's paintings, produced at different stages of her career as a professional painter, are on display. On top of the piano, a social marker of middle-class life, stand two formal graduation photographs depicting the other Miyada children.[22]

The material culture of this room presents the Miyadas as a happy modern middle-class family to the outside world. However, the Miyada family is not exactly the stereotypical harmonious Japanese family. Cohesion and dispersal are part of their everyday family. The Miyadas live the reality of a traditional home in transition. Four adults, each with their personal project, live together under the same roof. Gender and generational differences are at the base of dysfunctional inter-family relationships. Kaufmann, who conducted a study among couples in Paris, reveals that through everyday practices such as doing the laundry individuals negotiate the construction of a family identity (Kaufmann 1998: 83). In the Miyadas' home, material culture is, similarly, employed to mediate between the ideal notion of family and individual projects.

The idealization of the division between work and home lies at the base of most of the Miyadas' inter-family conflicts. Rosenberger describes how the household portrayed as the 'centre of harmony and nurture, and the workplace, the centre of competition and stressful human relations', rooted in samurai ideology, is still an aspiration for many Japanese (Rosenberger 1997: 156). Mrs Miyada is a full-time housewife, whose primary duties have been described as managing the home, mothering and caring, but as Imamura puts it, 'other activities may be permitted so long as they do not make her less effective as a nurturer' (Imamura 1987: 19). Mrs Miyada keeps a strict daily schedule of washing cloths, cleaning, shopping and preparing food because it enables her to engage in multiple activities outside the home. In spring 1999, she was, for instance, engaged in choral practices, Japanese-style painting classes, karaoke lessons and T'ai Chi classes.

The mixture of handiwork produced by Mrs Miyada is a major decorative feature in the house. This is a first example of how the Miyadas mediate individual projects within the family context. Most of these items were fabricated in special courses

22. See Halle (1993: 104) for a discussion of the display of formal and informal pictures in the home.

teaching home decoration. These hand-made items are a pretext for enjoyment outside the home and they also confirm Mrs Miyada's needs as an individual. By placing her handicrafts in the interior of the home they become tangible expressions of her commitment to family life.

Mrs Miyada told me she is afraid she will have to give up her free time after her husband retires. Mr Miyada himself does not really look forward to the event either. All his life he has contributed to the household through his work and the prospect of being at home all the time causes great anxiety. Gullestad points at a similar dilemma regarding the wife's independence and the marginality of the husband to the home in working-class families in Norway (Gullestad 1993: 141). Mr Miyada tries to negotiate – with variable success – the tensions in the home with material culture. He proudly told me he likes to relax in front of the TV and has placed a wide-screen TV with video in all the rooms in the house. This indicates his conservative interpretation of the home as a place for relaxation where his own needs are prioritized. Often each family member watches TV in another room. Livingstone has, for example, shown that placing a TV in different rooms may encourage individuality and actually enable family dispersal (Livingstone 1992: 1).

Another topic rooted in the ideal notion of family that causes much distress is marriage. The fact that two unmarried daughters in their thirties still lived at home is clearly a nuisance for both parents. Kaori, who is thirty-six, works part-time for Amway. She helps her mother with homework, but also spends a lot of time in her room watching TV, reading women's magazines or talking on the phone with friends. The Miyadas tried several times to talk Kaori into an arranged marriage but she has rejected all candidates. Thirty-four-year-old Naoko faces less pressure to get married because she suffers from chronic health problems. She lived in Tokyo for nearly twelve years, where she studied Japanese-style painting at a top university for the Fine Arts in Japan and is a successful artist. Romance and intimacy is not part of the traditional Japanese marital relationship, and the rather reserved Miyada couple exemplifies this. However, Kaori and Naoko, like many young Japanese women, have other hopes. The popularity among the younger generation of Japanese of Christmas, which celebrates the couple and romantic love (Moeran and Skov 1993: 114–15), for example, should be seen in this light.

Japanese women have always been central to the conflict between tradition and modernity in Japan. On the one hand they are active consumers, but, on the other hand, they are constrained by the traditional image of women as housewives and mothers. I agree with Skov and Moeran's view that messages of individuality and freedom in the media encourage women to consume and to enjoy themselves, while in reality there are strong social pressures to conform to married life and motherhood (Skov and Moeran 1995: 34). However, as Goldstein-Gidoni has stressed, often Japanese women collaborate in their own objectification as repositories of traditional values (Goldstein-Gidoni 1997: 159).

As Kaori nears forty, the Miyadas seem to have given up all hope of a marriage and expect her to move. However, Kaori has never lived on her own and continues to postpone the big step. As an incentive the Miyadas bought her a condominium in a new apartment block opposite the bay. However, the new purchase did not bring about the expected results. Instead, it became a 'good excuse' for both daughters not to return home in the evening. Mr Miyada is very strict about their relationships with men, and the condominium enabled the girls to stay out late or to bring home a boyfriend. Kaori also attempts to negotiate her refusal to marry with material culture. She supplies the family with Amway products employed in everyday practices such as cleaning, cooking or bathing. A range of soaps and body care products are displayed in the bathroom and toilets, while vitamins end up in the middle of the kitchen table. These products objectify feminine caring values.

Next, I will introduce my second case study, which focuses on the Moris, a young urban family who had the opportunity to built their new home from scratch. The Moris will provide us with an example of family life that is not modelled after the traditional family ideal. This family values the individuality and creativity of each family member and the material culture of their home expresses this.

The Mori Family's Dream House

The Mori family lives in Itami city, a small suburb between Osaka and Kobe. Mr Mori works downtown in a pharmacy. Mrs Mori is a full-time English teacher at a local high school. Both are in their late forties. He is originally from rural Kyushu in southern Japan but moved to Osaka more than twenty-five years ago to study pharmaceutical sciences in a top university. Her parents, who also migrated from the countryside, founded their own home in Itami. The Moris have two daughters who still live at home. Keiko who is nineteen is studying to become a chiropractitioner. Yoshiko is fifteen and in her last year at a local Junior High school.

During the Kobe earthquake of January 1995 the detached two-storied traditional prefab house the Mori's bought when they got married suffered severe structural damage. The Moris were fortunate to have the resources and the knowledge to design their new dream house. Mr Mori took a minor degree in architecture and drew the entire house plan himself. Less than six months after the quake the family moved into their new house, akin to the ideal middle-class model home discussed above.[23] Convenience, safety and storage are the three keywords in advertisements

---

23. The fact that the Mori's had the means to rebuild their house in six months shows that they are a wealthy, upper-middle-class family. After the quake most builders or carpenters were fully booked for the entire year. The train station in Itami city, for example, which was totally destroyed only reopened in the summer of 1998.

promoting model homes. The same principles guided the Mori family when they built their home. The interior of the house was entirely chosen from a catalogue. The Mori house cost approximately 60 million yen (£300,000). A standard house costs one-third of that, but the Moris opted for the most durable and safe materials. The whole house has wooden floors with floor heating and oak doors bigger than standard Japanese size. Mr Mori told me that when he designed the house the main limitation was the space available and storage was another important issue. All rooms in the house have big built-in closets and shelves. For additional storage space, a loft was built under the roof, which can be reached via stairs in Mr Mori's room.

Mrs Mori did not care much about the interior of their new home. She told me that the house was entirely father's project. She had expressed just three wishes. Firstly, she requested a place for the cupboard made by her father, which holds her collection of teapots. Secondly, the kitchen should not separate her from the rest of the family during meals. This point was also made by Mrs Miyada and repeated in advertisements for model homes. Thirdly, she wanted a veranda on the second floor to let the futons dry outside. The first request shows her concern with an object made by her father who was a carpenter. It is one of the few things she kept from the old house. I will return later to this cupboard when I discuss other objects in the house made by members of the family. In Livingstone's view, women stress the utility of domestic technologies linked with their everyday domestic practices (Livingstone 1992: 120). According to Mrs Mori, the material culture of her home should facilitate her housework (the veranda) and make domestic practices more enjoyable (the open fully equipped kitchen). High-tech equipment such as a fully automatic heating system for the bath and a highly intelligent washing machine were also installed for this reason.

The Mori family's central room, like the Miyadas', is the dining–kitchen. It is a brown wooden veneer built-in kitchen equipped with a American-size fridge, a dishwasher and a microwave oven. One wall has a built-in cabinet with glass doors where Mrs Mori keeps trays, dishes, glasses and other tableware. In this family the preparation and consumption of food, instead of watching TV, is highly appreciated. In the middle of the room stands a big wooden table that can seat at least ten people. Every day, at around six o'clock when Mr Mori comes home, the family has dinner together. The openness of the Mori home and family life is striking. Friends of the children or mother or some neighbours might come by for tea, and every so often the Moris hold huge dinner-parties. The Miyadas have a special parlour for guests, but Mrs Mori stresses that she did not want a special room to receive visitors because she thinks

it is quite ridiculous I would have to serve somebody tea in another room saying 'ocha wo dōzo' [Here you are, your tea] [with an high pitch voice imitating women that serve customers tea]. Anyone can enter our kitchen.

The family is involved in several foreign-exchange programmes and regularly foreign guests are staying in their home. Next to the hallway is a small room with a piano and a bed that can be turned into a bedroom for guests. It is decorated with paintings: three of Yoshiko's paintings and two abstract paintings received as gifts. The top of the piano functions as a display area for a collection of porcelain figurines.

The inter-family relations of this household are comparatively harmonious. The gendered division between home and work is blurred. Both parents have a full-time job and Mr Mori often returns home in the afternoon to work in his room. The couple's relationship is more affable and relaxed. Both teenage daughters are content, study hard and are committed to family life. The parents encourage them to be creative. Yoshiko, the youngest daughter, loves to design and display objects. It can be argued that these girls are too young to experience the same social pressure to marry as the Miyada daughters, but discussions with both parents indicate that above all they want their children to be happy. Twenty-year-old Keiko, for example, has a boyfriend whom she occasionally brings home.

The Moris appreciate Japanese aesthetics. Mrs Mori, for example, is learning the tea ceremony and flower arranging, both children practice calligraphy, and all of them like to wear kimono on festive occasions. This confirms the point made above that Japanese women actively participate in their role as keepers of tradition. It also shows how mothers socialize their daughters into traditional values (Goldstein-Gidoni 1997: 106). The Moris create their familial identity with elements of Japanese aesthetics such as *tatami* rooms and tea sets, but other items of material culture such as abstract art, a piano, French wine and electrical appliances carry similar importance. This is another piece of evidence that supports the argument that 'Japanese' and 'Western' should be seen as different consumer choices which can be easily mixed.

The remainder of this chapter will study the material culture of the Japanese-style room and the decorative alcove. Both elements are central in the discourse about the elegant Japanese house. In short, the Japanese-style room covered in *tatami* mats is depicted as the model of minimalist harmonious living, while the few objects displayed in the alcove express the taste and sophistication of the inhabitants of the house. We have argued that the Japanese-style room should be interpreted as a part of a certain style that consumers use in the ongoing construction of their identity. It can embody different things for different groups in contemporary Japan. For upper-class families, mostly homeowners, the *tatami* room, reminiscent of the houses of the Tokugawa elite, may express a sophisticated form of Japaneseness (Moeran 1995). The notion of the *tatami* room as a place for nostalgic relaxation fits in with the strict division of work and home idealized in contemporary Japan. However, *tatami* rooms are also common in suburban rented accommodation. In these living arrangements associated with lower income groups *tatami* are an efficient tool to combat crammed living conditions (Enders 1987). *Tatami* mats are multi-functional: during the day people can sit on them around a low table while in the evening a futon can be rolled out to sleep on.

The two families studied further elucidate the equivocal role of the Japanese-style room in the contemporary dwelling. Originally, the Miyadas' family house only consisted of *tatami* rooms. The multi-functional mats enabled three generations to live together under one roof. The current generation of Miyadas replaced two *tatami* rooms with a convenient Western-style dining kitchen and a parlour. Other *tatami* rooms such as the parents bedroom were transformed into Western-style rooms by covering the *tatami* with carpets and placing furniture such as beds, closets and desks on top. The Moris' dream home, on the other hand, consists mainly of Western-style rooms with wooden flooring. This family has one *tatami* room in their house, but Mr Mori complained that there was not enough space to incorporate another one. The *tatami* are partly covered with a carpet on which bamboo chairs and a table are placed.

We have seen that the *tokonoma* was one of the main style elements of the idealized *sukiya*-style dwelling of the Tokugawa elite. Originally it was a display area in which one or more scrolls were hung. Before the scroll 'three objects used in Buddhist ceremonies', namely an incense burner, a flower vase and a candle-holder were set out. In *Contemporary Japanese Design* (Evans 1991), for example, the *tokonoma* is depicted as the epitome of Japanese aesthetics of simplicity that in turn is an emblem of the lives of the household members. Thus, the aesthetic and the social ideal of harmony is supposed to merge in the *tokonoma*. The fact that many contemporary Japanese dwellings actually contain a Japanese-style room with a *tokonoma* has been used to add depth to this argument. Above, I have discussed the discrepancy between the social ideal of harmony and practices in two Japanese homes. The following analysis of the aesthetics of the Japanese-style room and the *tokonoma* of the same homes will challenge the aesthetic ideal.

Aesthetic Practices in the Japanese-style Room

1. Inherited Objects, Formal Gifts and the Long-Term Family Identity

From the Miyadas' dining–kitchen two sliding doors open onto a six-mat Japanese-style room with a *tokonoma*. In the middle of the room several cushions to sit on are arranged around a low table. In the evening Mr Miyada or Kaori often watch TV in this room while lying on the mats or sitting in a low Japanese-style chair. Sometimes visiting relatives or acquaintances are entertained in this room. Figure 10.1 illustrates the abundance of objects that decorate the room.

Apart from a calendar with pictures of Buddhist statues, a yearly New Year's gift from a local temple, all ornaments hanging on the wall were made by Mrs

Figure 10.1. Clutter in the Miyadas' Japanese-style room

Miyada. These are a big painting of a tiger and four framed pieces of embroidery depicting flowers. A wastepaper basket, next to the TV, is also covered with embroidery. As we have seen above, these decorations imbued with feeling are expressive of Mrs Miyada's role as caretaker of the household. The presence of these hand-made decorations in every room hints at her aesthetic control over the house (Forrest 1988: 216). Gullestad has linked women's responsibility for housework with their control over people and objects inside the home (Gullestad 1993: 141).

Against the same wall stand two wooden *chadansu*, literally cupboards for tea things. In the *Dictionary of Traditional Japanese Objects*, *chadansu* is defined as

> A small cupboard in which tea cups, bowls and other small items used in everyday life are stored. It doubles as a display shelf, often doll cases are placed on top of it. (*Nihon mingu jiten* 1997: 348)

Mr Miyada inherited both cupboards from his parents. Next to these cupboards stands a more modern-looking wooden chest of drawers that Mrs Miyada brought with her when she got married. Cupboards and other furniture to store away kitchen utensils, table ware and linen were part of the traditional dowry (*yomeiri dogu*, literally, tools of the entering bride) (Koizumi 1980: 274).[24] Furniture has been

24. These days the woman's parents will supply the couple mainly with new electrical appliances and furniture, but some traditional items such as kimono remain important elements of the dowry. Both families discussed are collecting kimono for their daughters.

depicted as the main embodiment of family lineage. In nineteenth-century bourgeoisie France, for example, furniture was seen as an investment in the future. Each piece was inscribed with family history (Auslander 1996: 81).

The Miyadas' furniture is covered with decorative objects. On one of the shelves four inherited wooden trays made by local craftsmen are stacked. Two dolls in glass display cases placed on top of the inherited cupboards dominate the room.[25] One case holds a female doll clad in a red kimono (*hina-ningyo*), a gift from Mrs Miyada's family for the first doll festival of their eldest daughter.[26] Goldstein-Gidoni mentions the parallel drawn between Japanese women and dolls. The term 'daughter in a box' (*hako-iri musume*), for example, illustrates a link between the dolls in glass boxes and daughters. This expression draws on the use of wooden or glass boxes to protect treasured possessions to refer to a sheltered maiden protected by her family from the outside world (Goldstein-Gidoni 1997: 126–7). These Japanese dolls are hand made, and may be employed as expensive formal gifts. The other doll displayed, depicting a Kabuki actor, is a gift from the Miyadas' insurance company. Mrs Miyada told me she likes some of the dolls, but more often these gifts cause distress. She explains:

> I am troubled because one cannot throw dolls away. I have no place to put them, so, I just have to put them there, well, I have no other option.

During my study many people expressed similar concerns regarding dolls.

In Japan gift occasions follow each other fast, and most people receive an excess of gifts throughout the year. In general, people found it difficult to throw away disliked gifts, and many items end up in the interior of the home. Dolls put an extra burden on the receiver, because traditionally these objects are considered to possess a certain agency and they therefore need to be handled with care.[27] This point relates back to the argument, made by Miller and Hecht in this volume, that the material culture of the home may exert some kind of power over its inhabitants. However, I do not want to suggest that Japanese people are passive recipients of gifts. While conducting my research in Japanese homes I found many examples of people who developed strategies to cope with the excess of gifts received. The Miyadas, for example, have a storage room filled with gifts in the back of their home.[28] The Moris, who, as we will see later, display only a few gifts in the interior

25. In a Japanese-style room in the back of the house where the Buddhist house altar is kept three more dolls in glass cases, all gifts, are displayed.

26. Traditionally, the family of the wife would present their granddaughter or grandson with a doll on their first girls day (3 March) or boys day (5 May).

27. Temples throughout Japan regularly organize memorial services for dolls.

28. In the Miyadas' Japanese-style room, for example, the painting of the tiger, the Buddhist calendar and the scroll are seasonal items that are changed at regular intervals. In spring 1999 Mrs Miyada finished another painting depicting rabbits to replace the one made in the year of the tiger.

Figure 10.2. The Miyadas' *tokonoma*

of their home, store away their disliked gifts in a built-in closet and in their garden shed.

Figure 10.2 shows that the Miyadas have accumulated twelve objects in their *tokonoma*. This is an example of a *tokonoma* whose appearance is not 'simple' and does not aim at the 'elimination of clutter' (Evans 1991: 89).

The alcove contains the basic set of scroll (1), incense burner (8) and vase (5), but an array of other objects are on display as well. The items displayed are mainly inherited objects and formal gifts. A Buddhist statue (2), a big rice scoop (*shamoji*) (3) and a statue of a good-luck god (12) are inherited objects inscribed with the Miyadas' family history. A tea utensils set (4 and 7) part of Mrs Miyada's dowry, together with the chest of drawers discussed above, as well as the expensive vase Mr Miyada bought (5) express the contribution of the current Miyada couple to the inalienable family wealth. A formal picture of their only son, living abroad, on one of the cupboards further illustrates the stress placed on the continuity of the family lineage. Four items in the *tokonoma*, the scroll (1), a display table (6), the incense burner (8) and a good-luck statue (11), are formal gifts from the two main religious institutions on the island, with whom the Miyada family traditionally had a strong tie. One commemorative gift is linked with their bank (9) and another with their local food supplier (10). These gifts are employed in the construction of a familial identity. Chevalier (1999) looks at the appropriation of gifts through their incorporation in the décor. She holds that

> One personalises a gift one receives by utilising it for expressing one's identity by integrating it in one's decor. . . . appropriation of a gift means that one recognises one's place in relation to others, and accept to continue ties with them. (Chevalier 1999: 508)

The gifts displayed materialize formal social relations. These relational objects are appropriated through their placement in the *tokonoma*, which in turn shows that the Miyadas value the social information they contain. Ancestors, religious institutions and reliable service providers play an important role in the life of the Miyada couple.

The Miyadas are a family in transition. The family house and the majority of objects placed inside the Japanese-style room and *tokonoma* embody the long-term familial identity. The parents attempt to hold on to this ideal, but their children are more committed to individual projects. Their presence or absence, in the case of the son, continuously draws attention to the gap between dream and reality. If the material culture of the Japanese-style room materializes the parents' ideal notion of transcendent family, what are we to make of the existence of the formal Western-style guest room which represents the transient family to the outside world? Brian Moeran and Lise Skov have pointed at the coexistence of 'overlapping rhythms' of consumption in Japan, 'the quicker one indicating fast-changing "fashion items"', and the slower one a 'consumption of tradition' (Moeran and Skov 1997: 201). The coexistence of two display rooms that embody different values within the same house proves the point made above that contemporary Japanese mix different consumer styles to create their identity. Gullestad has argued in the Norwegian context that the more fragile the family's solidarity the more stress is placed on its symbolic unity (Gullestad 1993: 154). Both display rooms are relatively static, unused spaces that symbolize family solidarity. It is mainly in the dining kitchen in between both rooms that the dynamics of everyday family life are played out. It is here where the family spends most of its time and where material culture is employed to express or resolve problems.

2. Hand-Made Bric-a-Brac to Personalize the Home

Adjoining the Moris' kitchen is an eight-mat *tatami* room that can be closed off with two wooden sliding doors. Another set of paper sliding window-covers cover a big window that opens up into a tiny garden where father grows some vegetables and flowers. The room is very bright and all family members use it to relax. Visitors also enter this room, and it is the main display area in the house. They sit either on the *tatami* mats or on two low bamboo armchairs around a small bamboo table

Figure 10.3. An inherited cupboard in the Moris' home

placed on top of a carpet. The seat of these chairs is covered with cushions made from kangaroo-skin souvenirs Mrs Mori brought home from a trip to Australia. In the middle of the room stands a low robust table made of a 10-cm-thick rough slice of a tree trunk with four short legs underneath.

The wooden cupboard made by Mrs Mori's father, mentioned above, is the most important piece of furniture in the room (see Figure 10.3).

Mr Mori designed a special alcove for this sideboard with glass sliding doors in which Mrs Mori keeps her precious teapot collection. The majority of the pots were gifts from her father from trips to China. In contrast, Mrs Miyada collects coffee cups from all around the globe, which she keeps in a white closet with glass doors in the kitchen. Most pieces are gifts from relatives, but some are small gifts from shops (*sōhin*) or wedding souvenirs (*hidemono*). A traditional tea set, part of Mrs Miyada's dowry, which is never used, is placed in the Japanese-style room. Chevalier argues that souvenirs from trips evoke the donator and the place where they were bought. Often these objects become part of a collection. This kind of gift values to a certain degree the 'expression of individuality of the receiver above the relation itself' (Chevalier 1999: 510). Mrs Mori's teapots and Mrs Miyada's coffee cups are a good example of collecting as an individual creative act. However, both collections also express familial identity because they are part of the interior of the house and they are frequently used by family members (Auslander 1996: 88).

On top of the sideboard we see a display of dolls and several miniature objects. These are a slim, tall standing Japanese doll in kimono, a head of a doll with traditional decorative head-wear, a Barbie doll with long blond hair and blue eyes dressed in kimono, and three bigger Japanese children dolls in kimono. Mrs Mori told me that these are displays made by Yoshiko that are changed each month.

Figure 10.4 shows the Moris' *tokonoma* full of objects. An inherited traditional scroll (3) and a sacred talisman from a local shrine (8) are objects associated with tradition and religion. Two glass cases containing Japanese dolls (6 and 7) are gifts. A set of a girl and boy in traditional kimono (6) was a present from Mrs Mori's parents for the Doll's festival. A female doll weaving on a loom (7) was a present from a friend. All other items displayed are made – or grown in case of the plants – by members of the family. In the middle of the *tokonoma* hangs a large piece of calligraphy made by Keiko (1). On each side of the *tokonoma* hangs a long wooden board with calligraphy made by Mrs Mori when she was younger (2a and 2b). On the floor stand two glass cases with models of wooden pagodas from famous temples, made by Mr Mori (4a and 4b). In his room he displays a whole collection of models of famous Japanese temples and shrines. On top of one of the cases stands a small clay swan made by Yoshiko while still in elementary school (5). Finally, there are also several plants grown by Mr Mori (9). On top of the bamboo table close to the *tokonoma* stands a flower arrangement made by Mrs Mori's younger sister (10).

The *tokonoma* and the Japanese-style room can be seen as the showcase of the Mori family's identity. However, hand-made decorative objects made by all family members are displayed throughout the house. An exception is father's collection of framed reproductions of abstract Western paintings. A Miro hangs in the hall, another one in the lavatory downstairs, a Picasso in another lavatory, and a Kandinsky

Figure 10.4. The Moris' *tokonoma*

in the guest bedroom. Yoshiko's paintings are often hung next to these artworks. The literature about gift giving explicitly deals with hand-made objects. Cheal, for example, argues that objects made by hand 'are gifts of personal substance, of the individual's labour power, and are recognisable as such' (Cheal 1987: 158). A hand-made object, infused with the person who produced it, has a strong 'reminiscent dimension' and is 'imbued with affective qualities' (Chevalier 1995: 33). The inherited scroll and the dolls in the *tokonoma* and the cupboard made by Mrs Mori's father in the interior of the Japanese-style room are the only expressions of lineage and long-term familial identity. The abundance of material culture produced by all members of the family indicates that the Moris value their identity as an affectionate nuclear family unit. It is noteworthy that Mr Mori also actively participates in personalizing the home with his plants, pagoda models and art works.

Conclusion

I began this chapter with the abstract, fragmented imaginary of the elegant Japanese house. I have attempted to put people back into the picture. The majority of Japanese people probably never lived in orderly homes. I have shown that the discourse surrounding the Japanese dwelling draws on an aesthetic and social ideal of order associated with the elite in feudal Japan. The ideal of social harmony based on gendered, framed identities continues to be cherished. However, in practice social relationships in the home, as in wider society, are dynamic and experiential rather than static. Material objects are expressive of these dynamics relationships.

My ethnographic observations illustrate that real, lived-in Japanese homes are complex and cluttered. My first case study illustrates the discrepancy between the Miyada couple's desired project for the future and everyday practices that contradict it. A mixture of objects associated with tradition and long-term formal social networks placed in the Japanese-style room embodies the ideal notion of the transcendent family. The Western-style guestroom evokes the image of a modern middle-class family to the outside world. However, everyday inter-family relations are fluid and material culture items are used to mediate problems. The Moris, in my second case study, aim to realize a short-term familial identity that values individuality and creativity within social networks. They occupy a new house devoid of family history, which they personalize with an excess of affectionate items made by each family member. Both families discussed, and many others I visited, display an abundance of transmitted, given or hand-made ornaments in their home. As we have seen above, the exterior and many elements of the interior of Japanese houses are standardized. Small decorative items that evoke memories and events but also a network of formal as well as personal relationships are employed in the interior to create an identity for the home.

There is an important concluding note to be made here about Japanese social relations. In Japan, as elsewhere, individuals as well as family units continuously reinvent themselves in relation to different social contexts. Japanese social relationships are not by definition hierarchical nor do they automatically suppress individuality in favour of the group. Personal relationships and agency play a far more important role than has hitherto been thought. All our lives are made up of series of temporary, changing relationships within certain frames in which we adopt different behaviour, but the Japanese, if I may borrow Moeran's words, 'are very aware of the ways in which each frame functions to affect their social behaviour. Indeed, they consciously mould both space and time to fit in with these frames' (Moeran 1996: 267). The clutter of objects in the home objectifies a network of changing social relationships that constitute the family and, to various degrees, the individuals within.

References

Attfield, J. (1994) 'Inside pram town: a case study of Harlow house interiors, 1951–61'. In J. Attfield and P. Kirkham (eds.) *A View from the interior: Women and Design.* London: The Women's Press.

Auslander, L. (1996) 'The gendering of consumer practices in nineteenth century France'. In D. Grazia (ed.) *The Sex of Things.* Berkeley: University of California Press.

Bognar, B. (1989) 'The place of no-thingness: the Japanese house and the oriental world views of the Japanese'. In J. Bourdier and N. Alsayyad (eds), *Dwelling, Settlement and Tradition.* New York: University Press of America.

Cheal, D. (1987) 'Showing them you love them: gift giving and the dialectic of intimacy'. *Sociological Review* 35:150–69.

Chevalier, S. (1995) 'The anthropology of an apparent banality: a comparative study'. *Cambridge Anthropology* 18: 25–39.

—— (1998) 'From woollen carpet to grass carpet: bridging house and garden in an English suburb'. In D. Miller (ed.) *Material Cultures: Why some Things Matter.* Chicago: University of Chicago Press.

—— (1999) 'Destins de cadeaux'. *Ethnologie Francaise* 28: 506–14.

Clammer, J. (1997) *Contemporary Urban Japan – A Sociology of Consumption.* Oxford: Blackwell.

Cram, R. (1982 [1905]) *Impressions of Japanese Architecture.* Tokyo: Charles & Tuttle.

Cwiertka, K. (1999), 'The Making of Modern Culinary Tradition in Japan'. Unpublished PhD thesis, Leiden University, The Netherlands.

Daniels, I. (1999) 'Review article: Japanese material culture and consumerism'. *Journal of Material Culture* 4: 231–40.

Enders, S. (1987) 'Wohntypen'. In R. Herold (ed.) *Wohnen in Japan.* Berlin: Erich Schmidt Verlag.

Engel, H. (1964) *The Japanese House.* Rutland: Charles & Tuttle.

Evans, S. (1991) *Contemporary Japanese Design.* London: Collins & Brown.

Fawcett, C. (1980) *The New Japanese House: Ritual and Anti-Ritual Patterns of Dwellin.* London: Granada Publishing

Forrest, J. (1988) *Lord, I'm Coming Home: Everyday Aesthetics in Tidewater North Carolina.* Ithaca: Cornell University Press.

Goldstein-Gidoni, O. (1997) *Packaged Japaneseness: Weddings, Business and Brides.* Richmond, Surrey: Curzon Press.

Goodman, P. (1992) *The Japanese Home Stylebook.* Berkeley: Stone Bridge Press.

Gullestad, M. (1993) 'Home decoration as popular culture: constructing homes, genders and classes in Norway'. In T. del Valle (ed.) *Gendered Anthropology.* London: Routledge.

Halle, D. (1993) *Inside Culture: Art and Class in the American Home.* Chicago: University of Chicago Press.

Hanley, S. (1997) *Everyday Things in Premodern Japan — The Hidden Legacy of Material Culture.* Berkeley: University of California Press.

Hoover, T. (1988 [1978]) *Zen Culture.* London: Routledge.

Imamura, A. (1987) *Urban Japanese Housewives: At Home and in the Community.* Honolulu: University of Hawaii Press.

Ito, T. (1969) *The Elegant Japanese House.* New York and Tokyo: Walker/ Weatherhill.

Jackson, S. and S. Moores (1995) *The Politics of Domestic Consumption: Critical Readings.* London: Prentice-Hall.

Jeremy, M. and M. Robinson (1989) *Ceremony and Symbolism in the Japanese Home.* Manchester: Manchester University Press.

Kaufmann, J. (1998) *Dirty Linen: Couples and their Laundry.* London: Middlesex University Press.

Knight, J. (1997), 'The soil as teacher: natural farming in a mountain village'. In P. Asquith and A. Kalland (eds) *Japanese Images of Nature.* Richmond, Surrey: Curzon Press.

Koizumi, K. (1980) *Kagu (Furniture).* Tokyo: Kondo Shuppansha.

Kurokawa, K. (1988) *Rediscovering Japanese Space.* New York: Weatherhill.

Livingstone, S. (1992) 'The meaning of domestic technologies'. In R. Silverstone and E. Hirsch (eds), *Consuming Technologies: Media and Information in Domestic Spaces.* London: Routledge.

Löfgren, O. (1994) 'Consuming interest'. In J. Friedman (ed.) *Consumption and Identity.* Chur, Switzerland: Harwood Academic Publishers.

Miller, D., P. Jackson, N. Thrift, B. Holbrook and M. Rowlands (1998) *Shopping, Place and Identity.* London: Routledge.

Moeran, B. (1995) 'Reading "Japaneseness" in Katei Gaho: the art of being an upper class housewife'. In L. Skov and B. Moeran (eds), *Women, Media and Consumption in Japan.* Richmond, Surrey: Curzon Press.

—— (1996) *A Japanese Advertising Agency: An Anthropology of Media and Markets*. Richmond, Surrey: Curzon Press.

—— (1997) *Folk Art Potters of Japan*. Richmond, Surrey: Curzon Press.

—— and Skov (1993) 'Cinderella Christmas: kitsch, youth and consumerism in Japan'. In D. Miller (ed.) *Unwrapping Christmas*. Oxford: Oxford University Press.

—— and L. Skov (1997), 'Mount Fuji and the cherry blossoms: a view from afar'. In P. Asquith and A. Kalland (eds) *Japanese Images of Nature*. Richmond, Surrey: Curzon Press.

Morse, E. (1886) *Japanese Homes and their Surroundings*. London: Sampson Low.

Nishi, K. and K. Hozumi (1985) *What is Japanese Architecture?* Tokyo: Kodansha International.

Nute, K. (1993) *Frank Lloyd Wright and Japan*. London: Chapman & Hall.

Ochiai, E. (1997) *The Japanese Family System*. Tokyo: LTCB International Library Foundation.

Orvell, M. (1989) *The Real Thing – Imitation and Authenticity in American Culture 1880–1940*. Chapel Hill: University of North Carolina Press.

Parker Pearson, M. and C. Richards (1994) 'Ordering the world: perceptions of architecture, space and time'. In M. Parker Pearson and C. Richards (eds) *Architecture and Order*. London: Routledge.

Rao, P. and J. Mahony (1988) *Japanese Accents in Western Interiors*. Tokyo: Shufunomoto.

Rosenberger, N. (1992) 'Images of the West: home style in Japanese magazines'. In J. Tobin (ed.) *Re-made in Japan*. New Haven: Yale University Press.

—— (1997) 'Interpretations of nature and the legitimation of gender differences'. In P. Asquith and A. Kalland (eds), *Japanese Images of Nature*. Richmond, Surrey: Curzon Press.

Silverstone R. and E. Hirsch (eds) (1992) *Consuming Technologies: Media and Information in Domestic Spaces*. London: Routledge.

Skov, L. and B. Moeran (1995) 'Introduction: hiding in the light: from Oshin to Yoshimoto Banana'. In L. Skov and B. Moeran (eds), *Women, Media and Consumption in Japan*. Richmond, Surrey: Curzon Press.

Slesin, S., C. Stafford and D. Rozensztroch (eds) (1987) *Japanese Style*. London, Thames & Hudson.

Sōgō josei rekishi kenkyūkai (Comprehensive Women's History Study Group) (1992) *Nihon josei no rekishi – sei, ai, kazoku* (A History of Japanese Women – gender, love, family). Tokyo: Kadakawa Shoten.

Sōgō josei rekishi kenkyūkai (Comprehensive Women's History Study Group) (1993) *Nihon Josei no rekishi – onna no hataraki* (A History of Japanese Women – a woman's labour). Tokyo: Kadakawa shoten.

Taira, K. (1993) 'Dialectics of economic growth, national power, and distributive struggles'. In A. Gordon (ed.) *Postwar Japan as History*. Berkeley: University of California Press.

Taut, B. (1958 [1937]) *Houses and People of Japan*. Tokyo: Sanseido.

Wright, G. (1981) *Building the Dream: A Social History of Housing in America*. New York: Pantheon Books.

Yagi, K. (1982) *A Japanese Touch for your Home*. Tokyo: Kodansha International.

Yoshino, S. (1994) 'The Japanese home: a grab bag of tradition, trends, and high-tech'. In A. Ueda (ed.) *The Electric Geisha*. Tokyo: Kodansha International.

Dictionaries

Daikangorin (Chinese Character Dictionary) (1992) Tokyo: Daishukan shoten

Japan, an Illustrated Encyclopaedia (1993) Tokyo: Kodansha.

Nihon mingu jiten (Dictionary of Traditional Japanese Objects) (1997) Tokyo: Gyosei.

Index

Index